Roy & Lois

MERRY CHRISTMAS !!! 1996

We thought you might enjoy this book
about Elder Boyd K. Packer. There is a story
in it on pages 183-84 in which he tells of an
experience in Western Samoa while we were
there. He mentions Mark a couple of times in
the story.
    Mark has related the experience several times
to most family members but we thought you might
like to read Elder Packer's account also. We have
heard him refer to it a couple of times in his talks.

Hope you enjoy it!

Love,
Mark & Marilyn

BOYD K. PACKER

A WATCHMAN ON THE TOWER

BOYD K. PACKER

A WATCHMAN ON THE TOWER

LUCILE C. TATE

Bookcraft
Salt Lake City, Utah

Library of Congress Catalog Card Number: 95-79003

ISBN 0-88494-997-4

2ND PRINTING, 1996

Printed in the United States of America

Contents

Preface

The imagery of *watchman* is fitting for those fifteen men who have been called by the Lord as prophets, seers, and revelators, who have been sustained as such by the Church, who have been anointed of the Lord, and who serve as His special witnesses.

They have been so designated by the Lord in the various dispensations of time. They are found in the Old Testament, the Book of Mormon, and the Doctrine and Covenants, identified as those who are to watch over His Church.

The term *watch* helps to define their roles which, in part, are: to be attentive to trends, drifts, and conditions within and without the Church; to be vigilant and alert to dangers from the archenemy, Satan; to guard, tend, heed, and warn as in the following scripture passages.

> Again the word of the Lord came unto me, saying,
> Son of man, speak to the children of thy people, and say unto them,
> When I bring the sword upon a land, if the people of the land take a
> man of their coasts, and set him for their watchman;

If when he seeth the sword come upon the land, he blow the trumpet, and warn the people;

Then whosoever heareth the sound of the trumpet, and taketh not warning; if the sword come, and take him away, his blood shall be upon his own head.

He heard the sound of the trumpet, and took not warning; his blood shall be upon him. But he that taketh warning shall deliver his soul.

But if the watchman see the sword come, and blow not the trumpet, and the people be not warned; if the sword come, and take any person from among them, he is taken away in his iniquity; but his blood will I require at the watchman's hand.

So thou, O son of man, I have set thee a watchman unto the house of Israel; therefore thou shalt hear the word at my mouth, and warn them from me. (Ezekiel 33:1–7.)

And now I say unto you that the time shall come that the salvation of the Lord shall be declared to every nation, kindred, tongue, and people.

Yea, Lord, thy watchmen shall lift up their voice; with the voice together shall they sing; for they shall see eye to eye, when the Lord shall bring again Zion. (Mosiah 15:28–29.)

And set watchmen round about them, and build a tower, that one may overlook the land round about, to be a watchman upon the tower, that mine olive-trees may not be broken down when the enemy shall come to spoil and take upon themselves the fruit of my vineyard (D&C 101:45).

Boyd K. Packer is one of those fifteen watchmen who have been called, sustained, and anointed, and is a witness to the world. These men are of varying backgrounds, abilities, and temperaments. Their individual stories are unique to themselves. But in some things they are alike. Each has been trained, tested, and tempered over many years. Each has a sure witness that Jesus is the Christ, the Son of the living God. And each is committed for life to be obedient to His will—no retirement because of illness, infirmity, or personal burden. They simply carry on.

As with the others, Boyd K. Packer's life is unique to himself. This book tells his story.

Of his reason for its writing, President Packer has said: "On several occasions Elder LeGrand Richards expressed his desire to me that Lucile Tate, who had written his biography, *LeGrand Richards: Beloved Apostle*, also write mine. Several years after Elder Richards died, I began to admit to myself, with some nudging from my wife, Donna, that we could no longer ignore the wish of that venerable and senior Apostle and friend who had had such a profound influence upon us. Except for my responsibility to be obedient to Elder Richards I would not have agreed to have my life's story written for publication. But an equal influence was the complete trust that Donna and I had developed in Lucile Tate, now in her eighties. In her we could confide our deep personal feelings, our experiences with our family, and the events relating to the sacred calling which had come to us."

As noted in the text, he has not kept a journal, but has stated that, collectively, his talks are his journal. Many of these have not been published. In lieu of journals as a source of information for the writing of this book he made available all of his published and unpublished talks, his books and booklets, and his pertinent personal papers, letters, and memorabilia. He also gave generous time for personal interviews over a period of several years, and he arranged interviews with family, friends, and members of the Quorum of the Twelve. Further, he approved author visits to all local and British sites pertaining to his life and lineage.

These extensive source materials and the author's long-standing association with him have made possible a careful assessment and a faithful portrayal of his and his companion's many-faceted lives and his public and private ministry.

The Lily and the Rose

The Tudor rose from the family coat of arms represents the English Packers. The sego lily symbolizes the American family branch that, like Joseph in the Old Testament, was "a fruitful bough, even a fruitful bough by a well; whose branches run over the wall" (Genesis 49:22), for they crossed the sea and took root in the New World.

When the Mormon pioneers entered the Salt Lake Valley in 1847 it was late in July, too late to sow and reap. In those hungry days they found that the bulb of the sego lily was edible. This beautiful white flower with a yellow center and deep red markings grew among the sagebrush. The pioneers dug the small bulbs to stave off their hunger. The flower became a symbol of triumph over adversity.

About the time the Packers arrived in the West, one young pioneer took his wife to settle in southern Utah. She was a woman of refinement and could not bear the hardships of pioneering in that semi-desert country. One day she announced to him that she was going back. The distraught young husband pleaded with her to stay. Finally she set a condition. "If you can show me one beautiful thing about this country, I will stay."

That night when he came from the fields he thrust into her hand a small bouquet of sego lilies. She stayed. (From *On Footings from the Past: The Packers in England,* by Donna Smith Packer.)

Chapter One

His Time and Place

 Boyd Kenneth Packer was born on 10 September 1924 in Brigham City, Utah, the tenth child and fifth son of Ira Wight Packer, a thirty-nine-year-old garage mechanic, and Emma Jensen Packer, a homemaker, aged thirty-six.

The year of Boyd's birth was one of portent. On a world scale, seeds of unrest were germinating in turbulent soil and they would flower into World War II just as Boyd reached manhood.

Abroad, 1924 began with the death of Lenin, architect of Russia's revolution and its first communist head of state. Stalin survived and forced all opposition leaders to surrender. Thus he became the undisputed master of the Soviet Union.

In Italy in 1924 Mussolini abolished non-Fascist trade unions and annexed Adriatic lands.

Found guilty of high treason in April 1924, Adolf Hitler, Nazi leader in Germany, was sentenced to prison for five years. There he began writing his book *Mein Kampf*.

In London, Prime Minister Stanley Baldwin appointed a new Conservative cabinet in 1924.

That year the government of Japan protested the barring of its immigrants to the United States.

At home, the death of former President Woodrow Wilson in February 1924 ended his dream of creating a league of nations that would "make the world safe for democracy."

Despite flourishing businesses and increased production in the United States during the 1920s, workers' wages and purchasing power declined. Five years after Boyd's birth the stock market crash plunged the nation into a deep depression.

The historic ocean-crossing flights by Americans in the late 1920s and the round-the-world attempts in the 1930s marked advances that would reach a level of supremacy in air power during the coming World War II.

Thus the period of Boyd K. Packer's birth and childhood was marked by events out of which that war evolved.

In contrast with the global scene of political change and power struggle was the peaceable community of Brigham City, Utah, a town of approximately 5,500 people. This small city had its roots in pioneer colonizing that began almost as soon as the pioneers entered the Salt Lake Valley in 1847.

William Davis, the first settler, took his family there in 1851 together with two other families, later to be joined by still others. They built a row of log rooms by the forks of Box Elder Creek. Two years later the settlers were ordered to move their log cabins into fort formation as protection from the Indians.

In 1853 Brigham Young called Elder Lorenzo Snow of the Quorum of the Twelve to select fifty families who would further colonize this Box Elder site, and then assigned Elder Snow to preside over the new community. Some of the families selected were Scandinavian; others Elder Snow had converted in England. They came a few at a time and were housed in the fort. A year later a second Scandinavian company arrived. The colony continued to grow.

Elder Snow wisely chose men of faith, devotion, and ability—teachers, masons, carpenters, blacksmiths, shoemakers, and other skilled and conscientious workers who would ensure the community's economic success.

Lorenzo Snow had been taught the principles of the united order

*Pioneer Stake Tabernacle in Brigham City, Utah; restored in 1987
and rededicated by Elder Boyd K. Packer*

by the Prophet Joseph Smith. With his appointment to colonize and direct the development of Box Elder came the opportunity to put a cooperative plan into operation.

The Brigham City Mercantile and Manufacturing Association was formed in December 1870. Lorenzo Snow was elected president in January 1871, with seven directors. Boyd's great-grandfather, Jonathan Taylor Packer, was one of them. Within four years of its incorporation virtually the entire economic life of this community of four hundred families was owned and directed by the cooperative association. Fifteen or so departments were later expanded to forty branches of industry. These included a woolen mill, a tannery, a shoe factory, a hat factory, cattle herds, dairies, a cheese factory, sawmills, as well as tailor, furniture, blacksmith, wagon, and tin shops.

The success of the Brigham City cooperative sprang largely from the leadership of Lorenzo Snow. He fostered it only in the sense that most of the people owned some stock in the corporate enterprise.

The cooperative was not, however, to interfere with a member's domestic affairs—one's home and land were separate and apart; only one's business was held in common.

For all that, the cooperative community functioned by united order general rules. These directed that members not take the name of Deity in vain nor speak lightly of sacred things. Prayer was fundamental to family and personal life. The Word of Wisdom was to be observed. Children were to be treated with kindness, and quarreling was to be avoided. Charity was encouraged and selfishness disapproved.

Families were to foster home production. Apparel and deportment were to focus on simplicity and appropriateness. Economy and prudence in the management of property were enjoined. Members were expected to be virtuous and honest.

Had the order's rules been made specifically for the Packer family, they could not have been more fitting. These personal standards were part of the traditions brought to that generation from four great-grandparents, Jonathan Taylor Packer and Lyman Wight and their wives.

The Packer family knew and honored their pioneer heritage. The cooperative's traditions were the unspoken code by which they lived. Not that the rules were preached at home; rather, the principles were taught by example and by the parents' quiet expectations that family members would be as obedient and good as their forebears had been.

Chapter Two

His Ancestry

Boyd K. Packer's ancestry linked two families—one British, the other Scandinavian.

His British Packer line has been traced back to 1460 to Thomas Packer through nine generations, the first six of which include two clerks of the Privy Seal of England: William, and his son John. John's son Philip inherited Groombridge Manor in Kent; and Philip's son Philip was the immigrant from Ireland to America in 1683.

The American Packer line descends through three generations who settled in Pennsylvania. One served in the colonial army during the Revolution. The third, Moses, became a member of the Society of Friends in Pennsylvania and later migrated to the western frontiers of Ohio.

The fourth descendant from Philip the immigrant was Jonathan Taylor Packer, Boyd's great-grandfather, who was born 26 July 1817 in Perry, Richland County, Ohio. He was twelve years of age when his father, Moses, died. The family resided in central Ohio, not far from Kirtland, where they heard of the newly organized Church of Jesus Christ of Latter-day Saints. Having investigated its doctrines and being convinced and converted, Jonathan and his two brothers joined the Church—Jonathan at the age of eighteen. He walked the eight hundred miles to Missouri, where he cast his lot with the Latter-day Saints there. Through their expulsion from Missouri and Nauvoo and their crossing of the plains, Jonathan arrived in the Salt Lake Valley with the second pioneer company in the early fall of 1847.

Jonathan's first wife, Sarah Ewell, died, leaving him one son, Nephi. He next married Angeline Avida Champlin, who would bear him nine children. He later married Christiana Petrina Sundby, and was living in Fort Herriman, about thirty-five miles southwest of the Salt Lake settlement, when their son Joseph Alma, Boyd's grandfather, was born on 13 January 1859.

When Joseph Alma was about eighteen months old the family moved to Brigham City. It was here that Jonathan became one of the first directors of the Brigham City Cooperative and Manufacturing Association. He was called to settle the community of Cannonville, Utah, and became its first bishop. He later left with other Saints for Safford, Arizona, where he died 29 January 1889 at age seventy-one.

At the last, Jonathan was tenderly cared for by his daughter-in-law, Mary Ann Packer, in her home. On 17 January 1889, twelve days before his death, she had written to his daughter Martha: "Your Father says for you all to be faithful to the principles of the Gospel and asks the blessings of Abraham, Isaac, and Jacob upon you all and bid[s] you all good bye until he meets you in the morning of the resurrection."[1]

At age fifteen Boyd's grandfather Joseph Alma began to work in the Brigham City cooperative blacksmith shop. After serving his apprenticeship for six years he married Sarah Adeline Wight in the Endowment House in Salt Lake City on 11 October 1880.

Joseph Alma built a blacksmith shop on First North and Second East in Brigham City but later moved his shop to near the courthouse. For thirty-five years he followed that trade, one which greatly influenced the life of his son Ira Wight Packer, Boyd's father.

In later years Joseph Alma served two missions to the Indians in Montana. His wife, Sarah Adeline, and their daughter, Vida, accompanied him on his last mission (1916–1918).

Ira was born 6 April 1885. He grew up helping in the blacksmith shop and learned much of what was known then about metal. He knew how to weld and drill, to fix and cut, to bolt and shape.

Ira's first years of school were spent in Brigham City, but when he was thirteen his father moved his blacksmith and wagon shop to Corrine, Utah, a few miles to the west. There Joseph Alma bought 265 acres of land, built a home, and purchased twenty-five cows and twenty-four horses. He eventually closed the shop and farmed full-time.

Ira's teen years were spent working on the farm. In the home his sister Vida helped loom rugs, stuff straw mattresses, churn butter, and make ice cream using ice cut from the river in winter and stored in sawdust. Garden produce and dairy products were traded for store commodities.

The Packer home received occasional visits from gypsies as they passed through, and Indians were a familiar sight in the town. In spring and summer, work was heavy and never-ending. In fall and winter there was school, though the children stayed away when snow fell deep and drifted.

Home-talent programs, picture shows accompanied by a player piano, and dances were held in the Opera House. Ira first met Emma Jensen, Boyd's mother, at one of these dances.

Emma's father, Peter Simon Jensen, born in 1860 in Tyvelse, Denmark, married Amelia Anderson on 16 August 1882. Amelia, born in 1861, came from Usolkattan, Loreig, Sweden.

This couple's first child, Boden, died within two months of birth. The second, William Peter, immigrated to America with his father when his parents joined the Church. Father and son settled in Malad, Idaho, where other relatives had preceded them.

As soon as Peter Simon was able to send for her, Amelia joined him and their son in Malad. Four other children were born to them

Boyd Kenneth Packer

Ira Wight Packer
1885–1958

Emma Jensen
1888–1965

Joseph Alma
Packer
1859–1941

Sarah Adeline
Wight
1861–1934

Peter Simon
Jensen
1860–1943

Amelia
Anderson
1861–1894

The ancestry of Boyd K. Packer

in that place. Boyd's mother, Emma, born 14 May 1888, was one of them. Charles and Laura lived, but James Oscar died as an infant.

Emma was four when her father moved his family to Sandy, Utah. On the way they traveled through sagebrush along a poorly defined road, stopping the first night in a little log cabin. (When Boyd was a teenager, his mother pointed out to him the cabin, which stood in a field west of the highway between Malad and Plymouth, Utah, and was still there until recent years.) The Jensens' trip took several days to complete. Thereafter Emma's father found work at the Magna smelter.

The family had been in Sandy only a year and a half when Emma's mother died of typhoid fever. Peter Simon came near dying. His stepmother, Sophia Jorgensen Jensen, came down from Bear River, Utah, and took the children back home with her. Laura lived with the Ole Hansens until she was grown. Emma's brothers, Charlie and Will, stayed with other relatives until their father recovered from his illness and came for them. Charlie, ill with heart trouble, lived at Ira Anderson's home in Elwood (a neighboring community) until he married. Will and his father went to work on the Brigham City cooperative farm in Corrine.

Meanwhile Emma stayed with Grandmother Jensen, who spoke no English. Emma's childhood was rich in Danish tradition but poor in material advantages. She was expected to help both with farm labor and heavy housecleaning. One of her tasks was to help roll up the rug, carry it outside, hang it on the clothesline, and beat the dust out of it. She swept up the straw padding and carried it out to be burned. She scrubbed the rough, uneven floorboards, then helped carry clean new straw and spread it so thick that, after the rug was again stretched and tacked down, the furniture leaned back against the walls until continual walking in the room leveled the matting evenly.

The young motherless girl also had other challenges. On one occasion her grandmother cooked bean soup. The beans had become damp and had started to sprout, but the thrifty grandmother had to make do with everything there was, so she made the soup. Emma could not eat it. She thought the bean sprouts were worms.

Emma occasionally missed school because of a nervous

condition, possibly the result of unhappiness. In her later years Emma seldom spoke about the hardships of her childhood. She did, however, express her unhappiness about a teenage worker's behavior in the orchard where Emma was picking fruit with others. The girl mimicked a spastic cripple who lived in the community. While others were amused, Emma was indignant. The trials of her childhood had developed within her a deep sympathy for the unfortunate.

When Emma was eighteen her grandmother suddenly left to live with her daughter in Preston, Idaho. With no place else to go, Emma moved into her father's home. He had remarried, and Emma spent most of her time hiring out, cooking for men who worked on the canal or picking fruit and garden produce to earn money.

Emma grew to womanhood with a great love of nature. She often told about wandering along the banks of the Bear River in the early evening, listening to the plaintive and beautiful call of mourning doves. Whenever she heard their call later in life she would remember those lonely years and say, "I love to hear the song of the doves."

Perhaps his mother's love of birds was quietly transmitted to Boyd. Certainly his love for them has been lifelong. His mother also loved flowers, as he does, and she had a gift for both growing them and arranging them.

As Emma grew to womanhood she participated in the simple entertainments the small community of Corrine offered. One evening she attended a Church dance at the Opera House and there met Ira Wight Packer. Emma was short, full-figured, with dark hair, clear skin, a happy smile, and kindness in her eyes. Ira was large of stature, gentle of touch, and even-tempered. He had a quiet sense of humor and a look about him that invited trust and confidence. When he met Emma, he was already skilled in his trade as a mechanic.

The two were immediately drawn to one another, became friends, then sweethearts. After a brief courtship they traveled by train to Malad, Idaho, where they were civilly married on 16 February 1907. The couple returned to Corrine and at first lived in part of the home of Ira's father, Joseph Alma. In April that year, when the weather permitted, they traveled to Salt Lake City, where in the temple they were sealed for time and eternity. The next day they returned to the temple to do the temple work for Emma's mother, Amelia Jensen.

Having been only six when her mother died of typhoid, Emma's memories of her were indistinct but loving. She grieved all her life that the location of her mother's grave in Sandy had never been found.

Whatever unhappiness Emma had experienced in her childhood and youth was compensated for in the personal fulfillment and joy she found in her marriage to Ira. She was home-centered and deeply committed to their eternal marriage, thus ensuring for their children not only that kind of daily example but also the love and security for which she, as a child, had longed while deprived of both.

Chapter Three

His Parents

In coming home to each other in marriage, for Ira and Emma Packer the wells of contentment ran deep with commitment. Their love existed for one another, but it also extended to having a family, thus magnifying their roles as husband and wife to those of father and mother. Their children would not be disruptive intruders into their personal relationship but welcomed additions to their intimate family circle.

Perhaps Emma's love of her wife-mother role stemmed from her lonely growing-up years, when she had lived and worked in the homes and fields of others. Now in her own home, with a good husband and with children coming along, she had the deep satisfaction of managing her small world as she wished. And being thrifty and creative from long practice, she was content with whatever Ira was able to provide.

Family traits and attitudes that would characterize Ira and Emma throughout their lives had begun in their youth and continued to develop through their marriage. After their wedding the couple stayed a few months in the home of Ira's father, Joseph Alma. From there, Ira took Emma to Ogden, where he worked as a traveling salesman for an implement company. Emma cared for their boardinghouse rooms and anxiously watched for Ira's return from sales trips. He soon tired of being away from her, and when he was offered a mechanic's job in the railroad yard he took it. Thereafter he was home each night.

In the spring of 1908 the couple moved back to Corinne, where they lived in a three-room house on Joseph Alma's farm near Bear River. Ira then worked to buy the house and a portion of the farm.

During that same summer the Packers' first child, Verna Emma, was born in that home, which also was the birthplace of the four children that followed—Opal Delores, Ronald Ira, Nona Ruth, and Adele Lorenis.

Aiding Emma in the care of her family was the spiritual perception that guided her throughout her life. While she and Ira were living on the farm, the following incident occurred:

> One Monday morning Father came in from the field. He had broken the plow. "I must go into Brigham City," he said, "and get some welding done. Would you like to go?" Mother was washing, but she hastily set things aside and prepared the youngsters for a trip to town. The big copper boiler was lifted from the range, the buckets of hot water were set off the stove into the bedroom. Mother took the youngsters to the front gate, where Father soon appeared with the white-topped buggy. As she put her foot onto the step, she paused and said, "Dad, somehow I think I shouldn't go with you today."
>
> "But why not? . . ."
>
> Mother finally said, "I just *feel* like I shouldn't go."
>
> "If you *feel* that way, Mother," he said, "perhaps you should stay home."
>
> She lifted the youngsters out of the buggy, and you can well guess what they started to do. Dad shook the reins, the buggy pulled down across the bridge, up the opposite bank and out of sight. . . .
>
> She busied herself with her washing again, and in a moment or two she smelled smoke. Everything they owned, much of what they had prayed for, was in that modest little home. She didn't find the fire until the ceiling of the bedroom burst into flame, a ceiling made of muslin, sized with glue and wallpapered. A rusted stove pipe had permitted a spark to fall and settle in the dust atop the ceiling. A bucket brigade from the back pump, and the fire was soon out.[1]

The couple had been saving to pay for their portion of the farm, and that money, along with every household thing they owned, would have been destroyed had Emma ignored the prompting and gone with Ira.

Throughout his life Elder Packer has treasured his mother's words: "We have the right to be prompted and inspired, and if we are righteous and are prayerful, the Lord will guide us."[2]

In 1916 Ira sold his share of the farm and moved to a house on what is now Washington Street in Corinne. The following year he purchased a home on Colorado Street in that same town. Another son, Leon Claren, was born there.

In their new location the Packer family had more opportunity for activity in the Church and the community. Ira was superintendent of the Young Men's Mutual Improvement Association. In winter he and Emma bundled up their children and pulled them on a sleigh to attend their Church meetings and activities. The youngest would often sleep during classes, programs, or dances. The couple kept alive their love for dancing, in later years attending dances with their grown children.

It was during their struggles in Corinne that Emma's Danish temper flared. Boyd tells of it:

> One morning, my mother answered a knock at the door and was confronted there by a large frightening-looking man, who asked her for money. She said, "We have no money." . . . He pressed his demands, insisting that she give him some money, finally saying, "I am hungry; I would like to get something to eat."
>
> "Well," she said, "if that is the case then I can help you." So she hurried to the kitchen and fixed him a lunch. And I am sure it was the most modest of provisions.
>
> She could tell as she gave him the lunch at the door that he was not pleased. . . . She watched him as he went down the lane through the gate and started up the road. He looked back, but he did not see her standing inside the door, and as he passed the property line, he took the lunch and threw it over the fence into the brush.
>
> . . . In that house there was nothing to waste, and she was angered that he was so ungrateful.
>
> The incident was forgotten until a week or two later; she answered

another knock at the door. There stood a tall, raw-boned teenage boy, who asked about the same question in essentially the same words: "We need help; we are hungry. Could you give us some money; could you give us some food?"

"No," excusing herself, "I am sorry. I am busy; I cannot help you. . . ." What she meant was "I won't. I won't. I won't be taken in again."

Well, the young man turned without protest and walked out the gate, and she stood looking after him. It wasn't until he passed through the gate that she noticed the wagon, the father and mother, and the other youngsters, and as the boy swung his long legs into the wagon, he looked back rather poignantly; the father shook the reins and the wagon went on down the road. She hesitated just long enough so that she could not call them back.

From that experience she drew a moral by which she has lived and which she has imparted to her children . . . "Never fail to give that which you have to someone who is in need."[3]

During the harvest season prior to 1915 Ira bought one of the first gas-driven tractors and threshing machines in the area and did custom threshing on farms in the region. Amos Hatch, one of the crew members and the son of Ira's cousin, remembers: "This threshing machine had at least one breakdown a day, but with a master mechanic as boss, we didn't get long rests because of the breakdown. Ira started to whistle, soon found the trouble, and improvised a broken part—sometimes with barbed wire."[4]

If a more complicated breakdown occurred he could build a fire and, with an anvil and bellows, fashion the needed part—a skill he had learned from his father.

Boyd's father was generally a patient, mild-mannered man who was pleasant to work for, but like his wife, Emma, he was capable of anger. Also, like his wife, he usually drew a lesson from a flare-up.

One day the threshing crew was hurrying to complete their harvest before an oncoming storm. One of the workers was a middle-aged Japanese man. It was his task to drive the teams. Ira had warned him about turning a corner of the field too abruptly but the man thoughtlessly did the very thing he had been told not to do, and the header bar broke. That meant a trip to town and loss of a day or more of harvesting.

Ira was angry. He climbed down from the tractor with some harsh expletives poised on his lips for the Japanese crew member. But before he could reach him the small man came to face him and bowed with great respect. "Sir, I am so incredibly sorry. I could not put in words shame for my feeling."

In the face of this, the best Ira could do was mutter something like: "Oh, that's all right. It could happen to anybody, and we'll fix it."[5]

Ira never forgot how that man's soft answer had turned away his wrath. It was a lesson that helped him in guiding his boys and in his business associations.

That harvest season the Packers and their five children lived in a large tent-wagon, where Emma cooked three hot meals a day for her family and the threshing crew of eight to ten men. One among the crew was a Colorado youth, Jack Dempsey, who became famous as the "Manassa Mauler"—the world heavyweight boxing champion.

After their daughter Adele Lorenis was born, Emma no longer worked with Ira on threshing jobs. Then with the advent of World War I male help was difficult to get and Ira could no longer contract for this kind of work.

There were other hardships incident to World War I. As it intensified, the Packers felt the impact. The government called for horses from the rural areas, and its agents took the best of the Packers' animals.

When the flu epidemic spread through Utah the family caught the dread disease. In later years Ira said of the experience: "We were all down with it. The only reason that we didn't die was that we didn't know we were supposed to."

In 1917 Ira was hired as foreman of the Corinne project to lay 212 miles of tile to drain out the alkali and reclaim the land for agriculture. While on this project he nearly lost his life. After a disturbing dream about him one night, Emma warned him to be particularly careful at work that day. He had occasion to remember her words. While he was leaning over to adjust a tiling machine on the tramway of the project his clothing caught in the gear and he found himself being pulled into the mechanism. Ira braced himself as the machine tore off his clothing and broke several of his ribs. As his belt broke he was thrown clear of the machine and tramway. In great pain, and with only his raincoat to cover him, he drove home.

Ira later sustained an even more serious injury. After the tile project was finished he worked as shop foreman for the J. A. Stewart Motor Company in Brigham City, repairing farm equipment and tractors. One day a fellow worker accidentally put a tractor in gear at the wrong moment. It jerked forward and pushed Ira against an oil pump. The pump broke and Ira was crushed.

His pelvic and hip bones were broken. It appeared that he might be permanently crippled, but Dr. R. A. Pearse, Brigham City's rugged, swearing medic, said, "Hell, Packer, we're not going to leave you this way." Dr. Pearse set the bones and fitted a seventy-five-pound cast to his satisfaction. The cast, he instructed, was to stay on for six months. Even with Emma's help it was a hardship for Ira to move. They managed until near the end of the six months, when Ira decided he had had enough. He took a pocketknife, cut off the cast, and went back to work. In time he was completely healed.

Both the Packers' second son and sixth child, Leon Claren (March 1917), and their third son and seventh child, Lowell Wight (March 1919), were born in Corinne. In November of that year Ira was elected to the office of councilman in that city for a two-year term. During the intervening summer, measles broke out in the family. Emma was concerned about the possible aftereffects of the disease and kept Nona and Adele in the living room with the shades drawn.

After the disease had spent itself the girls were allowed to play outside. Emma saw that they just leaned against the supports of the swing their father had made, not even trying to take turns. Alarmed, she and Ira took them to the doctor in Brigham City. He found them both suffering from serious heart damage. Since the summer was extremely hot he advised Ira to get his family into the cool of the canyon.

Ira immediately moved Emma and the seven children (Lowell was only a few months old) to a camp in Box Elder Canyon. He set up a large tent with an oil stove for cooking. He devised a cart to hold Nona, age six, and Adele, four.

By then he was working for a garage in Brigham City. All through that summer, as well as doing his daily work, he drove to

Corinne, fed and milked the cow, and took milk and supplies to the family.

The cool mountain air and frequent rests proved beneficial to the sick little girls, and by September Nona was able to start first grade. With the family back in Corinne, by mid-year she was down again to rest with Adele, missing half of the school year. During their months of illness Nona read books and played with Adele. To help their hours of enforced rest pass more quickly Ira fashioned a sandbox they could play with on their bed.

The Packers' eighth child, Donna Zola, arrived in June 1921. That fall the family moved to Brigham City, where they lived for a few months at 144 South First West. While they were there Nona attended Central School and completed three-quarters of that year. Soon after the fourth-grade class began she was tested and allowed to rejoin her own age group.

For a time the family settled in another rented home located at 30 West First South. Emma painted and papered inside and planted and tended flowers in the yard.

It was while living in that rented house that Ira determined to have a business of his own. When the Ford dealership in Brigham City went broke he recognized an opportunity, but to take it he would have to obtain a loan. Elder Packer tells the story.

> My father . . . went nervously into the bank in Brigham City to ask for a loan to start in business. He was asked about collateral. He had none beyond his willingness to work and some mechanical aptitude.
>
> The banker, in turning down his request, happened to ask Father where he lived. "In the old box house on First West," was the answer. The banker passed that corner on the way to work. He'd watched the transformation in the yard. He'd wondered who lived there, and admired what they were doing.
>
> Father got the loan to start in business on the strength of the flowers that Mother had planted in the yard of a very modest adobe house they were renting.[6]

Initially Ira set up a business partnership with his brother Lyman, but when the latter moved to Salt Lake Ira rented a building at 146 South Main Street and thereafter operated his own business. He

The Packer garage on Main Street in Brigham City

remodeled a large touring car into a wrecker and answered every call, day or night, to rescue travelers from breakdowns, accidents, or slidings from icy roads. He obtained a heavy-duty sewing machine with which he made canvas tops for the early automobiles, and he installed their isinglass windows. When glass took the place of that material, he learned to cut and install it as well.

In the spring of 1923 Ira purchased a large red brick home at 627 South Main Street. This home, more than any other, would be remembered as the family home, and Emma loved it. She appreciated the increased space for her growing family. She loved its fruit and shade trees, garden area, and places for flowers of every domestic variety.

During the move to that home Emma was expecting another child, and on 26 May 1923 she gave birth to her fourth son and ninth child, Doyle Lamont. Much of her time was thus spent caring for the new baby while she settled into the new home. And for a brief time Adele and Nona seemed a little better and responded favorably to their new surroundings.

Nona tells that early that summer she and Adele rode their stick horses into the corn patch for imaginary campouts, with their twelve-year-old brother, Ronald, watching out for them. Their bedrolls were gunnysacks; their lunch, small bottles of cherry juice and cookies. On irrigation days, when they could not enter their customary trails, the girls collected bricks, boards, empty cans, and pieces of broken dishes and created a playhouse.

Nona also remembers that at Sunday School Adele once slipped away from Emma and went up on the stand to Bishop Alma Jensen, who held her on his lap for the balance of the meeting.

Adele Packer,
Boyd's older sister,
who died of rheumatic
fever at age eight

Nona's and Adele's energy soon lagged again, however, and they were back in bed over the Fourth of July in 1923. Three days later, July 7, Adele crawled from her bed and weakly made her way to the kitchen. There she collapsed onto the floor, struggling for breath. Terribly alarmed, Emma called Dr. Pearse. He came immediately, examined Adele, and knowing that she had only minutes to live, left on the pretext of picking up medication for her. He felt too tender toward her to witness the end. She was gone before he returned.

Adele's brothers and sisters have warm memories of this gentle, lovable sister who spent most of her eight years patiently resting and quietly playing. She left an indefinable influence on each family member, not only those who knew her but, through them, also on the two who would follow—Boyd Kenneth, then William Lamoin.

Whether Ira and Emma had lived in part of his father's home, a thresher's wagon-tent, a temporary summer camp in the mountains, a small or a large house, or an apartment over Ira's garage, they had the knack of making it feel like home. Mother Emma was there to love and care for the children, and Father Ira was near in field, shop, or garage.

Once Ira had purchased his own garage he kept a twenty-four-hour, seven-day-week service for motorists. Then as his sons became old enough they took turns at night and also on Sunday evenings so

The Ira W. Packer family in 1938

Ira could attend evening sacrament meetings with Emma and any family members not "on duty" at the garage. But he carried the daytime shifts so that his boys could always be in Sunday School and priesthood meeting.

In the Packer home the gospel was taught by example. Respect for Church leadership was a family attitude. Whether bishop, stake president, Apostle, or Church President, each was spoken of with respect, and it was counted a privilege to shake his hand or to hear him speak.

Home and family were the Packers' closest link to God. Children were a sacred charge, with Church organizations serving as adjuncts to their training. Prayer and moral and spiritual values were stressed more than church attendance.

The Church, of course, provided crucial priesthood ordinances of blessing babies, baptism, priesthood ordinations, administration of the sick, and temple marriage. These were not to be neglected in the Packer family.

Family home evenings were not planned for special nights, nor were formal lessons taught; rather, the family gathered from school, play, or work each evening to be nourished by what they found at home. After the evening meal and cleanup, Ira would stretch out on the floor briefly to rest. Emma would fold clothes or mend as she watched the children entertain themselves with wood and paper and needle and thread. The children often thumbed through *The Source Book*[7] for patterns of birds or animals, instructions, or answers to questions about the world around them.

Money was scarce; even necessities were hard to come by. Waste was unknown to the Packers. Any material item was pressed to its furthest possible utility. Whether food, fabric, paper, wood, metal, or tool, it served many times over, creatively adapted to new forms and fresh uses until it became completely used up, worn out, or beyond repair. Meager table scraps were fed to chickens and pets; tattered clothing was cut into strips for braided rugs; paper scraps and stubs of pencils were used to draw or write with; worn-out auto parts became, under Ira's inventiveness, the seat of a swing, a sandbox, or a play-house; and scrap wood or metal was used to fashion toys, create miniature farms and animals, or build cages for birds.

Instead of developing a spirit of discontent, the very sparseness of materials fostered in the family members a hunger to create beauty out of near-nothing. Thus the lack of material things fostered creativity in a way only possible in a climate of encouragement and love. In both the lack and the love, each family member found his own level of fulfillment.

There were times when the family was under quarantine for contagious diseases. The health officer posted quarantine signs on the front window. When illness or trouble struck, Emma knew the comfort of having Ira nearby. Frequently these parents worried over a child with heart disease, scarlet fever, pneumonia, polio, or crippling arthritis—ailments that struck down one family member or another. The worry and the care for their ailing ones drew them closer.

Home was a purposeful place for the large family. Ira taught the boys his trade, because he needed their help. Mostly, he taught by showing; then, letting them try for themselves, he corrected their mistakes as they learned.

Emma also taught her daughters. The girls were quick to learn and observed that Emma loved her role as wife and mother. Thus, by showing and encouraging, Ira and Emma taught their children to work.

The Packer home was not a closed circle, however. Emma encouraged her children to bring their friends home, but her children's best friends were their own brothers and sisters.

In all, they were fun-loving and full of spirit. Discipline for the flare-ups and mischief common to growing up consisted of an occasional spanking from Emma. She usually sent the offending one to cut his own switch. But more often a word of parental disapproval carried the full weight of a reprimand. Such discipline engendered respect.

They learned not only respect from their parents but also compassion. When Grandmother Sarah Adeline Packer died in 1934, a room in the crowded home was thereafter given to Grandfather Alma Joseph. There he lived for the seven remaining years of his life. Nor was the Packers' concern limited to relatives. One evening a young man walking his girl home paused by the lamppost in front of the Packer home. A reckless driver hit and critically injured him. Ira and his boys carried him into the house. Emma nursed him for weeks until he could be moved to his own home.

Boyd tells of another instance of his mother's service:

> In elementary school I learned this great lesson. In our school were several youngsters from a family not blessed with an attentive mother at home. During the school year they were afflicted with impetigo, a common disease of the skin that is now very easily cured. Because they were not bathed and because their clothing was not clean, the infection quickly spread across their bodies.
>
> The principal asked my mother, who was the room mother for our class, to visit the home in the hope that she could encourage the type of care that these children so badly needed. "The woman's touch," he said, "will be most helpful there."
>
> Although she responded to the request, she failed in her mission, for she found circumstances in that home pitiable.
>
> Well do I remember the assignment to bring these little youngsters home from school with us. And, I remember, they were bathed, medication was applied to their little bodies, they were dressed in our clothing;

and in the early evening they were sent to their own home, to return the next day for the same treatment.

Night after night after night I remember my mother scrubbing end-lessly with a bottle of disinfectant and then boiling clothing against the possibility that her own family might become infected.[8]

Boyd's parents had faced life's tough realities; illness, accident, death, and material privations had bonded them ever more tightly together. And their children were deeply influenced by their examples.

Chapter Four

Childhood

It was four-fifty-five in the afternoon of Wednesday, 10 September 1924, when Boyd Kenneth Packer was born. His mother, attended by Dr. A. D. Cooley, had safely brought forth the tenth of her eleven children and her fifth son. It was her first child to be born in a hospital, a converted two-story home.

Holding her new babe, she must have been aware of the shimmering autumn day set between two brief periods of storm.[1]

From what we know of the family, the older children would have cared for the home and the younger children in Emma's absence. Yet she was a little impatient until she could rejoin them.

On 2 November 1924 the new baby was blessed and given a name by D. H. Matthews—Boyd Kenneth Packer.

His next older brother, Doyle, had been born with a skin disease that was often fatal in children aged about five or six. The layers of Doyle's skin were not laminated properly, and any irritation would cause large blisters to form over his body. To protect him from bumps he had a round walker which allowed him to move around safely. A soothing ointment, Poslam, also helped him.

Boyd at age three

On 7 September 1927, when Boyd was nearly three and Doyle four, Emma gave birth to her eleventh and last child, William Lamoin. No longer the baby, Boyd liked to look after him. Bill, who has been a bishop and a high councilor in Brigham City, says, "Boyd has never stopped looking after me."

At the time of Bill's birth their sister Verna was nineteen. She had a natural sense for style, which apparently was perceived by the manager of the local J. C. Penney store. He invited her to work at the store. At that time she and Opal worked at the cement plant sewing sacks. Clerking in a store sounded much more appealing, so Verna accepted his offer. She later became buyer for the women's department.

Verna developed her skill as a seamstress, all her life finding joy in sewing for family members. In an early effort to make short pants for Boyd and Doyle she forgot the front flies and made them the same front and back. The little brothers neither knew nor cared about her mistake as they posed for a picture. Verna also made pajamas for each family member for New Year's Day, a gift that became traditional over many years.

Boyd's sister Donna remembers him as "a happy child with plenty of smiles, and a bit of mischief." This happiness was rooted in the security of family and home. Shortly after his fifth birthday Boyd was stricken with a high fever. His legs gave way and he was placed on a cot near the large oak table in the living room. Old Dr. Pearse diagnosed his illness as pneumonia and prescribed the current treatment for it. The front room was closed off and its windows opened to the cold, fresh air. Bundled up to keep warm, Boyd stayed there for six weeks.

Wearing her winter coat, Emma sat beside him as often as she could. She talked and read to him. In the evening Ira took his turn. Each time he gave Boyd a few coins to save for new shoes when he was well. The fever finally subsided. He was allowed to get up but he could not walk; the sickness had been polio rather than pneumonia.

In the picture taken of Boyd after his illness and during the period there is a different look about him than before or after. There is an old look in a young face.

Years later when Boyd applied for flight training in the Air Corps, he reported on medical forms that he had had pneumonia. Had it been known that he had had polio, he would have been barred from military service. Actually, the disease was not accurately diagnosed until years later when Boyd suffered intense pain at night. He told his doctors of his bout with pneumonia and of having to learn to walk again. Total body x-rays then gave sure evidence of polio in the malformed bones of his knees and hip.

Boyd remembers the painful process of learning to walk again, crawling about on the floor, then pulling himself up to a chair.

After his illness he experienced fear that was new to him. It was something internal, apart from the security of home and family. Nightmares followed. He feels that these were partly due to the long illness and his struggle to walk again.

But there was more. A spiritually sensitive child, Boyd became vaguely aware of influences that existed beyond his safe family circle. Inner fear, then, became a reality to be reckoned with and eventually overcome. Fear finally left Boyd, but the feeling of inadequacy persisted.

During the summer after his illness Boyd walked with Doyle the four long blocks to the Brigham City Tabernacle for stake conference. It was Sunday, 29 June 1930.[2] Tired from his walk, Boyd sat with Doyle near the back under the balcony. When Elder George Albert Smith of the Quorum of the Twelve, the visiting authority, arose to speak, Boyd's attention became riveted. Later he would testify: "I have never forgotten him. . . . I don't remember what he said, but I remember how powerful was the witness that he was a man of God."[3]

Because of that early imprint upon his soul, Boyd Packer has a deep reverence for the capacity of a child to respond to the promptings of the Spirit.

Boyd as a first grader in the Central School in Brigham City

In September of that year, 1930, Boyd turned six and entered first grade at Central School, located across from the Brigham City Tabernacle. When the weather turned cold his mother provided him with a hand-me-down plush coat—a girl's coat. Sensitive about it, in fact abhorring it, he wore it and was embarrassed as only a child can be about such matters.

His report cards show that, overall, Boyd enjoyed school and did well.[4]

Boyd's teachers were Regena Jensen in first grade, Leola Seely in second, and Doril White in third. Because of Doyle's slow start and skin problem he was held back a year, and from then through high school he and Boyd were in the same grades. Their fourth-grade teacher was Leola Seely; their fifth, Miss Leona Cuthbert (who mixed up their names to come out "Doyd and Boyle"); and the principal, Mr. Frye, taught sixth grade.

Boyd liked geography, social studies, history, art. Phonics helped him to read and spell. He disliked mathematics, an aversion that continued throughout his military and university studies.

Report cards tallied times tardy, of which Boyd had none, and absences from school, of which he had from fifteen to twenty-eight per year—the result of contagious childhood diseases to which children were exposed.

Boyd scored well in deportment, but in early grades he seems to have had a short interest span. He admits to daydreaming and wishing to be out of doors. Records show that he was underweight for his age and height until the sixth grade.

At the end of each term Boyd's report cards were signed by "Mrs. Ira W. Packer." Doyle recalls that Emma always took an interest in her children's schoolwork, attended their school functions, and as a room mother made cookies and king-sized cakes for special events.

He also recalls that she initiated one of the first school-lunch

The old Central School in Brigham City, later destroyed by fire

programs for elementary grades. It began with small bottles of milk served with crackers, but it expanded to include a bowl of hot soup and a sandwich which she and other mothers made in their homes and delivered to school. Their efforts resulted in the building of a kitchen in the school basement. Thereafter, school lunches were prepared and served from there.

Emma also made sure that Church ordinances for the children were performed. Soon after his eighth birthday, on 1 October 1932, Boyd was baptized in the font at the Fifth Ward meetinghouse by Robert Francis Johnson, a priest. He was confirmed the same day by Elder Anthon M. Hansen.

About this time Boyd began drawing animals and birds. At first he drew them upside down—the feet and legs progressing down to body, neck, and head. As his powers of observation improved he drew his subjects right side up.

Boyd drew on newsprint, which Ira obtained free at the *Box Elder News*. He says that for the other Packer children "drawing was a disease to which they were exposed and of which they had mild cases, but with me it was a serious affliction."

Because of his natural aptitude and skill, Boyd's art helped to compensate for his lack of physical prowess and to give him more confidence among his fellows. Beyond this natural aptitude, other influences helped Boyd in his visual expression: keen powers of observation, an imaginative approach to play or work, simple materials and tools his parents provided, and their encouragement.

There was much to capture a child's imagination on the Packers' acre located at 627 South Main Street. The home faced west. Sidewalks were unpaved, and a ditch ran along the other side of the street. Their backyard ended at First East and was bordered by an irrigation ditch.

In the orchard to the east of the house there were pie-cherry, apricot, and peach trees. Scattered in large areas to the south of the home were Emma's cosmos, which grew taller than Boyd when he played there. The garden out back provided vegetables, with corn standing high in late summer and serving as a jungle for the children's safaris.

Along the board fence on the north separating the Packer and Glen properties were two rows of shasta daisies. A ditch ran between the rows, making a hiding place for childhood games. A gravel driveway extended from the street to the back of the house.

Packer home on South Main Street in Brigham City during Boyd's boyhood

Boyd remembers his mother's love for her flowers. In front were beds of black-eyed Susan, nasturtiums, petunias, larkspur, chrysanthemums, pinks, zinnias, pansies, bachelor's buttons. Emma's American Beauty rose bloomed to the left of the front porch, and a Talisman climber competed with Virginia creeper vines to reach the upstairs screened-in porch at the south corner of the house. Boyd liked to help his mother in the fall when Emma gathered the dried seeds and carefully marked them for replanting the next spring.

There was a sandbox at the back of the home, shaded by lilacs. The remodeled chassis of Ira's old Veelie automobile served for the children's playhouse. The attic of the wash-shed in the backyard became a hideaway for "cowboys and Indians."

During Boyd's childhood his playmates were his sister Donna and brothers Doyle and Billy. Donna remembers the small licorice babies purchased from the corner grocery. "We fashioned little wings for them and flew them around the lawn. We also made newspaper wings for ourselves and flew about in the pretend-stories we had made for the licorice babies."

Doyle too remembers their fascination with flying. He and his brothers made cardboard wings and were on their way to climb the billboards across the street for their trial flight when Emma intercepted them and, Doyle says, "probably saved our lives."

Donna recalls that on summer nights bats would fly about. Then the children would run after them singing, "Bat-bat, get out of my hat and we'll give you a slice of bacon; and when we bake, we'll make you a cake, if I am not mistaken." Also at night they would spread a quilt on the lawn and, sitting in the middle with their backs to the center, would draw up the four corners to cover them. There they studied the stars and the moon and saw nighthawks in the sky.

One of the older cherry trees had a limb which resembled a bicycle. Two branches came out of it like handlebars, and another two down below served as pedals. "With a little bouncing up and down," Donna says, "it almost seemed like we were riding. We all took our turns on that favorite limb."

All was not play for the Packer children, however, for each had his chores to do. But even in their work they devised ways to have fun. All took turns doing dishes in the free-standing sink with no draining board. And all helped to pick, peel, and can fruit in season.

One time their good spirits were dampened when the legs of the large kitchen table gave way and some fifty two-quart bottles of peaches shattered on the kitchen floor. Groans mingled with laughter as they counted the loss and then shoveled up the broken glass and cleaned the sticky linoleum.

Each boy teamed with a brother or two, chopping wood, cleaning the yard, irrigating, pulling weeds, picking vegetables and fruit, not only at home but also for neighbors.

One work experience was painful for Boyd. He and Doyle rode in the back of a truck to pick beans in Perry, Utah. When it was about to discharge its passengers Boyd jumped from the truck before it had completely stopped, injuring his weak hip. From then on he walked with a slight limp.

Ira gave the children coping saws and discarded glass-box boards from the garage. With these, their imaginations soared. They made guns from the boards, triggers from clothespins, and ammunition from rubber inner tube bands. Donna recalls: "We became cowboys and Indians. We shot at make-believe objects and at each other."

The boys spent hundreds of hours fashioning animals and birds with the coping saw. Boyd found he could carve his animals in bas relief and color them. To paint them he used dregs from paint cans a neighbor had discarded.

He recalls: "We played a lot with small wooden horses we made. And we created little farms, placed sticks in the ground, and ran strings through to make fences."

Boyd also experimented with a magnifying glass in sunlight to burn designs into his boards. One day the neighborhood bully, seeing him sitting on the lawn so occupied, demanded that Boyd give him the magnifying glass. When he refused, the boy knocked Boyd down and sat on him, holding the magnifying glass to the sun and focused on Boyd with the intent of burning him.

Hearing her brother's cries, Donna came around the house at a fast clip. Although younger and smaller than the bully, she tore into him with such fury that he let go and started to run. She chased him up the street, caught him on the Glens' front lawn, and gave him a sound thrashing.

Each spring the children looked forward to the sheep herds being driven from desert to mountain ranges. These passed half a block south of the Packer home in a noise-filled cloud of dust and were followed by barking dogs and by herders on horses. The excitement propelled Boyd and his brothers to chase after them. On one occasion Billy, the youngest, wandered off alone in the midst of the herd. A worried Ira rightly guessed where he had gone. It was one of the few times when Bill Packer remembers his father being angry. After rescuing him from the herd, Ira made sure that his son would never again leave without permission. Permission, however, was sometimes given for the boys to follow the herds to the foothills. At such times Emma packed a lunch for them and added her words of caution to be careful.

It was not only following the herds that drew Boyd to the hills. Bally Johnson's pond was a favorite place. Another pond, located on the Christopherson property, was surrounded by orchards. Fascinated by any living creature in this pond, Boyd found a giant water bug, small leopard frogs, tadpoles, and ducks. In the sage of the hillsides they saw rabbits and lizards, small desert swifts, and occasionally blue-tailed lizards that measured eight or ten inches long. These Boyd brought home and kept in a box covered with screen. His sisters sometimes complained about the "treasures" they found in his room.

His explorations in the hills once led him and a friend, Jimmy Potter, to danger. They climbed up the mountain to Slide Rock, an area which in ancient times had been cliffs but had since broken into large boulders. There they rolled rocks down the mountain. Tiring of this, they explored further and found an opening under one of the large rocks. Jimmy slid in and persuaded Boyd to join him. They found another opening below and, continuing, went deep under the large pile of boulders. Having a flashlight, they discovered a long-eared bat, which they caught.

Deciding that it was time to leave, they found that sliding into the cave was far easier than climbing out over the slick rock. Realizing that a shift in the rocks could crush them and that no one would be able to find them, they became frightened. With great care they helped each other up into daylight again.

In the Packer family, holidays were traditional events. For Easter they took picnics to Little Mountain, west of Corinne, or to Box Elder Canyon, where Emma and the children had stayed when her daughters were ill.

On Decoration Day they decorated family graves with flowers from Emma's garden or artificial flowers she and the girls had made. At these times Emma felt deep sorrow that her mother's grave was not there, because its location was not then known.

All of Brigham City celebrated the Fourth of July. The music of the band was stirring to a people whose lives were focused on home, church, and community.

Brigham City was a fruit-growing community, and its annual Peach Day parade was another event that drew the whole county. Residents exhibited handcrafts, artwork, and food items. Town dignitaries, as judges, gave prizes to winners. One year Boyd won a prize for his circus of carved wood animals.

Returning home from the town festivities, the Packers ate Emma's white cake topped with Opal's caramel icing and Ira's ice cream treat. To bake a perfect cake with no temperature gauge was an accomplishment. Emma tested the temperature by feeling inside the oven of the coal range with her hand. Opal hand-stirred the creamy frosting until it set.

Thanksgiving was a time to feel gratitude for home ties and for being together around a table set for family members and also for others who might be in need. The turkey or goose as well as other makings of the holiday feast were provided by Ira's customers in payment on their bills.

But Christmas was the crowning holiday of the year. Before the days of electric tree lights they placed small candles on the branches and watched so that the branches did not catch fire. Gifts, other than homemade, were usually provided by Verna. One of Boyd's most memorable presents from this Santa was a cast-iron circus wagon with a bear in it. Doyle's was its duplicate but held a tiger. Favorite Christmas treats included Emma's Danish jelly tarts, still a tradition in the homes of her children.

Whenever the Packer children performed in school or church Ira gave them a quarter and treated the family to ice cream.

The three youngest boys had parts in Central School's annual operetta *The Kitchen Clock*. Boyd was "Stew Kettle"; Billy, a "Dustpan"; and Doyle, a "Night Serenader." Doyle kept one of the programs. It is dated March 28, 1936. Upon seeing it for the first time in fifty-two years, Boyd immediately recited the lyrics of his song.

After Boyd and Doyle's sixth and final year at Central School their family met a time of change and challenge. To avoid the necessity of constant travel back and forth between home and garage for Ira and the boys, and to move his maturing children within blocks of their high school and town jobs, their father decided to remodel the upstairs floor of his garage building at 75 South Main Street into a large apartment. That floor had originally housed a wagon repair shop.

In place of its wide ramp that ascended from the backyard to the second floor, Ira built a narrower ramp which was to serve as the main approach to the apartment. Ira and his son Ron, a skilled carpenter and mechanic by that time, partitioned and finished eight rooms to accommodate the family, including Grandfather Packer. The front with its six arched windows became the living room.

The children watched the remodeling with mixed feelings. Gone would be the orchard, the garden, Emma's flowers, and their play areas. While the spirit of their home would remain the same, the uprooting would be painful. Each sensed in his own way that the move would begin a time of permanent change in all of their lives.

Chapter Five

As a Youth in Brigham City

William L. Packer says that consistency is one of his brother Boyd's most striking characteristics. "He hasn't changed a lot," Bill says, "except that after his service in the military he was more quiet than before and more devoted to the Church."[1] Bill's comment suggests that during Boyd K. Packer's childhood and youth he developed traits, interests, and skills upon which he simply continued to build.

One of these was his art. He created gifts for family members, many of which have been kept and treasured. Even his childhood sketches were collected by his sisters Verna and Donna.

When their friends Harold and Lillian Felt arrived at Brigham City in 1934 to establish a mortuary, Boyd's parents welcomed them into their family circle. Lillian describes the miniature farm and animals that teenage Boyd fashioned to amuse her children when he tended them one Christmastime.[2] If their make-believe world needed circus animals, he made them. For their jungle scenes he cut out birds from garage throwaway boards and painted them with residue from a sign painter's cans. Boyd's creative ability was possibly an extension of the Packer children's imaginative games. His brother Bill says,

"Boyd was always a character, a wit, and fun-loving, especially among those he knows well."

Despite the talents that gave him a measure of satisfaction, Boyd often felt inadequate. He was sensitive to things that set him apart from others. These same feelings plagued him in junior high school. His lack of physical strength resulting from polio kept him from participating in contact sports and made him dread gym.

Except for his feelings of inadequacy Boyd's memories of junior high are few. He remembers the school, four blocks east of the Packer apartment and garage. The junior high occupied three floors on the east end of the Box Elder High School building and used the old gymnasium in the basement. The high school had a new gymnasium and a football field across the street on the north. These were located where the old co-op tannery and hat factory had stood.

Boyd remembers that he liked science, but his A's were in English, geography, and art.[3] When Boyd began high school he made friends with Robert Baird, who was crippled from childhood polio and confined to a wheelchair. Later Robert learned to walk with crutches. At the time Boyd did not know that he too had had that crippling disease.

Robert raised pigeons, and Boyd determined to have some of his own. With his earnings from picking fruit and vegetables he began to purchase fantails and rollers, but only a few homing pigeons because their training cost money. At first he housed his birds in boxes. Later he built a coop for them out of old garage doors and wire screen.

"The pigeons became the center of my interest," he recalls, "and I think they were a great protection to me during those years. They kept me home a great deal more than otherwise I might have been." His civics class included a section on choosing a vocation. "I determined that I wanted to be an ornithologist and study birds all my life."

Boyd belonged to a pigeon club in Brigham City whose members offered their homing pigeons to help in the 1938 elections. The birds could bring returns from remote towns in Box Elder County that had no telephone service—Clear Creek, Stanrod, Kelton, Yost, Lynn, and Grouse Creek. For this project the boys fastened to the legs of the pigeons small capsules like those used by the military. Harold Felt

Boyd at age twelve with one of his pigeons

loaned his car for the transport of their birds over the four hundred miles involved in reaching the remote areas mentioned.

At the schoolhouse of each town where elections were held they left two pigeons—one bird as a backup in case the other should be killed by a hawk. Election officers wrote the returns on tissue paper, placed them in the capsules, and released the birds early the next morning. That election year, returns came in a full day earlier than in any preceding one.

For Boyd, pigeons also served as barter. He admired his brother Ron's ability as a hunter, and he longed for a .22 rifle. He remembered Ron's courage in saving his own life by shooting from his forearm a five-foot rattlesnake which bit him while he was fishing in the Blacksmith Fork Canyon in Cache Valley. Not having a knife, Ron had then shot through the flesh to cause bleeding and remove as much venom as possible until his friend found him, administered first aid, and brought him to Dr. Pearse in Brigham City.[4] Boyd was eight at the time.

So Boyd traded some of his pigeons for an old .22 rifle. Its sights were crooked and he had to compensate by aiming at somewhere else other than the target. "That way," he explains, "I was able to hit what I was not aiming at."

From their mother's example the Packer children developed the desire to beautify their surroundings. Bill tells how he and Boyd labored to satisfy their mother's longing for the green lawn and flowers of their former home. They grubbed and raked the hard-packed dirt behind the garage, planted lawn seed, and watched its green shoots come up. But the soil was so saturated with oil from old cars that the grass soon yellowed and died. Mother Emma shared their disappointment and contented herself with hanging baskets of geraniums across the wide back porch from which the entry ramp descended.

Two years before the Packers had moved to the apartment permanent changes had begun to take place which left deep impressions in family members. These set lifelong patterns in caring not only for their own but also for others.

Boyd was ten when Grandfather and Grandmother Packer came to the old home for Christmas dinner and stayed to visit and play table games before returning to their home. The next day, 26 December 1934, Boyd was alone with his mother, who was doing the laundry, when unexpectedly his father came in looking very serious. "Can you stand a shock?" he asked his wife.

Before he could go on, Emma said: "It's your mother. She is dead." His mother's spiritual perception and attunement made a lasting impression upon her son.

After the funeral, relatives crowded into the grandparents' small home. To lessen the congestion Emma sent Donna and her brothers Doyle, Boyd, and Billy home to stay until the company left. Donna remembers that cold December day. Their grandmother was dead and they were disappointed at having to leave the gathering. Donna bought canned soup for their meal, fired up the coal stove to take the chill off the kitchen, and did her best to cheer and amuse her brothers.

Back at the grandfather's home, serious discussions were held. Joseph Alma's health was poor and he could not live alone. Ron, the eldest son, who was planning soon to marry Hazel Olson, suggested a possible solution. He and Hazel could step up their wedding date, move in with the grandfather, and care for him until the apartment was finished, which would include a room for him.

Ron and Hazel cared for Joseph Alma in his home until the family moved into the apartment. Then he lived out the remaining years of his life with them, spending much of his time reading the scriptures. This example of caring for their own was thus set for the children to follow.

For Boyd the lesson was profound. One of his most frequent statements in recounting experiences or observations is, "From that I learned a great lesson."

Soon after their move to the apartment Boyd's sister Donna attended a genealogy class offered in the Mutual Improvement Association. She took Boyd with her. She was sixteen; he, thirteen. Both showed marked interest in the subject. Each began a book of remembrance and paid for small photographs of their ancestors to paste on their family charts. Grandmother Sarah's picture was one among the others. Their interest in family history has never dimmed.

When in 1937 Boyd began his freshman year at Box Elder High, he enrolled in seminary with his brother Doyle. Records show that they did not pay their seventy-five-cents-a-year fee in a lump sum, as did most of the students, but in five- and ten-cent installments.

The seminary for Box Elder High School was the second in the Church, that for Granite High being the first. The standard curriculum at Box Elder was the Old Testament, taught by Harold Nelson; the New Testament, by John P. Lillywhite; and Church History, by Abel S. Rich. No class in the Book of Mormon was then offered.

In seminary Boyd received his first real exposure to the scriptures. Because of the excellence of his teachers in presenting gospel subjects and the moral-spiritual values embodied in the scriptures, he has never forgotten them nor their teachings. From this beginning Boyd moved in a direction that would later determine his choice of a profession and eventually qualify him as a teacher of moral-spiritual values.

In his sophomore year of high school Boyd still struggled with his old feelings of inadequacy and was particularly vulnerable to thoughtless actions of his fellows. He remembers vividly an incident which could have redirected his life.

One Sunday morning he started for priesthood meeting dressed in his first suit, a pass-down from Leon to Lowell to him. Although it was a little large for him, he felt well dressed. He looked forward to meetings, especially to the hymns, which always drew him to church.

He entered the foyer of the First Ward, where other youths were gathered. A Church leader's son, who progressively had been in deacons, teachers, and priests quorum presidencies, greeted Boyd in words loud enough for all to hear: "Say, that's a fine suit you have on, Packer, but didn't they have one that would fit you?"

Stung by his words, Boyd turned quickly and left. Hurt, angry, and too stubborn to cry, he walked rapidly toward home, knowing as he went that he could not go in the house before meetings were over. He went to his pigeons for comfort. Over and over he relived his humiliation, vowing that he would *never, ever* go back to church again. He muses, "I can see myself having left the Church over that incident." Yet as vivid as the experience still is, he cannot recall what made him return.

Examining the influences about him during that period, it is not difficult to see how hurt and anger could be dispelled before they hardened into rancor. There was loyalty to mother and father. There were brothers and sisters, who suffered the same privations and embarrassments as he, yet helped each other through them. For instance, he remembers that his sister Donna had accepted an invitation to a formal dance, then came home in tears because she had no dress to wear—not just no dress that pleased her but *no* dress appropriate for the occasion. Then Verna, her creative gift heightened by love, fashioned from a bedspread a stylish dress that was admired at the dance.

So Boyd could not disappoint his family over a personal hurt. Besides, he needed to be an example for Billy. And the care of his birds occupied him, as did his drawing and making things with his hands.

His seminary teachers were another influence. Studying the New Testament under John P. Lillywhite, who was later to become Netherlands Mission president and subsequently stake patriarch, enlarged Boyd's understanding about dealing with provocation or persecution. Beyond these, Boyd had had an early witness of the Spirit that a visiting Apostle was truly a servant of the Lord Jesus Christ.

As Boyd began his junior year at high school he was more confident, wittier, and more fun-loving than he had been during those
more sensitive years. He inherited his quick wit and sense of humor
from his father.

Elder Malcolm Jeppsen tells about the triple date that he, Verl
Petersen, and Boyd had with high school girlfriends. They had taken
their dates home and were returning to the Packer garage to let Boyd
off. At the Brigham City Tabernacle they saw Carl Josephson parked
in his police car. As they passed him, Verl leaned out and gave a convincing imitation of a siren—a device that was illegal in a private
car.

"Sure enough," Elder Jeppsen says, "the police car whipped
around with its lights flashing and followed us to the garage, where
we stopped."

"All right, fellows," Officer Josephson said, "where's the siren?"

Boyd's cool answer was: "We just took her home."[5]

For some of their high school dates Boyd and Doyle used an old
Nash which their father had reluctantly purchased from a Japanese
man shortly before the attack on Pearl Harbor. The man had met
Ira's refusal with such persuasion and urgency that Ira had relented.
The boys called the car Shasta, because, they said, "Shasta be gassed;
Shasta be oiled; and Shasta be pushed."

During that year Boyd worked on Saturdays and after school as a
stock boy for J. C. Penney Company, a job Verna had helped him
obtain. Opal worked for Petersen Electric; Nona, for Compton's
Music and Photography; Ron, Lowell, and Doyle, for their father;
and Leon, for the Harold Felt Mortuary.

Verna, in particular, was sensitive to the dating needs of her
brothers and sisters. Boyd recalls that as he would leave home, she
might press a dollar in his hand to buy his date a treat. On another
occasion she fashioned a corsage from a garden iris so professionally
that Boyd was proud to present it.

While the younger boys were still in high school Leon joined the
air force, where he began flight training in April 1941. Harold Felt
then hired Boyd to take Leon's place at the mortuary.

Leon successfully completed his course and graduated at Sacramento's Mather Field on 12 December 1941. His parents drove to

California for the event. Boyd still remembers the Sunday afternoon of 7 December 1941, while his parents were gone. He was at a school-planning meeting when a student rushed in with the news of Japan's attack on Pearl Harbor.

"There was much rousing talk among the senior boys," Boyd recalls, "and it was our fear that the war would be over before we juniors had a chance to enlist and get into it. Perhaps we felt an exaggerated sense of patriotism, but little did we know the effect the war was to have on all of our lives."

After Leon's graduation he was given leave and came home for a short time. When he was ready to drive the old Plymouth back to Sacramento his parents suggested that Boyd go with him and then return by train. The brothers left in a snowstorm. Near Reno, Nevada, their car slid off the highway into a barrow pit. Leon hitched a ride back to town for a wrecker. Before he could return, a semi-truck stopped and pulled the car out with a tow chain.

Another tense moment came when, crossing Donner Pass in the Sierra Nevada mountains, they slid off the road into a heavy snowbank within feet of a steep canyon drop-off.

Sharing that trip with Leon, who now wore his pilot wings, created within Boyd a desire to follow his brother into the service. While the possibility of becoming a pilot seemed remote to Boyd, the desire to do so was strong.

He returned to school and to his work at the Felt Mortuary. As Leon had done, Boyd drove ambulance and hearse, did odd jobs, and tended the Felt children when Harold and Lillian were away from their upstairs apartment.

After Pearl Harbor there was much patriotic fervor at school. Boyd's yearbook, The 1942 Boomerang, reflects the tenor of the time. Six full-page color illustrations show the flag, the national capitol, the Statue of Liberty, an air force bomber, and so forth.

The war with Japan and Germany was gaining intensity and there was a serious note of unrest and anxiety, especially among the seniors. When the Brigham City National Guard left to join the armed forces, everyone gathered to see them off.

Boyd and his brother Doyle joined the Utah Home Guard, which had been reactivated by the Utah legislature on 22 September 1941.

They were issued uniforms and attended weekly drills and local maneuvers. Boyd spent part of a night with the local barber, Curly Burt, guarding the city water supply on Reservoir Hill east of Brigham City.

It was only a matter of time before the war would draw him and other family members and friends into military service. Even the limitation which had kept him from contact sports did not dampen his desire to enlist as a pilot cadet. "Although it might have been out of the question because of the stiff physical requirements," Boyd says, "my desire was to become a pilot like my brother Leon, and I could not let it go."

One night Boyd petitioned the Lord in the most fervent prayer of his young life. "I promised that if He would grant my desire to pass the physical examination and become an air cadet, I would do anything he wanted me to do for the rest of my life."

He continues: "That prayer was pivotal. There was no limit to the earnestness with which I prayed. It was an expression of beginning faith, and it was the beginning of developing some self-confidence."

In view of what would later follow it is noteworthy that among Box Elder High School's 1942 graduating class were Boyd K. Packer, who was to become a member of the Quorum of the Twelve Apostles; Dantzel White, the future wife of Russell M. Nelson, who likewise would become an Apostle; and Malcolm S. Jeppsen, who in 1989 would be called to the Second Quorum of the Seventy.

The war took on an even greater sense of urgency when Brigham City was chosen as the site for the army's Bushnell General Hospital.

Immediately after graduation Boyd went to work as a timekeeper for the plumbing-heating

*Boyd at the time of his
high school graduation*

contractor Lord and Loryea, from Portland, Oregon. Percy S. Lord was one of the owners of the company and the senior boss, but he was rarely seen on that project. His brother, George Lord, superintended the construction at the Brigham City site, and Boyd became a friend of his son, George, Jr. The office manager, Earl Everest, with whom Boyd enjoyed working, was his immediate boss.

Several times a day Boyd ran throughout the construction area to check with the plumbers. Mr. Everest called him Sea Biscuit after a famous racehorse.

One day in late summer Percy S. Lord came to the Bushnell site to see how things were going. Boyd had ridden his bicycle early to work and was staying late to handle extra details occasioned by Mr. Lord's visit. While he was thus engaged Mr. Lord came into the office and asked what he was doing there. Boyd told him that there was work he wanted to finish before going home. The man then asked how much he was being paid. Boyd told him.

The next morning Mr. Everest told Boyd that the boss had authorized a raise for him that nearly doubled his salary. Of this Boyd says, "From that experience I learned that the extra effort one puts into his responsibilities is an excellent investment, and it became quite an incentive to me."

His sister Donna also obtained work at the Bushnell operation, and the earnings of the brother and sister made it possible for them to help their parents financially. They paid for a new electric stove for Emma and purchased cases of canned goods against the time when food would be rationed.

Boyd finally applied for the air cadet program and, with two friends, went to Salt Lake City for the tests. A qualifying written exam was required before taking the physical. When his test was scored, Boyd was one point below the minimum for acceptance. His heart sank. The sergeant studied the test carefully. There were several two-part questions. He then said that they allowed for half of a two-part question. He found the two-part questions needed. One was, "What is ethylene glycol used for?" From working in his father's garage Boyd knew that it was used in automobiles as an antifreeze. He reflects, "Knowing that one thing made the difference on whether or not I was to become a pilot."

When one has examined the substantive aspects of Boyd Packer's childhood and youth, his brother Bill's assessment of him seems accurate. He has been consistent and has not changed a lot. Yet the assessment is incomplete; it does not take into account the growth that took place because Boyd learned early to tap the source of knowledge and power through fervent, faith-driven prayer. Thus the seeds of courage and calm were planted in his childhood and youth. As he had earlier learned to walk again, he would now learn to fly.

Chapter Six

Serving His Country

 In 1943 when Boyd K. Packer entered military service as a flight cadet, World War II's drain on the nation's manpower had caused the missionary program of The Church of Jesus Christ of Latter-day Saints to reach its lowest ebb since World War I. In 1941 there had been 1,257 missionaries called and set apart; in 1942, 629; and in 1943, there were only 261.[1]

Thus, like thousands of other young Latter-day Saint men of that time, the young Boyd Packer did not serve a mission for the Church. Had times been normal, however, he still may not have filled a mission, since the emphasis on doing so was not as great then as it became later. None of his brothers was called, and it would not have occurred to them to volunteer.

They did, however, volunteer to serve their country, which had been at war since Japan's attack on Pearl Harbor on 7 December 1941. His brothers Leon, Lowell, Doyle, and Bill all served in the military.[2] Only the eldest, Ronald, who had a family, stayed at home to help their father keep the family business going.

In addition the husbands of their sisters Opal, Nona, and Donna—Alfred Hansen Frye, John McLaren Funk, and Alfred

Stanley Swiss, respectively—served in the armed forces. And Verna, the eldest sister, met her future husband, Forrest Lester Beail, at Bushnell General Hospital, where he was stationed and where she served with the Red Cross.

Military service gave to Boyd and to them all many of the same opportunities for spiritual growth that missionaries have.

Boyd's desire to become a pilot like Leon grew with each of his brother's letters home, wherein he recounted his flight to England with the 93rd, the first bomber group to fly the Atlantic nonstop; the activation of the 96th Bomber Wing, to which he became director of operations; and his participation in dangerous low-level flights over the Ploesti oil fields in Romania, which supplied Germany's war machine.

During the course of the war Leon was to fly twenty-two combat missions and to be awarded ten decorations, including the Distinguished Flying Cross, the European-African-Middle East Campaign Medal with nine battle stars, and the Croix de Guerre with Palm from the French government. In time, Leon became a brigadier general.

Notwithstanding his great desire to follow in Leon's footsteps, Boyd's acceptance into the pilot cadet program came about perhaps by the slimmest margin on record, hanging on half a point in the written examination. As for his physical exam, he passed only because the requirements had been somewhat relaxed to meet the country's desperate need for pilots.

Only, that is, if his fervent prayer and promise as a high school senior are forgotten. But *he* does not forget. Rather he attributes both his acceptance and his subsequent successful performance as a pilot to that prayer and to his promise that if he was accepted he would serve the Lord in whatever capacity he might be asked to. During his military service he would be presented with all the challenges a missionary faces and more, including homesickness. For him it would be a forty-month preparation for that which was to come.

Boyd was to carry his home-longing with him to nine bases in the United States, to Hawaii, to the Philippines, to Ie Shima Island off Okinawa, and to Japan.

Like many who are called on missions, he left home with only a high school education and a belief—not a certainty—that the teachings of the Church were true. Seminary classes had given him an introduction to the Bible and to the history of the Church. Sunday School and occasional reading had provided him with an acquaintance with the Book of Mormon.

When he received his pocket-size servicemen's copy of the Book of Mormon he began a consistent search at every standing, waiting moment. His bold, colored markings show his study. He wore out its bent, water-soaked cover, then fitted and sewed another from the back of someone's discarded leather flight jacket.

Not only did his study feed his spirit but also, as he became acquainted with the accounts of ancient Book of Mormon generals waging defensive wars against brutal enemies, he came to understand the conditions under which war is justified of God. He read and marked: "Inasmuch as ye are not guilty of the first offense, neither the second, ye shall not suffer yourselves to be slain by the hands of your enemies. And again, the Lord has said: Ye shall defend your families even unto bloodshed. Therefore for this cause were the Nephites contending with the Lamanites, to defend themselves, and their families, and their lands, their country, and their rights, and their religion." (Alma 43:46–47.)

Boyd began his basic training at Camp Kearns, Utah, on 14 May 1943. It was his worst assignment. Because of his childhood polio he was not physically robust and was constantly afraid of being dropped from the program. During daily calisthenics he hid a painfully swollen knee. A fourteen-mile hike into the west mountains during July was hard, as was the daily chore of hauling stones from the practice field when each evening a tractor churned up the next day's allotment.

Boyd's miserable Camp Kearns experience was over in July 1943. From August to October he attended Washington State College at Pullman for intensive academic studies and crash courses in aircraft and naval-unit identification and in weather training. During that time each cadet was also given ten hours of introductory training in Piper aircraft with Franklin 65 engines—a method of screening out those who were considered unfit for *real* pilot training.

At the beginning of the program Boyd was assigned quarters in

As an air cadet

one large room of Stimpson Hall with seven other cadets. To Boyd they seemed a very intimidating group. All had attended or graduated from college. One, from a wealthy family in the East, casually mentioned the private schools he had attended and his family's summer vacations on the Continent. The father of another had been governor of Ohio and was then serving in the president's cabinet.

Each introduced himself. When it was Boyd's turn he told them: "I come from a little town in Utah that you have never heard of. I come from a family of eleven children. My father is a mechanic and runs a little garage." He added that his great-grandfather had come west with the pioneers.

"To my surprise and relief," he recalls, "I was accepted. My faith and my obscurity were not a penalty."[3]

Having been accepted by his peers at Washington State, Boyd now had to meet a far greater challenge—college mathematics. Now he must face competition from young men of greater academic background. Fortunately his teacher, a Dr. Schaefer, not only taught him what he needed to know but also strongly influenced his choice of a vocation.

Noting the difference in the academic backgrounds of his students, Dr. Schaefer indicated to begin with that the only stupid question was the question that wasn't asked when you needed information. He then said that for the beginners he would go patiently through the basics first. Because of his teacher's concern, Boyd mastered the needed material and passed the course with a grade among the highest in the class.

After completing their assignment at Washington State, his group was sent to Santa Ana, California—via Brigham City. It was a poignant moment for the homesick youth when his train stopped in his hometown about midnight. He remembers: "I hadn't been home for many months, and my parents didn't know we were just a few blocks away on the train. I remember seeing Carl Josephson, our city policeman, standing on the platform at the little station. I tried to get his attention, but he didn't see me, and our train rolled away."

During their three months in Santa Ana the cadets received intensive preflight training. Also during that period, having obtained a recommend from his home bishop, Boyd received his patriarchal blessing from the stake patriarch, J. Roland Sandstrom. It is dated 15 January 1944. Its blessings and promises were to sustain him throughout the remainder of his forty-month experience.

The blessing told him: "In the spirit world, you were valiant in the defense of truth and right. You made a free and willing decision to abide by the laws of eternal progress as outlined by our elder brother, the Lord Jesus Christ."

The blessing was prophetic: "The word of God shall speak through you as an authorized minister of the Gospel of Jesus Christ." Its promise of a worthy companion and "the blessing of fatherhood," wherein "you shall hold the esteem and honor of your wife and the love and affection of your children," gave him the assurance that his life would be preserved if he followed its counsel: "Always face toward the sunlight of truth so that the shadow of error, disbelief, doubt, and discouragement shall be cast behind you."

From Santa Ana, Boyd's unit was sent to Thunderbird Field No. 2 at Scottsdale, Arizona, for flight training. From February to April 1944 they flew old fabric-covered Stearman PT-19 trainers with open cockpits.

Boyd by a Stearman plane during basic pilot training at Thunderbird Field No. 2 in Arizona

Boyd remembers his first solo

flight from one of the auxiliary fields in the desert. Once he was actually aloft, he seriously wondered whether he could get the plane
safely back to the ground. Even more vividly he remembers the day a
classmate crashed and was killed. Immediately flight schedules were
intensified; this was war, and it was no time to let anyone get jittery.
That same afternoon the trainees were made to practice landings at
an auxiliary field. And at day's end Boyd was assigned to fly one of
the planes across the valley to the main field.

"Out of curiosity I decided to fly over the crash site," he recalls.
"It was plainly visible from the air. One could see the spot where the
plane had hit, burst into flames, and skidded across the desert floor,
burning the chaparral in a long sooty smear."

His curiosity satisfied, Boyd headed for the main base, and having been taught the maneuvers of stalls, loops, and spins, he put his
plane into a practice spin to lose altitude and enter the landing pattern.

Boyd continues: "In attempting a recovery from the spin, and
perhaps frightened by the thoughts of the accident, I was clumsy and
overcorrected. Instead of making a recovery, the plane shuddered
violently, stalled, and flipped into a secondary spin.

"Never have I known such panic. I found myself clawing at the
controls. I really don't know what happened. I think probably I let go
of the controls. . . . Finally the plane pulled out in a long sweeping
skid, just feet above the desert floor.

"I quickly recovered my composure and made a normal landing,
with the hope that no one had seen the circus performance!"

Unable to sleep that night, he confided to an LDS buddy, Louis
Merrill, what had happened and asked, "What did I do wrong?"

His friend told him that early in their flight training his instructor had warned his students against the singular danger of a secondary spin and had taken each student up and demonstrated how to
recover if it should happen.

Boyd felt intense resentment toward his instructor's negligence.
It had nearly cost his life. For the next few days he continued resent-
ful and angry. As a result he became extremely tense.

After a particularly bad flight one day, his instructor said:
"What's the matter with you, Packer? You're no good at this. Why

can't you loosen up? You keep this up and we're going to wash you right out of the program!"

"I was afraid to tell him what was the matter. And then he said: 'I have a special assignment for you this weekend. I want you to go into Phoenix and get good and drunk. You go get loosened up and relax, and maybe we can make a pilot of you.'"

Wanting those pilot wings more than anything on earth, Boyd saw them slipping from him. There was a great temptation to follow that advice. "We did go to Phoenix that weekend," he said, "but we sought the other kind of spirit in association with brethren in the priesthood and with members of the Church in worship service. There came an inspiration and a restoration of confidence. There came an assurance that has sustained me ever since."4

Boyd's unit left Thunderbird No. 2 for Marana, Arizona, for basic flight training in BT-15 Vibrator planes. During April, May, and June of 1944 he logged hours on the flight line. And while he waited his turns he read and marked his Book of Mormon or made pen-and-ink sketches on envelopes for his letters home. Week by week he drew nearer his goal—*wings*. One more three-month assignment and they would be his.

Illustrations on envelopes of letters he sent home from military service

That assignment was to Marfa, Texas, for advanced pilot training in UC-78 aircraft from July to September 1944. Boyd's sister Verna kept his letters from Marfa with their illustrated envelopes. When she gave them to him shortly before she died in 1969 she commented that the letters were brief. He told her that his drawings had used up most of his writing time.

On 8 September 1944 Boyd graduated from advanced pilot school and received his wings plus his first furlough home in fourteen months.

Boyd's arrival home on the eve of his twentieth birthday was reported in the *Box Elder News Journal* of 12 September 1944. About the same time the paper also printed a letter from Ira Packer to Editor Bill Long urging people to buy more war bonds. Few parents had a more profound reason to plead for patriotic support than Emma and Ira Packer, who had five sons and four sons-in-law serving in the military.

While in Brigham City, Boyd attended Peach Days and visited with high school friends—Malcolm Jeppsen, on leave from his navy medical training, and Verl Petersen, also on leave after graduating from advanced pilot training.

After his furlough Boyd was assigned to fly larger aircraft at Yuma, Arizona. And his next assignment was to a B-24 crew as co-pilot for training at Murock Army Air Base in California's Mojave Desert near Murock Dry Lake, the most desolate part of the state.

At Murock he became friends with an enlisted crew member, Leonard T. Saltysiak, a devout Catholic, with whom he spent much time and upon whom he would have a lasting influence. Saltysiak was the armor gunner, whose job was to care for the guns and bomb racks in the upper tier in the B-24, a four-engine, heavy bombardment plane of the Eighth Air Force.

Saltysiak was very impressed with the way Boyd handled himself, observing that instead of going with the other men for their beers he would be reading his Book of Mormon and marking it with different-colored pencils. He noted that Boyd always had a joke or a quip, and he seemed to be at peace.

As a practicing Roman Catholic, Saltysiak believed in Jesus and his redemption, so he and Boyd discussed religion, faith, and family.

On one occasion when Saltysiak was worried about life and the future, Boyd counseled him from the scripture, "But seek ye first the kingdom of God, and his righteousness; and all these things shall be added unto you" (Matthew 6:33). Boyd's elaboration on this principle meant much to the young man at the time.

Now an optometrist and the father of seven children, Dr. Saltysiak says that of all the people he has ever met Boyd Packer is one of the most remarkable and memorable. He had influenced the doctor's thinking about the importance of family and of integrity more than any other person.[5]

At Murock Field bomber groups were being trained for combat duty overseas. A points system was in effect that would indicate the top three bomber crews. Boyd's crew placed second, and with the other top two was not sent overseas just then but was reassigned to Langley Field, Virginia, to train in radar, a new, top secret innovation. They practiced over Chesapeake Bay and became so accurate that they could hit oil drums anchored in the ocean.

These crews were called "snooper crews," flying B-24 bombers that were painted black and with their bomb sights and navigation equipment operated by radar. In the course of their training they flew a nighttime target-finding mission over Montreal, Boston, New York, and points in between. This assignment gave Boyd his first view of the New England area.

While at Langley Field Boyd visited his brother Leon, then a colonel, who had been transferred from the European theater of the war to serve at the Pentagon on General Hap Arnold's staff. Boyd, on the other hand, was expecting soon to go overseas and into the thick of battle. He recalls: "We talked of courage and of fear. I asked how he had held himself together in the face of all that he had endured."

Leon replied: "I have a favorite hymn, 'Come, Come, Ye Saints,' and when things were desperate, when there was little hope that we would return, I would keep that on my mind and it was as though the engines of the aircraft would sing back to me."

"From this he clung to faith," Boyd says, "the one essential ingredient to courage."[6]

At Langley Field Boyd continued his advanced training, receiving his diploma on 23 June 1945. Primed for overseas duty, his crew posed for a picture.

Because of heavy demands upon U.S. wartime transportation, their unit was loaded into box cars. These had been fitted with narrow cots folded four or five deep against both sides of the car—actually, just bedsprings upon which to place their bedrolls. Another car with a dirt floor served as a camp kitchen where food was actually prepared over open fires.

Lt. Packer with his B-24 bomber crew

The group left the East Coast for California in July. On the first day out their car was separated from the luggage cars that carried their equipment, duffel bags, and changes of clothing. Thus for six days and nights they rode that crowded train through the hot southern route of Oklahoma, Texas, and Arizona without baths or changes of clothing. And to make them even more grimy the cinders from the engine blew into the cars, doors being left open for what air might be stirred up for breathing.

Arriving in Los Angeles the ten men bore small resemblance to a sharp bomber crew. Even before baths, however, they needed a good meal. Locating a fine restaurant, they pooled their money for a full dinner each. As they waited in line, a smartly dressed woman standing immediately in front of Boyd glanced back at him, lifted her nose, and made a cutting remark about their appearance loud enough for all to hear.

Boyd felt the grime, sweat, and dirt of that trip keenly; and though the crew had good reason for looking as they did, the thoughtless taunt embarrassed him. He wanted to be physically clean; but more than that, and at the deepest level of his soul, he determined always to be spiritually clean.

Boyd's crew was sent next, via San Luis Obispo, to Seattle, where they boarded a ship headed into the Pacific by night. He remembers lying on his bunk among the many men, reading his Book of Mormon. Many passages held special meaning for him.

In 1 Nephi 15:11 he read the promise: "If ye will not harden your hearts, and ask me in faith, believing that ye shall receive, with diligence in keeping my commandments, surely these things shall be made known unto you." When he reached the final promise in Moroni 10:4–5 he blocked it in solid red: "And when ye shall receive these things, I would exhort you that ye would ask God, the Eternal Father, in the name of Christ, if these things are not true; and if ye shall ask with a sincere heart, with real intent, having faith in Christ, he will manifest the truth of it unto you, by the power of the Holy Ghost. And by the power of the Holy Ghost ye may know the truth of all things."

Now on a crowded ship that was taking a horde of men into battle, he explained to the Lord that he wanted to know whether the Book of Mormon was or was not true. "I must know for sure that it is," he fervently prayed, "for if it is not true, then I'm not sure that it is important whether or not I come back, because things in the world seem to be all undone anyway." And so he continued to plead for an answer—an answer that seemed slow in coming.

Trained as part of the invasion forces against Japan, the men were first taken to Hawaii and billeted for several weeks in quarters at Barking Sands on Kauai, where they practiced ditching operations offshore. During free time Boyd swam, walked, and talked with his friend Leonard Saltysiak.

While stationed on Kauai, Boyd managed to go by military transport to Oahu, then hitchhiked to see the temple in Laie. While on Oahu that night he stayed at the LDS servicemen's home, Malamakoa, in Honolulu. Wandering about alone, he entered a small Chinese souvenir shop to buy a carved box for his sister Verna. Suddenly a man rushed in, gesturing, speaking in Chinese. The proprietor of the shop started shouting and pushed Boyd and the other customers out into the street, where pandemonium had broken loose. The screaming crowd were shouting that Japan had surrendered. It was 2 September 1945.

Boyd's first reaction was the overwhelming thought: "It's all over. We can go home."

That, however, was not yet to be, for his crew was to be part of the occupation forces in Japan. A few days later they boarded a ship, which set sail for the Philippines. In addition to those normally accommodated aboard there were six hundred men sleeping on deck in bedrolls. The vessel followed a zigzag course for wartime safety. Far out at sea it caught fire, and although the blaze was soon put out, Boyd remembers the fear the men felt. Finally landing on Leyte they stayed for six weeks.

During the long months of intensive training to become a good pilot, Boyd had fed his spiritual hunger with daily study and prayer. He had kept himself clean. And he had used every opportunity to join with other members of the Church to partake the sacrament and participate in services. Occasionally that participation was difficult, as when he and the other two Church members in camp had no private place to meet except a small clearing in the jungle, some distance away from camp, where a deep pit had been dug and left open with a heavy plank placed across it. On this plank the three men sat, prayed, prepared the sacrament from their C rations, partook, and then read to each other from the Book of Mormon.

Leaving Leyte, their group went first to Manila and then to Ie Shima Island off the coast of Okinawa. Ie Shima was to be Boyd's mount in the wilderness. His personal preparation and meeting with other members had deepened his belief in gospel teachings. What he yet lacked was confirmation—*sure* knowledge of that which he had already come to *feel* was true.

Counter to the peace of confirmation he sought, he came face to face with the hell of war against the innocent. Seeking solitude and time to think, he climbed, one day, to a rise above the ocean. There he found the gutted remains of a peasant cottage, its neglected sweet potato field nearby. And lying amid the dying plants he saw the corpses of a slaughtered mother and her two children. The sight filled him with a deep sadness mingled with the feelings of love for his own family and for all families.

Those emotions again tugged at him as he came at low tide to the rocky base of a thirty-foot cliff along the north shore of the island. There among the rocks, and floating in the shallow water about them, were parts of human bodies, washed from a landing craft—more innocents wasted in the senseless hell of war.

On 6 October 1945, while awaiting orders and arrangements for transportation to Japan, Boyd and a few others went to Nara, south of Okinawa, for a conference of LDS servicemen. Late that evening they returned to the north end of Okinawa, expecting to take a boat back to their island. They learned, however, that all ships had been ordered to port because a hurricane was approaching. Boyd and his companions finally persuaded the commander of a PT boat to take them back to Ie Shima.

All bombers and other aircraft had been ordered to Saipan, Guam, or other islands that were out of the path of the storm. Finally landing, Boyd and his companions took shelter on the forty-foot coral cliff in tents that were fastened to it with every piece of metal they could find.

All that night and all day Monday the wind blew fiercely against the tents. Rain poured through the roofs and walls in a torrent. Waves from the sea ascended the cliff to within feet of them. On Tuesday the eye of the hurricane passed over and calm returned for a short time, then it hit again. The storm's power had destroyed every building on the island save the hospital. The mess hall, built of eight-by-eight timbers set in concrete, was shorn off and blown away. Ships at sea were lost and many in port were wrecked and washed ashore.

Cold and wet, shaken and sober, Boyd and his companions were safe. He and a few others held study classes, and on Sunday they held a simple sacrament service. "It was then," he says, "that the Book of Mormon became a part of my very soul."

One night, soon after this, he could not sleep. He was unsettled in spirit. "I thought that I had no testimony to anchor me," he recalls. "I desperately wanted to know. I struggled with doubt and uncertainty. I wanted a testimony."

During the night I left my bed and went some distance to a secluded area where a makeshift bunker had been built. It was constructed of fifty-gallon fuel barrels filled with sand. There was a second row upon the first for the wall. Sand had been pushed up on all sides to the height of the top barrels. One lower barrel at the end was left out to allow a low opening into the bunker, which was perhaps six by eight feet in size. There was no roof.

It was a clear night. After some moments I determined to ask; to really ask for some consolation, some indication to strengthen me. I wanted a testimony. I had studied the scriptures; we had tried to teach one another. I had tried to perfect myself according to the meager knowledge I had. I felt a compelling inward need for some spiritual consolation.

Then I knelt to pray. Almost mid-sentence it happened. I could not describe to you what happened if I were determined to do so—and I am not! It was, as Brother McConkie often said, "beyond my power of expression." I knew it to be a very private, a very individual, manifestation. At last I knew! I knew! I knew for a certainty! I was still unlettered in scriptural studies and all else, but I knew! That which is most worth knowing I knew, for it had been given to me.

After some time I crawled from that bunker under a sky of brilliant stars. I walked, or floated, back to my bed and spent the rest of the night in a feeling of joy and awe.

I did not accept it as a commission or a setting apart. It was a testimony, a witness, *the* witness. From that time to this, my challenge has not been with obedience, nor with resolution or diligence; it has been with restraint! The challenge has been to temper myself and bridle my impulsive Danish personality. It has been to keep sacred and keep private that which each of us must learn for one's own self. Such an experience is at once a light to follow and a burden to carry.[7]

On another night, still waiting for orders that would take them to Japan, Boyd sat alone on that same cliff pondering long about what he should do with his life should he survive his tour of duty with the occupation forces in Japan. The moon was full and his thoughts turned to home and family, presumably safe under the same moon.

Thus pondering the words he had so boldly marked in Jacob 1:19 about the responsibility of "teaching . . . the word of God with all diligence . . . by laboring with our might," Boyd determined to become a teacher. It was the same kind of determination that had led him against many odds to become a pilot. In so choosing, he knew it meant turning aside from other things that he might do or might have, including high monetary rewards. It did not matter. He would pay whatever price his choice would require. That choice, made so far from home, became a milestone of immense consequence.

Waiting for their flight to Japan, his unit was caught in limbo. They were ready to go, but unsent. Boyd rebelled against living out of duffel bags, never unpacking, never knowing how long he would be in that place, living from hour to hour and day to day, waiting, waiting for the next assignment. Finally he decided: "This isn't the way it is going to be. So I unpacked and arranged everything around the thin old mattress I'd picked up somewhere and settled in as though we were going to be there a long time. I adopted that as a practice."

When the move came it was made by plane with his bomber crew to Atsugi Airfield, Yokohama. There, armed with his new resolve, he immediately unpacked and settled down in the barracks as if "for the duration." This practice for the rest of his service career and then in civilian life made the difference between misery and happiness and has contributed to his and his family's feeling of stability ever since.

In Japan, as in other assignments, there were within reach the undesirable aspects of military life—smoking, drinking, immorality, and profane language—which Boyd learned to shut out by running through his mind the words to hymns and by associating with other LDS men who were also determined to live the gospel.

They often held meetings on weekday evenings, for flight duties were not cancelled on Sundays. Groups usually were small, often numbering only two or three. The men came to believe the scripture "Where two or three are gathered together in my name, there am I in the midst of them" (Matthew 18:20).

The influence of these men upon Boyd was profound. An occasional returned missionary provided invaluable help to the less experienced ones. Though they were without lesson manuals and supplementary literature, the small servicemen's *Principles of the Gospel* with its instructions, hymns, and explanations of gospel principles provided further instruction.

As Boyd moved from base to base, the personalities changed but the influence did not. Because they studied together, many servicemen must be credited with helping him to prepare for what would come later in his life. He admits, however: "I am not a good veteran. My mind and direction are ever moving forward and not back. While these associations were important, even crucial for their time, they were passing ones, and few contacts have continued over the years."

LDS meetings were held in Tokyo in the Meiji Building across from the palace, spared when most of Tokyo was destroyed. He now knew what was most precious to him—that God and His Son Jesus Christ lived, that Joseph Smith was their prophet, and that the Book of Mormon was true. His testimony is handwritten in his military record book in English; in Japanese, written in Roman letters; and, with help, in Japanese Kanji-character writing.

Boyd pondered the immense gift of a sure witness. He deeply wished to give something in return. He desired to become a true disciple of the Savior and to please God the Eternal Father. Not certain how this should be done, he reasoned that *disciple* involved self-discipline. That brought him face to face with a profound test. Of most value to man is his agency. How much of it was he, Boyd Packer, willing to yield? How much was he capable of giving away?

"It had become critically important," he said, "to establish this intention between me and the Lord so that I knew that He knew which way I had committed my agency. I went before Him and said, 'I'm not neutral, and you can do with me what you want. If you need my vote, it's there. I don't care what you do with me and you don't have to take anything from me because I give it to you—everything, all I own, all I am.' And that makes the difference."[8]

Boyd flew an overnight mission in December to Chitose Air Base, near Sapporo, on Hokkaido Island. While he and his crew were there, snow began to fall, and it did not stop for eight days and eight nights. The men were snowbound from the storm, the length and intensity of which actually swallowed up Christmas. Cold and uncomfortable, with no communication from loved ones, they spent the holiday in a white world, with only a small stray dog to lighten their spirits.

Many years later, when he compiled his military record book, he wrote on the back of a snapshot of himself with the little dog: "2nd

Lt. Boyd K. Packer, age 21, Chitose Air Base, Hokkaido Island Japan, Dec. 1945. No wife, no degrees, no 10 children, no Apostle, but a missionary nevertheless."

In early spring of 1946 Boyd and a fellow pilot, Ted Lysak, were given a week's rest leave at the beautiful Nikko Kanko Hotel on Lake Tyuzenzi in Nikko National Park on Honshu Island. This was Boyd's first leave since returning to Brigham City after earning his wings.

On duty again and now stationed in Tokyo, Boyd was assigned with his crew to take a B-17 bomber to Saipan Island and

On leave at the Nikko Kanko Hotel

then on to Guam to pick up a much-needed beacon light for the base. Postwar flight-safety procedures not yet being established, the crew was not aware that just as they left Tokyo heading south a typhoon of major proportions was forming out in the central Pacific. This made islands difficult to see from the air, since shadows of clouds could look like islands and islands like clouds.

After a time the navigator said, "If we're on course, we should be over Iwo Jima," and he began countdown to zero, the signal to tip the plane for a visual sighting. They were right on course at that point.

Boyd remembers: "Finally, after several hours, the navigator said: 'Something is wrong. We're off course.' We dropped down through the cloud cover. There were terrible winds. The ocean was white with waves. He said, 'I don't know where we are.' Then, the radios went out!"

Lost, they began to fly a square-search pattern so that they would cover new territory each time and not fly in circles. They flew a long course on the compass.

At one point the other pilot said, "Let's turn." But for some reason Boyd said, "Hold it just a minute."

They were just a few thousand feet above the water. Then they could see a long line of white waves washing over rocks sticking out of the ocean. Nearby was an island. With no idea whether they were over the rocks south or north of it they made a prayerful turn and in about five minutes could hear voices on the short-range radio. They were over Tinian Island, which had an airfield. As they landed the B-17 and taxied down the runway the engines sputtered one by one and then stopped. Their last fuel had been used up on the runway.

"During the last hour of that flight, when I sat there wondering if we would or wouldn't make it, my patriarchal blessing kept coming to my mind. It said, 'You will be warned of danger, and if you heed those warnings you will be privileged to return to your loved ones.'"

Boyd's last assignment was as operations officer for a search and rescue unit at Itami Air Base, near Osaka.

> Just when I was scheduled to go home, my commanding officer called me in and told me we were opening a new flight at Osaka and that I was to be the operations officer. Well, I expressed myself to him. . . . I think I'll even admit I used a few scriptural terms out of context. He listened very patiently, and when it was all over with he said, "Well, that's all right, Packer; you're still going." And so it was.
>
> That afternoon, on a C-47, with all my gear and the others who'd been assigned, I sat bitterly grumbling over the fact that it would take months, it wouldn't be just an assignment of a week or two. Then I pled with the Lord, saying, "Why is it?" I had never wanted anything so much as I wanted to be home. I'd prayed for it, I'd tried to earn it, I'd tried to deserve it, I'd tried to behave myself, and then, when it was within my grasp, the very thing I wanted most was denied me.
>
> Somehow, I don't remember how, I took hold of myself; but looking back now, I can say the Lord was answering my prayers then. There came from that experience, from things that happened in those few months, lessons essential to the preparation for the calling that is now mine. I couldn't see that far ahead, but by those tests or trials that we receive, ofttimes the Lord will prepare us for what He has in mind.[9]

As he filled new flight assignments he became acquainted with an educated Japanese gentleman, Tatsui Sato, a Christian, who had been taught the gospel by Ray Hanks and C. Elliott Richards. Both Tatsui and his wife, Chio, knew that what these men had taught them was true, and shortly after Boyd's arrival in Osaka they accepted

*Tatsui Sato, Chio, and son Yasuo on the day of their
baptism, with Boyd, Norton D. Nixon, and
C. Elliot Richards in Osaka*

the challenge to be baptized. A spirit of kinship immediately existed
between Boyd and this man's family. Boyd felt the potential of Tatsui
in service to the Church. The Satos' young son, Yasuo, told his father
that Boyd would some day be a great man in the Church.

The Satos' baptisms—the first in Japan since 1924, when the
Japanese mission was closed—took place 7 July 1946, after the morning session of conference. About 150 LDS servicemen and a few
Japanese people came fasting to the meeting. At its close they went
out from the city of Osaka to Kansagakwin University, which had
been largely destroyed by bombs. There stood what was left of a
once-beautiful swimming pool and enough bathhouses intact for the
participants to change into white clothing.

After a poolside service Elliott Richards baptized Tatsui and Boyd
baptized Chio. From that time the Satos always called Elliott and
Boyd their sons.

Tatsui Sato, that choice convert to the Church, was later to
retranslate the Book of Mormon into Japanese and to translate into

The baptism of Chio Sato at Osaka

that language other standard works, several books on Church doctrine and history, numerous tracts, pamphlets, and manuals, and the temple ceremonies for the Hawaiian Temple. He also served as President Harold B. Lee's interpreter on his visit to Japan.

It is not common for Japanese people to display emotion at funerals, weddings, or other touching times in their lives, but when Boyd left Osaka to board a train to Yokohama for his long boat journey home the Satos mingled their tears with his. He recalls: "We had learned to love them, and they, us, officers of a conquering army. We were taught a remarkable lesson among the Japanese people. After all our training and instructions to demean them, to subdue them, we found that they were a good people and as individuals they were worthy of the gospel. They were seeking light, and even in their terrible circumstances they had many virtues that we might emulate."

Their terrible circumstances were evident to Boyd on many occasions. One was while he was stationed near Osaka. He and other crew members went one day to the waterfront in Kobe Bay to look for a suitable dock for the boat of their air-sea rescue squadron. Kobe Bay itself looked something like a burned-over forest, with the masts of sunken ships sticking above the shallow water of the bay. "Virtually everything had been destroyed," he recalls.

> The road went around a fairly sizable tidal basin that at low tide was only about waist deep at the deepest part. We noticed a number of Japanese women and children wading in the water. Oil from the sunken vessels was captured in this tidal basin at low tide. It was very cold. We stopped to see what they were doing and found that they were gathering the thick oil scum as it washed onto the shore line. They were molding

it into small balls, squeezing the water out of it, and putting it on boards to dry in the sun. Obviously it was for fuel against the cold winter that was coming.

As I looked at them, soaked and filthy with oil, cold and underfed, a scripture came to my mind: "Inasmuch as ye have done it unto one of the least of these my brethren, ye have done it unto me" (Matthew 25:40). I thought, "Surely, these are the least of all of those spoken of in that scripture."

Another sad incident happened on Boyd's train journey to Yokohama. The station, or what had been left of it, was cold. Starving children were sleeping in the corners, the fortunate ones with a newspaper or old rags to cover them.

Boyd had undressed for the night and was sleeping fitfully in a bunk that was too short for him when, in the bleak dawn, the train made a brief stop at a station. Aroused by an insistent tapping on the window, he raised the blind to see a small boy of six or so dressed only in a ragged shirt-like kimono. He was emaciated from hunger, his head scaly, his jaw swollen and a dirty rag binding it. He held a beggar's cup out to Boyd.

> When I saw him, and he saw that I was awake, he waved his can. He was begging. In pity, I thought, "How can I help him?" Then I remembered. I had money, Japanese money. I quickly groped for my clothing and found some yen notes in my pocket. I tried to open the window. But it was stuck. I slipped on my trousers and hurried to the end of the car. He stood outside expectantly. As I pushed at the resistant door, the train pulled away from the station. Through the dirty windows I could see him, holding that rusty tin can, with the dirty rag around his swollen jaw.
>
> There I stood, an officer from a conquering army, heading home to a family and a future. There I stood, half-dressed, clutching some money which he had seen but which I could not get to him. I wanted to help him, but couldn't. The only comfort I draw is that I did want to help him.
>
> That was thirty-eight years ago, but I can see him as clearly as if it were yesterday.
>
> Perhaps I was scarred by that experience. If so, it is a battle scar, a worthy one, for which I bear no shame. It reminds me of my duty.[10]

Boyd went aboard ship with other servicemen for the long voyage to Seattle and his mustering out at Fort Lewis. En route he thought of Verna, the sister who had been so good to him since babyhood. He dreamed about her, a dream fraught with darkness. He determined to visit her in Portland, just a bus ride away.

He found her very ill from crippling arthritis. She asked for a blessing, and in faith Boyd and her bishop blessed her. Soon after, her doctor discovered that she had a large tumor they had not known was there. Surgery was performed and her health improved.

Again going home! This time to Brigham City, to his parents, and to a changed and expanding family. They were changed as years and new experiences change people, but unchanged in the love and loyalty that had always bound them.

In this beloved climate of home, a new desire was born. Unashamedly, he determined to be good—a good son to his Father in Heaven as he had tried to be a good son to his parents. Beyond this, he desired to claim the promises in his patriarchal blessing and, in the near future, find an eternal companion to whom he would be a good husband; and he would be a good father to their children as they came. To this end, and with this deep desire, he began a new chapter in his life.

Chapter Seven

Courtship and Marriage

Boyd Packer's return home from Japan to Brigham City required a period of adjustment. The comparative plenty about him and the abject misery within the conquered country he had recently left caused him distress. He was still haunted by the sight of starving children sleeping on the streets at night or huddled in alcoves with damp newspapers drawn about their soiled, emaciated bodies against the cold. He remembered still the stench of death.

To sleep in clean sheets under his father's roof, to sit at his mother's table for a home-cooked meal, to be with brothers and sisters—these were blessings made poignant by the contrast of the Japan experience.

When he had left home four years before, Ronald, Opal, Nona, and Lowell were married. During his absence Verna, Leon, and Doyle also had found their companions. Now only Boyd, Bill, and Donna remained at home, and in October of that year (1946) Donna would marry Alfred Swiss. Each of the children had married, or would marry, after the Packer tradition, choosing companions not from backgrounds of wealth or prominence but from homes with strong family ties, with deep roots in Christian principles, and with firm adherence to integrity and the work ethic.

Boyd was now free to spend time out of doors, to hunt and fish and hike. He learned some taxidermy in order to preserve some birds for study for his paintings.

And also Boyd looked ahead. Having committed himself to become a teacher, he must obtain an education. Again, following the lead of his brother Leon, a former student body officer at Weber College in Ogden, Boyd entered that school. He lived at home and, not having a car, rode to school each morning with a neighbor who worked in Ogden. After classes he caught a bus to North Ogden and then hitched a ride home to work at his father's garage during the afternoon. Not being mechanically inclined as were his brothers, he kept the books and tended the gas pumps up front.

Since most of his and his brothers' military allotments had been sent home to help remodel his father's garage and establish his Chrysler dealership, Boyd's savings were meager. But along with other returning servicemen he received funds under the G.I. Bill of Rights that paid for tuition, books, and a small subsistence allowance. He bought a few civilian clothes while making use of his officer's gabardine slacks and their matching shirts, from which he removed the epaulets.

To his satisfaction he found that his military discipline, his consistent study habits, and his fixed purpose to become a teacher gave him an edge in his classes. From the beginning he did very well.

He also began to date with the intent of finding an eternal companion. Entertainments were simple: hikes and outings, school and Church dances, ice cream treats, sacrament meetings (then held in the evenings), reading, and discussions.

That fall Boyd attended the annual Peach Days Ball with a girl from his ward whom he had dated before his military experience and during his leaves at home. As was the case with him, she was dating others, and they soon found themselves drifting from rather than toward one another. It was at the ball that he heard the name of the new Brigham City Peach Queen announced—Donna Edith Smith—and saw her crowned. Boyd then remembered having seen her walking along the north side of Forest Street to junior high as he walked the south side to high school. He had noted how very pretty she was.

Despite her shyness, Donna had been persuaded to enter the queen's competition. After that competition the Brigham City Corporation and others pressed her to enter the Miss Utah contest. Bending to their wishes, she agreed. In this competition, held at the Utah State Fairgrounds in Salt Lake City, she became one of the ten finalists. Of the experience she says: "As I walked across the stage the thought came that there were other things ahead for me that were far more important than becoming Miss Utah. I count that

*Donna Edith Smith,
Brigham City Peach Queen*

evening's prompting concerning the purpose of my life as one of my early spiritual experiences."

About that time Boyd was working up front in the garage one afternoon when Bishop Lewis S. Wight of the Third Ward, a distant cousin, a fruit grower and dairy farmer, came to get gas in exchange for the milk he regularly delivered to the Packer apartment upstairs. He asked Boyd to speak at a Sunday evening sacrament service at the old Third Ward chapel with its stained glass window of the First Vision. Donna was in attendance. Her father, William W. Smith, served as counselor to Bishop White. Her grandfather Rasmus Julius Smith and his family had worshipped here.

When Boyd was introduced and came to the pulpit he was prompted to speak on obedience. He then urged Church members to willingly respond to calls that came to them. Donna Smith, who was dating several young men, one rather seriously, listened intently to Boyd Packer. She thought, "Now, this is the type of man I would wish to marry."

After the meeting the bishop told Donna he had a calling for her. Inspired by the message of Boyd's talk, she said yes.

The next day Boyd walked to the circulation desk at the school library and found Donna working there. It was the first time they had spoken. Her opening words gave him a start: "You have caused me a very serious problem."

"How is that?" he asked.

"Following sacrament meeting last evening, Bishop White called me to teach Junior Sunday School, and after your counsel about accepting calls, how could I refuse? You are responsible for my having to go home every weekend now."

Her words pleased Boyd. He began arranging for Donna's rides to Brigham City each weekend.

On their first date they went to a dance at Harper Ward, a one-room stone chapel north of Brigham City. It served as meetinghouse and, with benches placed against the walls, as recreation hall.

A later date held elements of frustration, especially for Boyd. Donna was an attendant to the county queen for the Days of '47 celebration sponsored by the Daughters of Utah Pioneers. The county queen was to be crowned at a formal centennial ball at the Brigham City armory. The event drew practically every adult in town, including Boyd's parents, brothers, sisters, and their partners.

The president of the Daughters of Utah Pioneers that year insisted that the queen and her attendants should not appear on the dance floor until they were announced for the inauguration ceremony late in the evening. This meant that the less-than-enthusiastic escorts of the contestants were required to stand around most of the evening and wait for this event to take place. For some time thereafter Boyd could never see that DUP president without grinding his teeth a bit.

When the ceremony was over he introduced Donna to his family. Then, before he could have even a single dance with her, his father, brothers, and brothers-in-law each claimed her for a turn. She took it with good grace.

By then Boyd knew that this was the girl he wanted to marry. Her lack of affectation strongly appealed to him, as did her ready smile, her thoughtfulness, and her uncomplaining nature. He had a sure eye for beauty and an innate taste for goodness. In Donna he found beauty and goodness in a perfect blend. Always he would honor her with the simple words, "Donna is perfect."

Then as he became acquainted with Donna's parents and three younger brothers, he loved them as well. Her mother, Nellie Jordan Smith, gave careful and devoted attention to her four children and her home. She had filled a full-time mission for the Church, and at the time of Boyd and Donna's courtship she was president of the North Box Elder Stake Young Women's Mutual Improvement Association.

William W. Smith, second counselor in the bishopric, was a good father. From his various business ventures he provided well for his family.

As with Boyd's parents, Donna's had come from faithful convert stock who had sacrificed everything for the gospel of Jesus Christ and His restored church. And each family had its roots deep in the communal beginnings of Brigham City, which had given to them a strong sense of place. Boyd and Donna shared a love for their hometown and its pioneer heritage.

While Boyd commuted to Weber College daily during the school year, Donna lived in Ogden at the home of Lydia Tanner, retired head of the Home Economics Department. From her she learned homemaking skills beyond those taught by her mother. In addition to her work in the library Donna was an active member of La Dianaeda girls sorority and president of the Whip Club, the Weber College service organization. She was greatly admired and much in demand for special school activities.

In late March of 1947 the sorority sponsored the school's Easter Prom, and Donna was responsible for theme and decorations. She confided in Boyd that the assignment weighed on her. His willingness to create Easter-theme drawings and to help decorate were just what was needed to relieve her concern.

Following the Easter Prom, Boyd gave Donna a diamond ring, its small stone set in solitaire. He would later replace it with a larger gem, saying of the first, "It was hardly big enough to be noticed, but it was enough." Donna adds, "Boyd did not actually ask me to marry him, but he did indicate that I was the one he wanted for eternity."

Both sets of parents were very pleased. Boyd's mother wrote to Verna in Portland that Donna was "a grand girl."

The dance had been held on Saturday, 5 April 1947. The next morning found the couple seated on the north balcony of the

Tabernacle in Salt Lake City for general conference. That day they saw Elder Henry D. Moyle sustained as an Apostle of the Lord Jesus Christ.

Donna recalls receiving a sure witness that Elder Moyle had indeed been called of God. Boyd received that same witness. But in addition, he had the soul-shaking impression that one day he would be called from the audience to speak at that pulpit. This witness and his love for the girl beside him caused him to say in solemn retrospect, "I suppose I had some small interest in what was being said at the pulpit that day."

That witness placed upon him a heavy burden. When the impression was repeated as the years passed, he says, he would immediately "throw a rock on it and move ahead." But from that time on the Lord would tutor, test, and season him.

Between their engagement in early April and their marriage in late July, Boyd and Donna spent every moment they could together. The need to work and to finish that school year allowed them only small blocks of time, but they made the most of them.

Boyd recalls how Donna would watch for his shadow to appear at the opaque window of the side door to the Home Economics Department. Seeing him there she would slip out and, like a line in a poem he had read, send him on with a "cookie and a kiss."

They read the book *Discourses of Brigham Young* together, and they attended school functions and dances. For one of these occasions the only available vehicle for Boyd to use was his father's homemade wrecker. Ira had cut off the back of an old heavy-duty touring car, brought the back forward, and welded it to the front to create a one-seater. On the heavy back-frame he had built a hand-crank wrecker from gears of cars and tractors. Boyd describes it as "pure ugly."

He cleaned it thoroughly, thinking as he did so, "If she'll ride with me in this, we can go through life with few problems." Dressed in her best, Donna took his arm and stepped into the wrecker as unconcerned as if it were up to the standard that Boyd desired for her.

Donna's lack of concern about riding with him in the old wrecker gave him confidence to negotiate with a local realtor on the purchase of an old, run-down home in the southeast part of the city.

It had been owned by a bachelor who had recently died. The house captured Boyd's interest as a place that he and Donna could restore and beautify. It was financially feasible and would be well within a teacher's income.

Thinking about this house led them to serious discussion about their future family. Donna wanted a dozen children, and Boyd, who knew the richness of life in a large family, agreed. That goal set, they decided that their mutual occupation would be their family, and that no activity would take precedence over it. Whatever he did to provide for them would be secondary to their mutual responsibility to their children.

They also decided that, since children must always be somewhere and doing something every waking moment, one or the other of them would always be with the children

To Boyd and Donna these commitments made previous to their marriage were as binding as were the eternal covenants that would follow in the temple.

During this period, few notes or letters passed between them, but Donna has treasured one from Boyd that said in part, "When I think of you, and all that we can accomplish together, when I see the dreams of eternity unfolding before us, . . . it is as though my heart were crying tears of thankfulness."[1]

About that time Boyd was presented with a test that was much more serious than Donna's challenge of riding with him in the wrecker. Donna's father, an enterprising and generous man, had successfully built several homes and was in the process of building two directly through the block from the one where he and his family lived. One of the new homes had been sold. The other, Donna's father told them, was to be his wedding gift to them.

His words touched something that was deep and elemental to Boyd's nature and made him resolutely say to himself, "We cannot do that." With all his heart he desired to provide for his bride himself, and he felt entirely capable of taking that responsibility. Thus that desire and the anticipation of fixing up the old home for them warred against the proffered gift, creating within Boyd a distinct crisis. He struggled with it, rejecting even the thought of the gift. Finding no peace, he went to his father and asked what he should do.

Ira listened with understanding. After deliberating, he said: "Son, what if in the future you should want to do this for one of your own children? Do you think that would be in order?"

Boyd was forced to answer, "Yes."

Ira continued, "Well, why is it out of order for Brother Smith to want to do this for his only daughter?"

It was a hard lesson for Boyd to learn: Even when you definitely do not want it, sometimes you must accept a gift from another so that the giver might receive the joy of giving.

Finally he yielded *his* will to the counsel of his father and Donna's and moved ahead. His willingness to submit to counsel helped to qualify Boyd for leadership in the family he and Donna hoped for. And his obedience to his earthly father advanced him a step along the path of his commitment to be obedient to his Father in Heaven.

The couple set their wedding date for 28 July 1947. Verna would travel from Portland. Leon would return from his military post at the Pentagon. And Boyd's parents would be home from their Centennial "pioneer trek" from Nauvoo, Illinois, to the Salt Lake Valley.

This trek was to be a great experience for Boyd's parents. Ira, an active member of the Sons of the Utah Pioneers, said: "One of the officers of the Sons of the Utah Pioneers came and told me there would be nine men selected from Box Elder County [and] one of them should be a mechanic [and] also have the necessary background for pioneer requirements. I explained that both of my grandmothers were handcart pioneers and both of my grandfathers had lived at Nauvoo prior to having been driven out. My grandmothers walked the entire distance from the Missouri River to Salt Lake City."

He added, "Two or three times I talked myself out of going, but it seemed to grow into a necessary trip."[2]

Ira and Emma first traveled to Detroit, where they picked up a new Chrysler and drove to Nauvoo. There they joined the other trekkers, creating canvas wagon covers for their cars and cutting out and painting plywood oxen for their front fenders. Elder Spencer W. Kimball and his wife, Camilla, were among the large group making the trek.

Following the route of the 1847 pioneers the trekkers entered the

Salt Lake Valley through Emigration Canyon on July 22 and stopped at the new *This Is the Place Monument.* It had been a hundred years since Brigham Young declared from his makeshift bed in Wilford Woodruff's carriage, "This is the place."[3]

Packer children were among the thousands who gathered to greet the trekkers. It was a memorable day for them and their parents, who were full of stories about their unique pioneer experience.

Also there to welcome the pioneers were state and local dignitaries and leaders of the Church. Noticeable among these were President George Albert Smith and his counselors, President J. Reuben Clark, Jr., and President David O. McKay.

July 24 found Ira and Emma and available family members gathered about the "pioneer wagon" in front of the Packer garage. Before leaving for the reception and dinner to honor the trekkers that day,[4] Ira took brush and paint and "branded" his plywood oxen I.W.P. for him and E.J.P. for Emma. Then, standing back to survey the effect, he said, "The best team that ever pulled together this side of eternity."

Inspired by this team-ideal of pulling together, Boyd years later carved an ox with a yoke as the model that became the Packer family emblem. Copies cast into brass door-knockers mark the homes of Ira and Emma's descendants.

With Boyd and Donna's wedding just four days away, there was much to be done. Their reception was to be held in the garden at the home of Donna's parents. To block off the street view from the south lawn of the Smith home Boyd built a sectional lattice-work fence six feet tall and twenty feet long from lath Donna's father had salvaged from a building he had demolished. Boyd painted it white, and his sister Verna trimmed it with window-display flowers.

On 28 July 1947 members of the immediate family traveled to Logan in Ira's new Chrysler and William Smith's older LaSalle. As they were about to enter the temple, a distant relative came from his home across the street to inquire about the honeymoon car they might be taking. Suspecting a prank, Boyd pointed to the LaSalle, then walked with the others into the building.

Within the sacred precincts the sealing ceremony that would forever bind Boyd and Donna together was spoken by ElRay L. Christiansen, president of the Logan Temple. That same day Elders Joseph

Wedding day 28 July 1947

Fielding Smith and Spencer W. Kimball of the Quorum of the Twelve were in the temple, going through a session with their wives. The wedding party had the privilege of shaking hands with these brethren with whom Boyd would later serve.

As the party left the temple, they found the LaSalle labeled "Just Married" and decorated with tin cans and streamers. Boyd and Donna drove away in the Chrysler. The two sets of parents picked up the wedding cake in Logan and drove to Brigham City. They laughed for weeks over the astonished looks of drivers who drew near to see the newlyweds and saw, instead, two older men up front and their wives in back balancing a wedding cake.

The night of the reception was clear, with a full moon lighting the garden. Friends and family filed by to extend congratulations and then to linger and visit.

Upon their return to Brigham City from a brief honeymoon, Boyd arranged for his final year at Weber College, from which Donna had graduated that spring. Donna's father had painted and papered the unfinished rooms in the home.

Before school started, the couple cleared the yard of gravel and rocks and planted lawns, front and back. By then Boyd was content about the matter of the home, and when Brother Smith later faced some financial reverses Boyd was able to help by taking over the payments.

Of their beginnings Boyd said: "We were as happy as could be with one another. And neither one of us would have cared where we lived as long as we could be together." And so began their married life, near the Smith home where Donna's life had begun.

Chapter Eight

Donna

Donna Edith Smith's grandfather Rasmus Julius (Smidt) Smith was given to know and impressed to say to another young granddaughter, Nelda, "Someone in our family will work with the prophets."

He continued: "Now, I do not know who it will be, whether it will come through the priesthood line or whether it will come through one of the girls. This promise could be fulfilled through you, or perhaps through your new little cousin, Donna."

Julius, as he was known, was short and slight of build, weighing one hundred twenty-five pounds. In his late years he wore a white beard and usually dressed in black. And although his eyes were kindly and his manner mild, granddaughter Nelda was just a little frightened of him. But she kept his words in her heart, and when the two cousins were grown she related them to Donna at a family reunion.

Donna treasures those words. They gave special meaning to a photograph of Grandfather Julius holding her, a six-month-old baby, at general conference on Easter day, 8 April 1928.

Although he died when she was but two, his words, the photo of her with him, and the records of his research and temple work inspired Donna to write the story of his life. In doing so she forged a bond between her and her grand-father.

Julius Smith stands as a spiritual bridge between his ancestors, who passed on without the blessings of the gospel, and his descendants, who have kept their sacred trust as members of The Church of Jesus Christ of Latter-day Saints.

Rasmus Julius Smith was born on 20 August 1843 at Foldbjaerg, Denmark, the only child of Juliane Sorensdatter. His father was listed as Rasmus Smidt, a lawyer-farmer, for whom Juliane worked as house-keeper.

Donna on the lap of her Grandfather Rasmus Julius Smith

The child Julius's life was difficult and lonely. During his early years he lived with Juliane's brother Friderich Christian Sorensen, a schoolteacher, who took the boy while Juliane found employment first at Ravnstrup in Orum Parish and then in Aalborg. When Friderich married and had children of his own, the boy Julius was cared for by other relatives.

Then in April 1853 he was reunited with his mother, who had accepted the message of the missionaries and had been baptized into the Church. She was determined to immigrate to Utah with other Saints and to take her son with her. Accordingly they left Aalborg, first traveling to Copenhagen and then to Liverpool, England. There, with other Scandinavian Saints, they embarked on the *Benjamin Adams* on 28 January 1854, bound for New Orleans. Juliane was thirty-eight and Julius ten.

After a voyage of eight weeks the ship reached New Orleans on 22 March. Three days later Julius and his mother, along with their company, boarded the *L. M. Kennet*, arriving at St. Louis, Missouri, on 3 April.

Under the leadership of Hans Peter Olsen, this company joined another group of Scandinavian Saints from the vessel *Jesse Munns* and continued on to Kansas City, Missouri. There they were organized for the trek west under six captains, each responsible for ten of the wagons making up the train.

They began the journey on 15 June 1854, traveling only two miles the first day but averaging eight to ten miles daily for the rest of the journey. Young Julius, with others, walked the entire distance. Many died of cholera along the way. Julius and Juliane were among the survivors who arrived in the Salt Lake Valley on 5 October 1854. With other Scandinavian families they went directly to settle in Brigham City.

Juliane found employment with H. P. Jensen, who had confirmed her a member of the Church in Denmark.

Julius was baptized at age eleven on 30 March 1855. From then on he took the name of Smith. Through the years of his youth he worked as a farmhand, as an apprentice to a watch repairman and silversmith, as a rider for the Pony Express, and as a herder at Camp Floyd, Utah, at Fort Bridger, Wyoming, and then in Montana. During those years he was often lonely and sometimes hungry.

On the fringes of the army base and at various ranches he was exposed to worldly influences. Having been raised in Danish households, he had become accustomed to the array of pipes on mantel and hearth and to the smell of tobacco as the men smoked in the evening. Thus he naturally took to smoking a pipe himself.

One night in Montana he found himself alone at the ranch house where he lived, and while smoking his pipe he thumbed through his Book of Mormon. "It's a lie," he said emphatically. To his astonishment he heard a voice contradict him, saying, "It isn't a lie and you know it." Twice he repeated his denial, and twice the voice challenged him. The words of his denial and the answering challenge stayed with him but did not, at that time, change him.

In 1867, when he was twenty-four, Julius ended his lonely state by marrying Anna Anthony from Fort Hall, Idaho. To them was born a daughter, Berdina Anthony Smith, who with her mother died shortly thereafter. This was a crushing blow to his spirit.

While Julius lay desperately ill and weak he remembered his earlier denial and the answering voice and began praying fervently to the

Lord for forgiveness. He promised that if the Lord would restore him to health he would return to his mother in Brigham City and whole-heartedly embrace the gospel. Restoration did not come immediately, but some measure of hope did. During this illness he saw in a dream a desirable and lovely woman whose image he could not forget.

Still weak, he determined to go home. With the help of a friend he mounted his horse and began the trip south. As he rode the sage-brush trail his promise to the Lord came to his mind. He threw his pipe into the sage and rode on.

It was not long before the craving for tobacco overpowered him and he turned back to search for his pipe. He could not find it. He prayed for relief. It came. He rode from the place, never to smoke again.

Riding into the pleasant shaded streets of Brigham City to his mother's small home, a prodigal son was restored. Others came to rejoice with Juliane, to welcome Julius. One of them was Josephina Bernhardina Beckman, the young woman he remembered having seen in his dream.

He found employment mixing mortar for brick masons and stone masons, tending and harvesting orchards and gardens, peeling bark for the tanner, Mr. Hillam, and working in the Brigham City cooper-ative.

Financially prepared for marriage, he courted Josephina. He was ordained an elder in 1871 and soon took his bride to the Endowment House in Salt Lake City, where they were sealed for eternity.

The next year a son, Julius Junior, was born. He died the same day. To find solace, Julius sought a patriarchal blessing. It promised Julius that he would live a long life and have an inheritance among the fathers in Israel. He would also have enough of the world's goods that he would be able to feed many in times of scarcity.

Julius felt deep gratitude to the Lord for his blessings, and he expressed this in a letter dated 1 December 1896 to his Aunt Caro-line in Denmark: "We have a good land here, with fruit, wheat, pota-toes, and clear water . . . flowing down from the mountains to irrigate our gardens and fields, and our stock can get all they need. It is nice in summer and seldom as cold as is Denmark in winter. So the Lord has given us a good, pleasant land. And best of all, we are satisfied in our position."

Julius provided for his family of fourteen children and, beyond that, shared his time and means with others. He gave baskets of fruit and vegetables to the Indians as they came to him; in the market-place where he sold his produce he gave more than full measure.

At age thirty-nine he was called to work on the Logan Temple. This lightweight man shouldered a pack each Monday morning, then made his way on foot about twenty-five miles up and over the mountains, through Dry Canyon, and into Logan. On Saturday evening he walked back to Brigham City to spend the Sabbath with his family.

Of him, Elder Packer said:

> He was not a young man, just over five feet tall, and very slight in build. He was, nevertheless, assigned as a hod carrier. For the younger ones, I explain that a hod carrier would fill a V-shaped wooden box full of mortar or plaster. He would lift it to his shoulder and carry it to where the masons were working, often lifting this very heavy weight up long ladders.
>
> On the afternoon of 11 August 1883, Brother Smith was tending two plasterers who were finishing the ceiling a hundred feet above the ground in the northwest tower of the temple. Suddenly the scaffolding gave way, tipped to one side, and fell. The projections for the spiral stair-case had been installed. The three men tumbled through these projec-tions and landed amid the rubble. The record states that they were removed to their homes . . . and soon returned to their work, having sus-tained only minor injuries.[1]

As the masonry work was done, Julius received an honorable release. He cared for his crops and orchards, a half acre of raspberries, and two acres of strawberries. These he harvested, selling the surplus for cash to pay taxes and buy needed commodities.

At the end of the year he gathered his family around the kitchen table and allotted the money: first for tithing, next for the bills, some for the coming season, and some for each child as pay for his or her work.

When the Brigham City Tabernacle burned down in 1896 he interrupted his own work to serve as hod carrier in its reconstruction. That same year he was ordained a high priest.

As the years passed, his love for his forebears grew and his desire to do their temple work increased. Hence much of his time was devoted to searching out his Danish ancestors and doing their temple work. He also did the work for an Indian friend who had passed on.

In 1911 Julius wrote to his cousin Maria in Denmark that he was happy with his children; that the five oldest were married and well off; that of those left at home, one was a schoolteacher and five were still in school. The youngest of the fourteen was Donna's father, William Waldemer Smith, who was eleven years old at the time. William had been born on 6 January 1900, his birth welcoming in a new century.

William was a faithful son, and when in 1926 he married Nellie Jordan they rented a small house just east of the old family home on North Main Street. From there he helped care for his aging parents, who had celebrated their golden wedding anniversary five years before. When his mother, Josephina, passed away on 10 February 1928, William and Nellie moved into the family home to care for Julius during the remaining months of his life. Julius died the next year on 7 August 1929. He was eighty-six.

William was with him at the end, and Julius bore his last testimony to him. He said: "I did want so much to talk to you and tell you a few things. The first thing I want to tell you is that the gospel of Jesus Christ is true; I know it as I live. And I would like you to be more active in the Church. Go, take part, learn what you can about it, and be faithful in it. Pay an honest tithing. I always have and I have been blessed for paying an honest tithe."[2]

About four o'clock in the morning, as William sat by his side, Julius reached out his hands, saying, "Your mother has come for me." Moments later he was gone.

His father's testimony and the sweet experience of his passing had a profound influence upon William. All his life he had come under the influence of this humble, remarkable father. He had knelt in family prayer around the table with him; he had received kindly correction from him; he had attended church and heard his solemn public testimony to the truthfulness of the gospel; and from him he had learned to plant, tend, and harvest.

Donna Edith Smith

William Waldemer Smith
1900–1977

Edith Nellie Jordan
1901–1972

Rasmus Julius
Smith
1843–1929

Josefina Bernhardina
Beckman
1855–1928

Alvin Edgar
Jordan
1883–1933

Edith
Harman
1881–1960

The ancestry of Donna Edith Smith

As Julius Smith occupies a significant place in his granddaughter Donna's paternal line, so Edith Harman Hooper Jordan does in her maternal line. Edith Harman had her beginnings in London. She and her mother, Eleanor Sayer Harman, became dissatisfied with the Church of England. In 1905 they met the Latter-day Saint missionaries; they were baptized on 17 December that year.

At the time of her baptism Edith was married to Samuel Williams Hooper, a handsome man by whom she had a child, Edith Nellie, on 15 October 1901. They lived in the Hackney district of London. Samuel worked as a streetcar conductor but had difficulty in providing for his family. Edith, a skilled seamstress, was employed by day and brought piecework home to sew in the evening.

Both Edith and Samuel were very independent. Friction arose over finances, the number of children they should have, and especially over the hated "Mormon" religion, which Samuel felt Edith had been deluded into accepting. He determined to solve their problems by moving his family into his brother's apartment in Brixton, where his mother also lived. In Edith's mind this was no solution at all.

Despite her objections, when she returned from work one day she found that Samuel and Nellie had gone. He had moved all of their possessions to his brother's place.

Soon after that Edith and Samuel separated. Under English law he was given custody of Nellie, and Edith, with an aching heart, returned to the home of her mother.

Nellie was kindly treated by Grandmother Hooper, and when old enough she attended school in Brixton. At some point she also attended the Weston Maryland Point Infants Council School in Stratford.

Edith and her mother found employment as cook and housekeeper in the British Mission Home, which was known as Deseret. Members were encouraged to immigrate to America and settle in Utah, the gathering place for the Saints. Alvin Edgar Jordan, as presiding elder over the London Conference, was frequently at the mission home and no doubt encouraged Edith and her mother to join those who were preparing to leave.

Together Edith and Eleanor decided to go. They pooled their savings and prepared to join the others, praying for some way to take

Nellie with them. Before they could leave, however, Eleanor, Donna's great-grandmother, was stricken with cancer and taken to Chelsea Hospital for treatment. Knowing she could not make the journey, she exacted a promise from Edith to take their savings and leave for Zion immediately—with Nellie. How to bring this about was left in the hands of the Lord.

While Edith was visiting Nellie at school in September of 1909 the child clung to her and begged to go home with her. It was not that she was mistreated, for her father and Grandmother Hooper loved her, but she loved her mother and wanted to be with her. Without any preplanning, Edith yielded to Nellie's pleading and had the child follow well behind her until they were beyond Samuel's streetcar district.

She then took her directly to the mission home. The presiding elder took Nellie to a member's home at the seaside, the location of which Edith was deliberately not told.

When the child was discovered missing at the Hooper residence the alarm went out, and police were dispatched to investigate the mission home, where Samuel knew Edith was employed. Questioned, Edith could honestly answer, "I do not know where she is." That she was not believed is evident from headlines in the next day's newspaper, "Mormon Steals Girl."

Edith booked passage on the SS *St. Louis*, which would leave on 9 October 1909, under the assumed names of Anne Clark, age thirty-three (she was twenty-eight), and Ethel Clark, age ten (Nellie was almost eight). Edith became violently seasick and was forced to stay down for the entire voyage. Nellie managed on her own, roamed the decks, and made friends among the passengers. Her dark reddish-brown hair falling in long curls, dark brown eyes, and winsome smile created an appealing picture. Even the captain was taken with her, and on her eighth birthday he held a party for her. Her mother still lay seasick below deck.

They arrived in New York on Sunday, 17 October 1909, and were processed through Ellis Island the next day. Going through customs and immigrant lines was frightening. In the adjustment process Edith became, in her words, a "different person." She resolved that whatever lay ahead for them, she would rise above it.

As with Juliane, the mother of Rasmus Julius Smith, Edith was a lone woman facing a new country with her only child. She had no material resources and no husband to protect her and Nellie.

Edith and Nellie began the long journey west by train. While they rode instead of pushing a handcart or riding in an ox-drawn wagon, the same anxiety was theirs.

Nellie was fascinated by the kaleidoscopic views she saw from their window. Finally they reached Ogden, Utah, then continued on to Preston, Idaho, to the home of Walter P. Monson. Edith was to work temporarily as cook and seamstress in return for their room and board.

With no permanent employment, Edith accepted an invitation from the family of Leonard James Jordan, who lived in Enterprise, Oregon. He was the father of Alvin, former presiding elder at the British Mission Home. Before Alvin had left his field of labor, four months before Edith emigrated, there had been an understanding between them.

Donna Packer's mother, Nellie, and grandmother, Edith, were happy in the Jordan home. Nellie was baptized by Alvin's brother David on 17 July 1910. When Edith learned of the death of her mother, Eleanor, at the Chelsea Hospital in London on 25 October 1910 she was comforted to realize how happy Eleanor must have been to know that her dearest wishes for her and Nellie had been granted.

Alvin and Edith were married in the Salt Lake Temple on 4 October 1911 and had Nellie sealed to them.

A daughter, June Emily, was born to them in 1913 while they were still living in Oregon. They later moved with Alvin's parents to Howell, Utah, where Alvin's brother David had purchased a farm. In 1915 Alvin and Edith's son Walter Alvin was born. Other children soon followed.

Alvin and his father took over 640 acres west of David's farm. The land was mostly sagebrush, but there were irrigation rights for eighty of their acres. Mosquitoes, drought, severe winters, and insufficient water all limited the productivity of their land.

Conditions at the Jordan farm gradually improved. Eventually Edith became postmistress in the store that Alvin came to own. She played the piano for Church services and socials.

Meanwhile Nellie worked hard, set worthy goals, served in the Church, and learned the power of prayer. "It was evening, nearly sundown in Howell, Utah," she recalled. "I went alone to get the cows that were in the pasture over a mile from home. The mosquitoes were terrible. The cows were acting wild. . . . I didn't think I could get them home, so I prayed. A strong breeze came up, and the mosquitoes were blown away, the cows settled down, and I was able to bring them home before dark."[3]

That early experience remained with Nellie. Throughout her life she relied upon the Lord, knowing that He does answer the sincere prayers of humble hearts.

While in Howell, Nellie served in various Church callings. She appeared in plays and took part in the Fourth of July celebration at which her father would give an oration, a skill for which he had some reputation. The band consisted of her mother at the piano, a trombone, and a coal-bucket drum.

Nellie rode horseback the five miles to school for her seventh and eighth grades. She continued her education at Brigham Young College in Logan, where she lived with her Grandmother Jordan. She returned home for summers, then boarded in Brigham City, going on to graduate from Box Elder High School in 1922.

The year before graduation she had received a patriarchal blessing at the hands of J. P. Christensen of Garland, Utah. It was spiritually tailored to her own potential. She would "be able to battle with the obstacles of life successfully." She was counseled to store her "mind with useful knowledge, study the scriptures," and make herself "acquainted with the organization of the Church and the order of the Holy Priesthood," because the time would come when she would have opportunity to explain the doctrines of the Church, to stand as a leader, to give counsel and encouragement, and to be an example to many. Hers would be the power of discernment, and "her faith and faithfulness" would enable her to come out victorious until her "mission in life [was] fully accomplished."[4]

The rich promises began immediately to unfold. In September 1922 she was called to serve in the Northwestern States Mission, the first missionary to be sent from the Howell Ward. A young woman of beauty and deep spirituality, she filled an honorable mission and returned home poised and lovely.

In July 1925 she entered Colorado State Agricultural College at Fort Collins for library training. She did well, earned her library certificate, and became librarian for Box Elder High School in Brigham City.

She taught the Gleaner class in Brigham City Third Ward and there became well acquainted with the MIA superintendent, William W. Smith, the enterprising young man who already had his own service station and farm interests.

Bill Smith had first seen Nellie years before as she and two of her friends stopped for gas at his service station just prior to her leaving for the mission field. He had never forgotten her beauty and sparkle. Now, when Nellie took part in the MIA roadshow, he was on hand to drive her and the other young people around the stake in his new Chevrolet. From then on Bill Smith courted Nellie Jordan in earnest.

In the meantime Nellie's father had moved his family to Coalville, Utah, where his children would have improved opportunity for schooling. He and his brother David took over the O. P. Skaggs grocery store there.

Four generations: Nellie J. Smith, Donna's mother; Edith H. Jordan, her grandmother; Donna S. Packer; and Allan F. Packer

When Nellie joined her family in Coalville for the summer, Bill Smith made many trips to see her. They were married in the Salt Lake Temple on 28 December 1926.

The couple rented the small home just east of his old family home in Brigham City and together cared for his aged parents. The William Smiths' first child, Donna Edith, was born in the Cooley Hospital on 20 October 1927 while they were still living in the rented home.

When Bill's mother, Josephina, died on 10 February 1928, Bill, Nellie, and baby Donna moved into the old home and lived with his father. The aging Julius was not content to sit idly by but shelled peas, chopped wood, and walked about to visit friends. He often held Donna, and he took pleasure in watching her take her first steps. It was during this brief time that he spoke those prophetic words to another granddaughter, Nelda. On 7 August 1929 Julius passed away.

Donna's father, always interested in building and in improving his surroundings, remodeled the old home to make it more comfortable for his growing family. Here his sons were born—Robert William, in 1929; Glen Alvin, 1932; Ronald Julius, 1935. This was the only home that Donna and her brothers would know until they married.

The family worked hard all morning at home, at the farm, at William's service station, and later at his motel.

So that they would learn to utilize time, Nellie taught the children to make braided rugs for their rooms while they listened to the radio. She took an interest in the boys' Scouting activities and helped them when needed. When Donna showed an interest in photography, she taught her how to use a camera and compose her pictures for better results. She was an effective teacher because she was kind and made work seem like play.

She and William expected obedience and good behavior. When discipline was necessary, a word from Father carried a lot of weight. Mother made her point by putting the offending party on a chair to think about his or her words or actions.

As the years passed, Donna's mother developed serious health problems.

Donna's father provided well for his family, but as the Great

Depression gripped the economy he experienced financial reverses along with others. But there was always milk and produce for the table, and extended family members who were alone or ill were cared for at home.

William's older sister, Millicent, joined his household in 1935. Nellie did not adjust easily to having another woman in the home, but she cheerfully accepted Millicent as she had earlier accepted the need to care for her husband's aged father. Optimistic by nature, she simply made the best of situations.

By her example Donna grew naturally into patterns of cheerful optimism and basic goodness of spirit. She was influenced not only by Nellie's example but also by the ordinances she received in her childhood and youth, which she recorded as most significant: "I was blessed 4 December 1927 by my father, William W. Smith; baptized 2 November 1935 by Aaron Snow; confirmed 3 November 1935 by Bishop J. Frank Bowring; and given a patriarchal blessing 28 December 1942 by William Horsley."[5]

Donna also records that when she was twelve she took a class in genealogy at the Brigham City Third Ward, and at age thirteen she did thirty-nine baptisms for the dead. From these experiences she gained a love for family history and temple service.

Donna's love of family and forebears also gave her an appreciation for the household items they had used and for the hand-crafted items they had made. Many of these things that might have been lost through neglect were preserved. In a sense, for Donna the people themselves lived on in such items as her mother's wicker trunk, the watch her Grandmother Edith won in a porridge contest in London, and the cushion Grandmother Jordan made for Donna's small rocking chair.

Donna at the time she received her patriarchal blessing

When Donna entered school she was shy, a trait against which she struggled throughout her youth. Nellie encouraged her to accept talks in Primary and Sunday School. Her mother also provided for violin lessons from Harold Felt so that, in sharing a talent, Donna might overcome her shyness. With her mother's encouragement, Donna eventually could speak or play her violin before people with a measure of confidence and could assume teaching and leadership assignments at school and church.

With three brothers, Donna received her share of teasing, sometimes to the point of tears. She also went through a period of teenage rebellion when, wanting to be independent, she resented even her mother's kindly preaching. Because she was teachable, a kind, corrective word from a family member changed her attitude.

Donna graduated from Box Elder High School in June 1945. Her progress in overcoming her shyness can be measured by her receiving the American Legion Certificate of Award for the "Outstanding Girl" in the senior class; and a scholarship in orchestra to Weber College.

This, then, was the "very pretty girl" Boyd Packer had seen walking to junior high and the very beautiful young woman he saw crowned as Brigham City's Peach Days Queen soon after his return from Japan. It was not surprising that he would court her; and that in their union the prophecy of the faithful grandfather Rasmus Julius Smith would be realized.

Chapter Nine

Brigham City Days

Boyd and Donna Packer began their life together with a practical understanding of the Father's plan for his children—a plan with which they were personally acquainted through the example of their parents. Although different in age and personality, each set of parents had held to the traditional roles of strong family-oriented father and equally strong home-oriented mother working together as a harmonious team.

Although Boyd and Donna could not at first have known what those traditional roles would entail (any more than they could foresee what having Donna's hoped-for dozen children would bring) it did not matter. They were committed to having their large family and to following their parents' example in the home.

Boyd's ambition in life was to be good: to be a good son both to his Father in Heaven and to his earthly parents; to be a good husband to Donna and a good father to their children; and to be a good teacher. All else would have to fit those priorities or be set aside. One thing mostly set aside during the raising of their young family and Boyd's obtaining an education was his art work.

Donna's priorities were to be a good wife: to willingly accept the responsibility of bearing and nurturing as many children as the Lord would allow them; and to help create a home of order and beauty. All other interests would be incidental. Together they decided that Boyd would preside; they would counsel together; and they would act unitedly.

The couple moved into their new home at 549 North First West in Brigham City in early August 1947. Their furniture consisted of a table, sofa, chair, bed, and dresser. They had no refrigeration, so on hot summer days Donna prepared meals that required none. After a time they purchased a Kelvinator refrigerator that has operated an unbelievable forty-four years without repair. She laundered clothes at her mother's until, at the beginning of winter, they could afford a used wringer-washer. She remembers hanging the wet clothes on lines and having them freeze dry. That winter was severe, and hungry deer came down from the mountains into the yards for forage.

Boyd was finishing his last year at Weber College, working at the Packer garage, finishing the basement of the house, taking his turn milking Brother Smith's cow for a share of the milk, and helping

Boyd and Donna's first home in Brigham City

Donna with household chores. She remembers an incident that touched her. Noticing a small gold safety-pin fastened to the palm side of his wedding ring, she asked about it. He said simply, "That is to remind me to be good to you."

This small reminder was but an outward expression of the deep gratitude he felt for Donna. From her he drew daily strength and joy. She had truly assuaged the sense of loneliness he had often felt throughout his youth.

One bitter day as he waited for a ride from Ogden he became wet and chilled and came home with the flu. It was apparent to him and Donna that they must get a car. Earning the money to pay for it required diligence. Finally they were able to purchase a secondhand Ford.

About this time Boyd was called to teach the elders quorum and co-teach the Gospel Doctrine class.

In June 1948 he graduated from Weber College with an Associate of Science degree. On July 7 of that year, after a long and agonizing labor, Donna gave birth to their first child, a son, Allan Forrest. Her mother, who was managing the family motel, was not able to be with her, but Mother Packer was there to give comfort and encouragement.

That fall Boyd entered Utah State Agricultural College in Logan. He persuaded his advisors in the College of Education to let him to do part of his student teaching in Brigham City seminary and part at Box Elder High School. Their permission to do so proved to be a distinct advantage in the sequence of events.

President John P. Lillywhite of the North Box Elder Stake, who taught in the Brigham City seminary, was the quiet, spiritual man who would later serve as a patriarch and was, Boyd says, "always patriarchal." His grey hair, dignified manner, and immaculate dress gave him the appearance of a leader. Twice he had presided over the Netherlands Mission.

On 10 April 1948 Boyd became assistant stake clerk in the North Box Elder Stake and set about organizing President Lillywhite's files. Seeing him so occupied one night, his bishop commented, "Boyd, you don't have to do that."

"No," answered Boyd, "I don't have to do it; I get to!" Boyd ever served because of covenants and in gratitude for the incomparable blessing of witness he had received.

Boyd learned many lessons from President Lillywhite, one being that of forgiveness. He was the John that Elder Packer later memorialized in his general conference talk, "The Balm of Gilead," which was to have untold impact upon many who heard or have since read it.[1]

During his student-teaching experience Boyd was closely observed by the seminary principal, Abel S. Rich. Brother Rich was president of the South Box Elder Stake. An enterprising man, he was considered the city's leading citizen: twice mayor of Brigham City, a county commissioner, and a member of the school board. He had also been president of the Canadian Mission.

From him Boyd learned lasting lessons about making decisions. He learned, too, that if you want to know the truth about a man you go to his friends, not to his enemies.

In her history Donna tells of an incident that shows the esteem these leaders were accorded by the Brethren in Salt Lake. Elder Harold B. Lee, as a member of the Council of the Twelve, had come to their stake conference while Boyd was assistant stake clerk. Donna wrote:

> We slipped away between the morning and afternoon sessions and took the children to my mother's so they could be fed, while Boyd and I went over to the Zundells' home near the Third Ward building for dinner with the stake president and clerks.
>
> Brother Lee, who had also been invited to dinner, had forgotten something so had walked out to his car to get it, and was just leaving the car as we drove up. We greeted him and, as he paused to shake hands, he made two important statements. "Never turn aside from learning from great men such as those inside" and, "my boy, someday you shall have great responsibility in the Church." That experience was burned into my memory because of the witness of the Holy Ghost.[2]

On 3 June 1949 Boyd graduated with a B.S. degree from Utah State Agricultural College, having completed it in three years with the help of credits from his military training. Consistent with the steady pace that had marked his maturing years, he planned to begin his master's program that fall.

The same evening as graduation, the *Box Elder News Journal* reported a community meeting held in the Brigham City Tabernacle which Boyd attended. The purpose of the meeting was to gain the support of the citizens for housing the Intermountain Indian School in the facility left vacant when Bushnell Hospital had closed its doors during the summer of 1946. Attending the meeting were Senator Arthur V. Watkins (R-Utah); Dr. John R. Nichols, Commissioner of Indian Affairs, from Washington, D.C.; Dr. George A. Boyce from Window Rock, Arizona, superintendent of Indian schools for the Navajo reservations; and civic leaders from various parts of the state. Arriving late was Church President George Albert Smith from Salt Lake City.

Each speaker had praised Senator Watkins for his work to obtain the Bushnell facility from the War Assets Administration.[3] The meeting was well under way when President Smith entered the building. The audience rose to its feet. As the President took his place on the stand, the speaker at the pulpit readily gave over his place to him. Boyd recalls the President's words:

> I regret being late, but I have come against the counsel of my doc-tor. I had to come because there is something I want to tell you. When the suggestion was first made that an Indian school be established in one of our Latter-day Saint communities, I wrote President of the United States Harry S Truman and urged him to use his influence and adminis-trative power to consummate this action. In this way the American people could redeem themselves from some of the injustices that had been heaped upon the heads of the American Indians during the history of our country.

President Smith promised the citizens of Brigham City that any-thing they did to help and bless the Indian people would be answered with blessings upon their heads. His words pierced Boyd's heart. He thought: "Here is the prophet of the Lord, and I am just naive enough to believe that what he says is true. And whatever I can do to help, I will do."

Community leaders decided to send a fact-gathering committee to visit the Navajo Indian reservation in Arizona and New Mexico. They selected J. D. Gunderson as chairman of the committee, and

Boyd, representing the younger citizens, was one of sixteen committee members slated to make the trip.[4]

While the committee was away, the *News Journal* of October 21 reported that President John P. Lillywhite had been called to preside over the Netherlands Mission for the third time. Soon after, Elders Albert E. Bowen and Henry D. Moyle released him as president of the North Box Elder Stake and installed Vernal Willie to succeed him. Boyd was sustained as assistant to the stake clerk Roland L. Gourley.

Upon Boyd's return from the Indian trip, the principal Abel Rich counseled him to apply for the position left vacant by Brother Lillywhite. Boyd wrote a brief letter to Dr. Franklin L. West, commissioner of Church Education, stating that he was acting at the suggestion of the seminary principal.

Two days later he received an equally brief letter from Dr. West stating that it was his intention to assign an experienced seminary teacher to Brigham City. If Boyd wished to, however, he might apply for assignment elsewhere.

Feeling that the letter was in error, Boyd could think of little else as he drove to school the next day. After classes he left Logan, turned off on a narrow dirt road, and found a secluded wooded place where he could go and pray. He left there with the assurance that he was going to receive the desired appointment.

While serving as assistant stake clerk he was also chairman of the building committee for the new Brigham City Seventh Ward chapel. As a fund-raising incentive he had made a small model of the proposed building. One day Bishop Lewis S. Wight, who was leaving for Salt Lake to confer with the Church Building Committee, invited Boyd to bring the model and come with him.

While they were stopped at the Packer garage for gas, the seminary supervisor, J. Carl Wood, caught up with them and suggested that, while they were at Church headquarters, Boyd should see Dr. West. This Boyd did, and the two visited briefly. His contract came in the mail a few days later.

He hardly had time to savor the good news before he and others of the Indian Committee were asked to report on their recent visit to the reservations. Boyd's comments reflected his deep concern for the

Indian people he had visited. His heart had been wrenched when he saw a small Navajo boy, wearing nothing but a thin shirt, playing barefoot in the snow. These were the same feelings that had haunted him when he had seen the hungry, poverty-stricken children of post-war Japan.

Following his report, Boyd turned his attention to his seminary classes. At the same time he continued his own schooling in Logan.

Not only was the seminary appointment a fulfillment of his teaching dream but also through it he became closely associated with another seminary teacher, A. Theodore Tuttle, who had been hired the year before. Boyd had first met him in the stake offices while Brother Tuttle was serving as stake mission president. After meeting with his missionaries in the high council room he stopped to visit with Boyd as the latter worked on President Lillywhite's files. There was an instant rapport between them. Their friendship lasted for the duration of Brother Tuttle's life and brought them closer even than brothers.

Boyd's sense of fulfillment in seminary teaching was all he had expected it to be. He would later say: "The satisfaction of teaching is self-contained and it's quiet. You know when you've influenced someone, and that person knows it. Generally, no one else knows. In a sense, teaching is its own reward."

One of his students wrote about the impact of Boyd Packer's teaching: "Coming from a home where gospel teachings were not included, I remember how impressionable I was, and to this day can very clearly picture Elder Packer teaching us about repentance and how, like a bar of soap, it cleanses souls. I was impressed with [his] example of purity and humility and his personal life."[5]

Of particular satisfaction to Boyd was his pilot Book of Mormon class for seniors who had already graduated from seminary. They could choose to attend the new class before school in the morning. The first year, about thirty seniors chose to do so; the second, nearly fifty. As a result of this response and the approval in 1953 of William E. Berrett, administrator of seminaries and institutes, Book of Mormon classes became part of the standard curriculum.

To aid Boyd's teaching and her own assignment as Primary in-service leader, Donna created a subject file in two drawers of their filing cabinet. In a third drawer she kept household accounts and seed catalogs for garden planning. In the fourth, two files for each child—one for his best efforts in writing, art, and schoolwork, and one for his vital records. These she kept until the child, out of interest, created his own book of remembrance.

On 25 January 1950 Boyd and Donna's second son, Kenneth William, was born. Donna's Grandmother Jordan came each day to help. During her visits Donna heard the stories about her mother's British beginnings and the Jordans' early days in Enterprise, Oregon, and Howell, Utah. These stories fired Donna's interest in British family history.

On 12 March 1950 Boyd was ordained a seventy by Elder Ezra Taft Benson; on September 23 he was called to serve on the North Box Elder Stake high council under Stake President Vernal Willie; and on December 11 he was ordained a high priest by Elder Joseph F. Merrill.

One of his first high council assignments was to represent the North Box Elder Stake in fostering the Intermountain Indian School program. J. Edwin Baird, a counselor in the stake presidency of the South Box Elder Stake, acted as his counterpart. Brother Baird, a friend of the Packer family since their Corinne days, had been in attendance when Boyd gave the talk that so affected Donna. Of it he said, "I have never forgotten the spiritual quality of that talk nor the impression Boyd made upon me. He was devout, earnest, and had great comprehension of the scriptures."

In connection with his assignment to the Indian school Boyd became acquainted with Elder Spencer W. Kimball of the Quorum of the Twelve and Elders Milton R. Hunter and S. Dilworth Young of the First Council of the Seventy, who constituted the Indian Committee of the Church.

After Boyd began a seminary class at the Indian school his frequent travels over the Navajo reservation made him acquainted with officials from the Bureau of Indian Affairs, LDS mission presidents, and Catholic priests.

At the close of the 1950–51 school year Brother Tuttle left Brigham City to earn his doctorate at the University of Utah. Having completed his course work, but not a dissertation, he accepted a teaching position at the Church institute in Reno, Nevada. When in 1953 William E. Berrett was appointed administrator over all the seminaries and institutes of the Church, Ted Tuttle became a supervisor. Boyd was offered the Reno position left vacant by Brother Tuttle but, wishing to stay in Brigham City, declined it.

Living in Brigham City was a many-sided blessing for Boyd and Donna. Since Boyd was next to the youngest in his large family, his brothers and sisters were generous with their children's outgrown clothing, strollers, or playpens, and Donna and Boyd welcomed these gifts. Both were adept in fashioning the new from the used.

The dedication of the chapel in Howell, where Donna's grandmother had lived, provided Donna with a lesson about giving one's best to the Lord. She wrote: "The one long wall in the cultural hall had been put up in brick, and when they got it finished it was not square and true. The contractor, when told that the mistake could be hidden in the cornice and no one would know, said, 'I would know.' At his own expense, the builder took it down and redid it completely, saying that the chapel was an offering to the Lord and it should be perfect."[6]

After a strenuous summer of canning and gardening, Donna gave birth on 24 September 1951 to their third son, David Alma.

One night, after the Packers had retired, Boyd received a telephone call informing him that he had been nominated at the Democratic convention to run for the city council on their ticket. Boyd hesitated; he would need to talk with the principal Abel Rich in the morning before he could return the man's call. He was not sure whether he was Republican or Democrat. Boyd went to seminary certain that Brother Rich would get him out of this. Instead, his principal said, "Well, I guess we'll have to do all we can to see that we get you elected."

When 2,000 of the 2,100 possible registered voters turned out, Boyd received more votes than any other candidate.[7]

As a city councilor Boyd helped put through bond elections and helped to bring Brigham City's first sewer treatment plant into being. He found himself cast in the role of a community leader. Although he had no wish to continue in politics Boyd worked hard, learned from his associates, and experienced considerable personal growth. He also learned about taking criticism.

Being sworn in as city councilor

A member of his high priests quorum had eight acres of land with a two-story home that had once served as the co-op farmhouse. The land had generous irrigation rights serviced by a ditch that flowed past Boyd and Donna's home.

The city council moved to put sidewalks in that part of town. This meant that the man's ditch would have to be piped. He wanted a bigger pipe than that proposed because, he said, it would never hold the stream he needed. The city engineer told him it would be more than adequate. The council members upheld the decision. Not only did the home owner threaten to sue the city council but he also went to Boyd's home and scorched him with harsh words. As it happened, the installed pipe was twice as large as needed. Proved wrong, the man was more aggravated than ever.

While Boyd was yet in school all of Brigham City was saddened at the sudden death, on 14 August 1952, of President Abel S. Rich, who fell while helping repair the roof of his son's home in Ogden.

On the twenty-fourth of that same month Church President

David O. McKay dedicated the Seventh Ward chapel. Having served as chairman of its building committee, Boyd gave the financial report during the service.[8]

By then Boyd realized that if he was to teach seminary in the way he wished he must emulate the Master Teacher. To understand how this could be, he determined to study the Lord's teaching methods and write his thesis about them. Certain faculty members objected to his choice of subject. Finally, however, Boyd received approval. Later his thesis[9] became the basis for his much-used book *Teach Ye Diligently*.[10]

Dr. Wilford W. Richards, director of the institute and one of the great men of Boyd's acquaintance, was a strong advocate for Boyd and for his thesis. When Boyd had begun teaching seminary, Brother Richards wrote Dr. Franklin L. West highly approving his choice.

After completing his studies and his thesis, Boyd met his examining committee in late spring of 1953, tense and anxious to perform well. One committee member, however, seemed intent upon undermining his confidence. He spoke of the great privilege it was for Boyd to have been accepted to that university's graduate program and to have been instructed by so notable a faculty.

In answer, Dr. Richards spoke mildly, respectfully: "As you say, Boyd Packer *is* privileged to be the recipient of these advantages, but we, too, are privileged to teach such a sincere, hardworking student. Where would our university be without students?"

His words put Boyd at ease; he passed his orals with distinction, graduated with honors, and was elected to Phi Kappa Phi.

Boyd's parents and other family members attended the awards and honors convocation on 1 June 1953. A prominent professor of philosophy addressed himself to a lofty academic subject. As they left, Boyd's father, Ira Packer, said: "Well, that was a wonderful talk he gave. I think I would have enjoyed it even more if I had understood what he was talking about." Ira, however, readily understood Elder Harold B. Lee's message when he also spoke at the graduation exercises.

On 19 June 1953 Boyd and Donna's first daughter, Laurel Edith, was born.

With four children and plans for more, Boyd knew he must

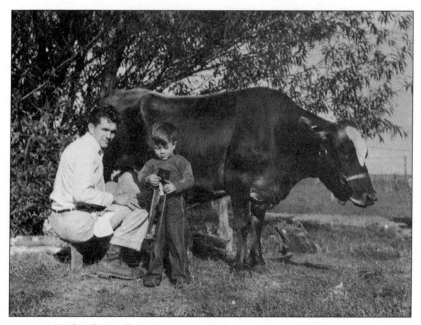

With Allan milking the cow in the pasture west of Brigham City

continue his education until he earned a doctorate. Only then could he qualify himself to increase his earning capacity. Thus he began the following school year to fill class requirements for that degree, distant though its attainment might be.

Boyd's focus on education was not limited to studies and seminary teaching but was also family directed. Realizing that a child learns best when he wants to know, he and Donna let no child's question go unanswered at the time of its asking. At one point he said, "If I were falling off the roof, I would stop in midair to answer one of the children."

On 23 November 1954 the Packers welcomed their fourth son, Russell LeGrand, into the family. And welcomed each child was, often hearing the parents say, "We are so glad you came to live with us," or "Without you in our family, there would be a big empty place."

Boyd is grateful for Donna's ability to create a spirit of peace to which the family gravitates. Always he could come *home*—home to orderliness, to a warm welcome, to a nourishing meal. No matter what riffles or problems might disturb the emotional climate in his outside world, he could count on a climate of peace at home. In turn Donna places a high value upon Boyd's support of decisions which she had to make in his absence; upon the power of his prayers; upon his wise family counsel, his skillful teaching, and his firm, kindly discipline of the children. They found that holding the children to a dependable schedule of naps, meals, play, chores, and bedtime helped not only in discipline but also in keeping them happier and more contented.

Boyd was not above learning from his children. "When our oldest son was a little fellow, he came in one day and in the course of conversation used, matter-of-factly, a profane word. It was worse than profane—it was a filthy word. I have always been grateful I restrained myself from spanking or punishing him in such a way that he never would forget the incident. Fortunately I said, 'Hey, where did you learn that word?' He told me he had heard it from one of the boys in the neighborhood. I said, 'That's not a good word.' He looked up at me in innocent surprise and said, 'It isn't? I didn't know that.' And he *didn't* know."[11]

Consistent teaching and guidance set proper bounds upon the children's behavior. To one who had spoken disrespectfully, Boyd would say: "Son, if you are in trouble with your mother, you are in big trouble with me. Do you understand?"

"Usually he would say yes, and I could tell him how we loved him and what a good boy he was. Then sooner or later he would prove it by changing his ways."

In appreciation, Donna tells how Boyd shared responsibility for the children's care. "If you have a new baby and another youngster cutting teeth, or one with a fever, you can be up and down twenty or thirty times a night. We finally divided our children into 'his' and 'hers' for night tending. I would get up for the new baby, and Boyd would tend the one cutting teeth. We schooled our ears to hear only the one over which we had charge and to sleep through the other's crying."

With five children the Packers found their small house crowded. Knowing of their desire for a yet larger family, Donna's father said one evening in early 1954: "I have heard that the owner of the old

Boyd and Donna's second home; the farm home built during the
united order days in Brigham City

co-op farmhouse is going to sell, and you two ought to have it. It
would be just right for you." The thought of its eight fertile acres, its
water rights, its orchard and garden, and the old historic house sent
Boyd and Donna's spirits soaring.

Its owner, however, was the man who had given Boyd that
tongue-lashing over the water pipe issue, and there was still tension.
Nevertheless Boyd lost no time in negotiating, and he succeeded in
pacifying the man into accepting his offer. Despite the lengthy time
it took to sell their small home, the family moved into the new one
in July in order to harvest the garden and orchard. And they loved it.
Even cleaning out the old basement was exciting. In it they found an
antique string of Swedish sleigh bells that has ever since hung on
their front door at Christmas.

Cleaning out the furnace room one day, Boyd, with a paper sack
over his head and his face blackened from soot, carried out buckets of
coal dust. Coming up the stairs he found Brother Tuttle and another
seminary supervisor looking at him in disbelief. His embarrassment
was washed away in their laughter.

That same year Boyd was selected by the Junior Chamber of Commerce as Brigham City's outstanding young man, and on 21 January 1955 he was given the Distinguished Service Award by that organization,[12] a fitting end to his term as a city councilor.

At school's end he and Donna were invited to a dinner for seminary teachers at Aspen Grove in American Fork Canyon. Not wishing to leave the children, they declined, but were told, "We think you should be there." During the event President Ernest L. Wilkinson of Brigham Young University took Boyd outside and told him that he had been selected to serve as a supervisor of Church seminaries and institutes with Brother Tuttle under William E. Berrett.

After talking it over with Donna, Boyd accepted the position. For the next year he commuted to Provo, a distance of nearly a hundred miles. He also traveled extensively to observe and oversee the seminaries and institutes and their teachers. At the same time he finished his assignments in the stake high council and at the Intermountain Indian School.

The Packers' Brigham City experience culminated on 8 January 1956 with President David O. McKay's dedication of the chapel for Indian students just north of the school. That month there was a warm spell when the ground dried enough for Boyd to mow the lawns' shaggy winter growth in preparation for the dedication.

Elder Spencer W. Kimball came with President McKay and spoke at the meeting. Indian students gave prayers and musical numbers. By then 2,300 Indian students were enrolled in the school. Several hundred were now Church members.

Boyd recalls: "President McKay and Elder Kimball had overcoats that looked identical. Somehow they mistakenly put on each other's after the meeting. The President's came almost to Brother Kimball's ankles, and the sleeves of Elder Kimball's barely covered President McKay's elbows. Both were rich in humor and made the most of the situation."

Chapter Ten

A Supervisor of Seminaries and Institutes

 When Boyd K. Packer accepted the appointment as supervisor of seminaries (and later of institutes) his opportunity to learn and serve expanded significantly. From local service in church, seminary, community, and the Indian school in Brigham City he was drawn into Churchwide religious instruction.

Of this change, he reflects, "When I began working under administrator William E. Berrett, I found myself paddling a canoe in a tributary that would later merge into the mainstream of Church administration."

With Boyd's assignment and the extensive travel it required, Donna found herself often paddling in home waters alone. The task of caring for their six, seven, eight, then nine children of the Lindon period fell largely to her, as also did much of the home's maintenance.

Taxed to their limits, Donna and Boyd underwent a process of struggle and growth. Each must support and strengthen the other. Only then could they be prepared to enter that mainstream.

In 1953 Elders Adam S. Bennion and Henry D. Moyle had consulted with William E. Berrett about a presentation for a meeting at the Assembly Hall in Temple Square as part of October general conference. A scholarly priesthood lesson on the Apostasy had proven difficult for priesthood leaders to teach. Brother Berrett assigned A. Theodore Tuttle, newly appointed assistant director of seminaries, to speak on improved gospel teaching for priesthood quorums. He in turn asked Boyd to demonstrate with a presentation on the Apostasy.

Boyd had earlier developed a lesson on the subject for his seminary students, in which he had created illustrations on a flannelboard, representing the Church with Christ as the cornerstone. To show how the Apostasy came about he had then removed the essential components that Christ had set in place. On the other side of the board he had reassembled the components to represent the restoration of the Church of Jesus Christ in the latter days. While his small visual aid had worked well in class, a presentation in the Assembly Hall would require a four-by-eight-foot flannelboard and figures drawn to scale. He enlarged the figures, mounted flannel on a wood frame, and carried it from Brigham City on the top of his car.

Brother Tuttle made his presentation on effective teaching of the gospel, then called for Boyd's presentation. When he had concluded, Elder Bennion came to the pulpit, put his arm about Boyd's shoulders, and invited questions from the audience.

One brother stood and said: "Surely you don't expect our Melchizedek Priesthood teachers to use such elementary things as if they were teaching Primary. Isn't that rather childish?"

Brother Bennion waited for Boyd to answer. He responded, "Perhaps the demonstration *is* rather childish, but should we not remember that except we become as little children we shall not enter into the kingdom of heaven."

This was greeted by approving laughter. Thus, as Boyd's service in the Indian program had come to the attention of Elder Spencer W. Kimball, his teaching skill and his ability to think on his feet came to the attention of two more members of the Twelve.

Although as a seminary supervisor Boyd received a modest raise in salary it was largely used up in his commuting from Brigham City to Provo. Accordingly he began to search for a home to buy in Utah Valley. Not finding one suitable for the family's needs, he determined to purchase a lot and build.

"I drove all over Utah Valley," he recalls, "and one evening I came into Lindon from the east and saw a beautiful lot on a corner. It had an old-fashioned Victorian iron fence on the north. There were large evergreens and other trees on the lot. Alternate sycamores and silver maples bordered it on the west. It appeared that a large home had once stood there."

He continues: "I learned from a neighbor that it was the site of the old Lindon Ward chapel and it was for sale. When I found the bishop, he quoted the price at eight hundred dollars."

Boyd made out an option to buy, paid twenty-five dollars earnest money, and called Donna to see if they could cover the check. She told him yes.

They rented a home near the building site and Boyd and the boys moved there on 14 August 1956, the day Donna's fifth son and sixth child, Spencer Gordon, was born in Brigham City's Cooley Hospital, where his father had been born. Because of a lung problem Spencer's life hung in the balance for some precarious days, and he was blessed and given his name at the hospital.

Children on horse at the home the Packers built in Lindon, Utah

Between his supervisory trips Boyd oversaw the construction of the new home. During the year it took to sell the Brigham City home they made its payments along with those for the Lindon house. They bought a cow, kept chickens and pigs, and in his absence Donna and their sons did the chores.

Since Boyd was often gone for a week or two at a time, Donna learned to depend upon her inner resources. Organizing time and work, she filled the days with never-ending tasks; taught the children to help; calmed her fears when a child took sick or hurt himself; and bore the long, lonely nights. "It was at this point in time," she recalls, "that I really grew up."

Shortly after arriving in Lindon, Donna was called as Top Pilot teacher in the Primary. When school started in the fall her kinder-garten, first-grade, and third-grade sons went at different times.

In the summer of 1956 Donna's father traded his Brigham City motel for a large cattle ranch in Wyoming and invited the older boys to spend each summer there. Located at Burnt Fork, forty miles from Mountain View, the ranch was a complex of former homesteads, with some of the old cabins still standing and old farm relics lying about.

Brother Smith divided his time between Brigham City and the ranch. In summers Donna's mother went to cook and help. The house had electricity but no telephone or indoor plumbing. Water had to be carried in from a spring located near the back door. A cabin bunkhouse stood next to the house, and there were a few sheds.

Donna's father ran both cattle and sheep and also kept horses. Downhill from the ranch house was a deep pond with a diving board. Between the house and the pond a town of prairie dogs thrived.

Happy to be there, the Packer boys carried water for Grandma and helped Grandpa mow hay, irrigate, fence, brand cattle, and shear sheep. As they grew older they operated farm machinery. They learned to work so well that their grandfather valued their help above that of hired men.

Whenever Boyd and Donna could leave for a weekend they drove to the ranch, taking welcome fruit and produce to the Smiths. On Sundays they attended church in McKinnon Ward's chapel, where families of ranchers came to worship. Friendliness pervaded

Children at Grandfather Smith's ranch at McKinnon, Wyoming

the meetings, and the Packer boys had opportunity to help prepare and pass the sacrament and occasionally to give a talk.

At home in Lindon, Donna made trips to her former doctor in Brigham City, in whom she had confidence. On 18 January 1958 in the Cooley Hospital their seventh child, a healthy second daughter, Gayle Ann, was born.

Boyd had always enjoyed being out of doors, but during the years when the children were young he gave up the hunting and fishing he enjoyed, because they took him away from the family. For the same reason, except for home beautification projects, he rarely painted or carved.

Whenever he was home, Boyd centered his attention on his family. He made a large sandpile in the sloping front yard where Donna could see the children from the kitchen window. He carved a bird weather vane for the garage. And with the help of his boys he built a small barn for the cow in the field adjacent to the home.

The cow provided a lesson for them. Bossy gave birth to a calf just before Boyd was to leave on a trip. She lay helpless, unable to care for her calf. The veterinarian said she had swallowed a piece of wire that had evidently punctured her heart and she would not survive the night.

That evening the son who had a special love for the new calf was asked to pray. Donna recalled: "He prayed about all the usual things in the usual way, asking that his daddy would be blessed in his travels and return to them in safety and that all would be well with them at home. Finally, near the close . . . he became most serious and fervent. One might say that he stopped merely saying prayers and began really to pray. 'Please Heavenly Father,' he pleaded, 'bless our bossy cow that she will get to be all right.'"[1]

Before leaving the next morning Boyd posted the number of an animal by-products company near the telephone, saying, "Donna, you'd better call these people and have them come and get the cow."

She did not make that call, however. When Boyd returned, Bossy was on her feet taking care of her calf. A little boy's prayer had been answered. Concerned that the children might expect such divine intervention for every emergency, Boyd made a point of teaching them that Father in Heaven must sometimes answer prayers with a no.

The Lindon period in the Packers' life was an innovative time for the family. Donna began a tradition which had a parallel in Brigham Young's statement about dealings with the Indians: "Better to feed them than fight them."

"When the children came home from school at four o'clock in the afternoon," she recalls, "they would mill about, drink milk, eat bread and jam, and lag over doing chores or lessons. I hit upon the idea of having their supper ready when they came from school. After a big bowl of stew, their milk, and plenty of bread and jam, they were settled. They accepted their chore lists and worked with a minimum of complaint. By evening they were ready for lessons, creative family activities, and a bedtime snack."

Donna made the children's winter coats with hoods, and she braided wool strips for a nine-by-twelve braided rug for the hardwood living room floor.

Inspired by the many birds that made nests in their trees, Boyd painted a mural for the east wall of the living room. He drew a spreading tree, painted life-size drawings of the birds on paper, cut them out, and with the help of the children pasted them on the branches. He taught the children each bird's name and habits.

Having earlier set the goal of earning a doctorate, he worked on it whenever he could crowd in time. His Brigham City experience in seminary and in the Indian program provided the topic for his dissertation.[2]

At one point, Boyd and Brother Tuttle were sent to Washington, D.C., to meet with the Commissioner of Indian Affairs, the Secretary of the Interior, and the Commissioner of Education. While they were there Secretary of Agriculture Elder Ezra Taft Benson invited them to lunch at his office.

Later Boyd was appointed to an advisory committee for the Bureau of Indian Affairs that met several times each year. In that capacity he visited all of the Indian boarding schools in the United States as well as the Blood Reservation in Canada.

During the summers, when the seminaries were closed, he continued to fill class requirements toward his degree. One of his last courses, educational philosophy, was taught by visiting professor Henry Aldous Dixon, president of Weber College and Utah State University. Boyd knew him from his student days at Weber College.

In the class were two students beginning the master's degree program and two doctoral candidates. Discussions centered on philosophic views regarding the source of ultimate truth. Boyd and the other doctoral candidate were at loggerheads on every point. The two younger students took sides, the first acting as second to Boyd; the other, to his opponent. During class Boyd and his adversary did verbal battle. Dr. Dixon encouraged the sparring.

Boyd knew his material, articulated his views clearly, but was regularly put down, defeated, and didn't know what to do about this. After a month, his adversary's second walked down the hall with Boyd.

"Do you know what's wrong with you?" he asked.

"I'd like to know," Boyd answered dejectedly.

"You're fighting out of context and are never going to win."

"What do you mean?" Boyd asked.

"Just what I said." And he walked away.

Boyd drove home puzzled, sat on the little bench under a tree, and analyzed. Finally he knew that what they had really been discussing was God, revelation, good, and evil. But in the context of philosophical terms, Boyd had failed.

Next time in class he slipped quietly into context: he dropped references to intelligence from some external, unidentified source and talked frankly about revelation from God and about the real forces of good and evil. From that point the tables turned and Boyd gained the ground he had lost.

Although fully conversant with the terminology of educational philosophy, Boyd had learned that it cannot describe things of the spirit. Only words of spiritual truth as they are presented in the scriptures by the prophets and by the Lord can do that. These truths became Boyd's context from then on.

In the institute program Brother Tuttle and Boyd were frequently challenged by a spirit of intellectualism that had spread under former administrators who had promoted men of such leanings over more orthodox religion teachers. One example will serve to illustrate.

During the first few weeks of his new assignment Boyd had attended a meeting of seminary and institute teachers who were holding an in-service training meeting. He sat with the teachers. One of their number was the debunker.

"He vigorously criticized the recorded history of the Church and some of the traditions that have been established. He listed a number of things that he alleged, from his careful, scientific inquiry, just weren't so. His words impugned the characters of some early leaders of the Church, and perhaps some of the present ones. He was presenting this material, he said, to make the teachers think! 'We've got to wake up and be more critical and selective.' The spirit of his presentation did little to engender faith."

After the presentation Boyd was invited to give a few closing remarks. He felt nervous before the experienced teachers, some of whom were many years his senior. He prayed earnestly for inspiration to know what to say to make the meeting come out all right. There came into his mind the image of the *Winged Victory*, a statue of which he had seen a picture as a boy. He now had his text. Said he:

The statue has endured many things. The head is gone; both arms are gone; the wings are chipped; there are cracks and scrapes here and there; a foot is missing; yet it is regarded as probably the single most valuable piece of artwork existing today. Why?

Well, among other things, it is hard rock—adamant, undeniable, irrefutable proof that somewhere, sometime, someone with supreme artistic genius took some stone and with his tools fashioned this statue. With all that has been chipped away, with all of the flaws, that truth remains. There is enough left to be a testimony of the inspiration of the sculptor.

Regarding the Church, I suppose if we look we can find flaws and abrasions and a chip missing here and there. I suppose we can see an aberration or an imperfection in a leader of the past or perhaps the present. Nonetheless, there is still absolute, hard-rock, undeniable, irrefutable proof, because the Church is what it is and because that someone, sometime, with supreme inspired spiritual genius set to work obediently under inspiration and organized it, and so it came into being. It is best that we should enlarge ourselves to appreciate the beauty and genius of it, rather than debunk and look for the flaws.[3]

Having publicly acknowledged his orthodoxy and having publicly defended the Church and its revealed truths, he grew in stature before the men he supervised.

Boyd became more aware of the situation when in 1954 he attended summer school on BYU campus. In the minds of the Brethren, there clearly had been a drift. Some seminary and institute teachers, having earned advanced degrees in eastern universities, were determined to lift their students above the pioneer heritage, thinking they were liberating them.

The First Presidency called the seminary and institute men to BYU for a summer course. They assigned Elder Harold B. Lee, a great teacher himself, to conduct a five-week course. He came well prepared, stating that the purpose of the course was to lift the shades of ignorance and allow the truth to enter.

Each student was assigned to write a fifteen-hundred-word summary of Joseph Fielding Smith's *Man: His Origin and Destiny*. There followed twenty two-hour lesson periods covering basic teachings of the Church, the lessons being given by either Elder Lee or other

General Authorities, including President J. Reuben Clark, Jr., and Elders Marion G. Romney, Adam S. Bennion, and Mark E. Petersen of the Twelve.

Elder Lee's comments on Boyd's term paper were both approving and prophetic. He wrote: "Brother Packer, With your engaging personality, your flair for detail, and your foundation of faith you should go far in giving leadership much needed in the Church today and in the future. I shall be watching your progress! Faithfully yours, Harold B. Lee."

The seminar confirmed Boyd's deepest commitments. President J. Reuben Clark's 1933 address entitled "The Charted Course of the Church in Education"[4] became for him a measuring rod for religious views, philosophies, and teachings.

The more liberally inclined teachers later indicated by their actions what their attitudes were concerning the seminar and President Clark's message. Some left the system of their own accord. Others fought to accommodate speculation in place of, or mingled with, revealed truths. These were, for the most part, good men who either did not know or had forgotten that spiritual things *can* be proven; but proof comes only by the Spirit and by obedience to the laws that govern the proof.

Another experience with an out-of-step teacher taught both Boyd and Brother Tuttle an important lesson. An institute teacher, among other things, was counseling young people that repentance was not required and that confession to their bishops for sin was an invasion of their privacy. Complaints from parents and leaders alarmed General Authorities, who called upon Brother Berrett to investigate.

He sent Brother Tuttle to interview the man and to make a decision about him. He and Boyd traveled part way together, then separated, Boyd to meet with teachers in Pocatello.

After Boyd's meetings of the next evening he returned to his motel at midnight. Without knowing why, he checked out of that motel the next morning and into another before going to his meetings. That night as he opened his motel door the telephone rang. It was Brother Tuttle. "Boyd, I need help!"

"How on earth did you find me?"

"I remembered there is a Utah Motel in Pocatello, so I rang that first." Then he said: "I'm terrified! As I've been praying over what I should do about this man, it is as though all of the hosts of the adversary are working on me. I need your help!"

Promising his best efforts, Boyd hung up, dropped to his knees, and prayed mightily for Ted. "No sooner had I begun to pray than the same heinous power attacked me," he says. "I felt that the room was filled with demons, and I knew that not only Ted's life but mine was in deadly peril." In faith, he continued to plead with the Lord in their behalf, exercising the power of the priesthood to curb and dispel the dark evil. Finally it left.

Anxious about Ted's safety, Boyd joined him as soon as possible. The dread attack upon their persons drew them even closer in spirit. Each had come to know for himself that the power of evil was real.

"Still shaken from our terrifying experience," Boyd recalls, "we determined on our return to Salt Lake to speak of it to Elder Harold B. Lee, our teacher and mentor. He was very sober about it. 'This is very, very meaningful. Perhaps this is prophetic of something that awaits one of you in a call.' At the next conference, April 1958, A. Theodore Tuttle was sustained as a member of the First Council of the Seventy."

For his part, Elder Tuttle respected Boyd for his spiritual insights. He later wrote: "Of all the fields in which he excels, it is as a teacher that he is a master among men. I know of no man who is his superior in teaching a gospel concept. He is blessed with unusual gifts. He has the capacity to translate an ethereal verbal concept to an understandable activity in everyday life. . . . You will soon discover that what is explained so clearly and obviously was neither clear nor obvious before he explained it."[5]

William E. Berrett said Ted and Boyd were a David and Jonathan in their friendship. He also noted that "they were in full agreement with my approach to supervision. Being blessed with the spirit of discernment, they hired men they could trust and support, men who filled their positions in such a way that they could solve their problems with the help of the Lord."

Without Donna's commitment to their early goals and her remarkable abilities Boyd could not have carried his responsibilities in the Church Educational System, nor in his subsequent callings. Boyd's appreciation and gratitude for her have been constant and ever-present. He will readily say, "Without Donna, I am nothing."

A personal delight came to them and their family with the birth of Kathleen Amelia, their third daughter and eighth child, born in American Fork 5 September 1959.

Several men Brother Tuttle and Boyd supervised have spoken of their teaching in terms of greatness, but they note differences: "Ted flashed that smile and warmed you with the simple truths of the gospel, its sweetness and joy, and the power of faith. He had a quick wit. Boyd did, too, but his genius was in putting things together as an understandable whole. This he did with such consummate skill that we marveled, as we did over his ability to draw. He was a master at the blackboard."

Berrett, Tuttle, and Packer made a rare team, according to their secretary, who called them "the awesome threesome."[6] Later, Brother Berrett jokingly referred to his office as a training ground for General Authorities.

Ted and Boyd, however, became concerned over the growing lack of confidence in seminary and institute men on the part of the First Presidency and the Quorum of the Twelve. As mentioned, this came about by letters from dissatisfied parents and stake presidents.

One day Boyd and Ted came to the office fasting and asked the secretaries to hold all calls until notified. Together they discussed the issue in depth and prayed in council about it. The simple, profound answer came by direct revelation: *Follow the Brethren.*

This answer simplified their supervisory roles by providing a standard against which to measure

Boyd K. Packer and A. Theodore Tuttle, supervisors of Seminaries and Institutes of Religion

every out-of-context view or argument. No matter how learned or how steeped in academic pursuits he might be, the Latter-day Saint teacher of moral and spiritual truths must stay within the province of the Spirit and follow the Brethren.

Boyd later stated this in an unpublished letter: "It is an easy thing for a man with extensive academic training to try and measure the Church with the principles he has been taught in his professional training. In my mind it ought to be the other way around. A member of the Church ought always to judge the professions of men against the revealed word of the Lord."[7]

Boyd continued to serve by special assignment from one or another of the Brethren. On one occasion President Hugh B. Brown was conducting a meeting for all stake presidents in the Assembly Hall on Temple Square. Having a presentation to make, Boyd sat on the stand next to him. After the meeting began, President Brown leaned over and said: "We should have taken a roll. I wish we had a clipboard or something to send around for them to sign."

Having met most of them in his supervisory work, Boyd replied, "I think I can make a roll." Beginning with the first row of the center section where the stake presidents were seated, he wrote the names of all but half a dozen.

One day Boyd returned home from a supervisory trip and told Donna, "While I was up in Idaho I found a rope."

Somewhat puzzled, she said, "That was nice."

Sheepishly, he added, "Well, there was a horse tied to the other end of it." They had no corral for a horse, but Donna said pleasantly, "Well, we'll have to make arrangements so we can keep it." It had been a gift to the children from an Idaho stake president. The horse, however, had not been broken, so before the children could ride it Reed Orton, an experienced neighbor, took over the task.

Aware that his father's health was failing, Boyd invited his parents to join him on a trip to Los Angeles, where he had a seminary convention. Leaving there, they drove up the coast road toward San Francisco, and although feeble at the time, his father enjoyed the trip. Boyd was grateful that he could spend that extra time with his parents.

On 11 December 1958 Ira Wight Packer passed quietly away in

his sleep at age seventy-three. The entire community mourned the loss of this beloved and friendly man.

In August 1961 Brother Tuttle, as a member of the First Council of the Seventy, was called with his family to serve a three-year assignment to Montevideo, Uruguay. Donna and Boyd helped them off. They received Elder Tuttle's letter from Barbados Island dated August 15. With smooth waters and much to capture their interest, the voyage was a vacation for them. One sentence in the letter says: "I presume you are surviving all the mundane matters that we left you with." These matters included the management of their house and property, located near the Packer home, just at harvest time.

That same month, at age thirty-seven, Boyd was appointed a member of the Administrative Council of Brigham Young University.

Missing his friend Ted, he continued his supervisory work. One night after an institute meeting in Logan at which Elder LeGrand Richards had spoken, Boyd saw the venerable Apostle leaving the campus in his car. Because it was snowing heavily, Boyd determined to follow him in case he had difficulty in getting through Sardine Canyon and beyond. It was still snowing heavily as they neared Salt Lake City after dark, but Boyd felt confident that from there Brother Richards would be all right.

Accordingly he turned west off the highway and drove up over the railroad tracks. Suddenly his car stalled, then skidded backwards a few inches. Out of the darkness and blinding snow came a piercing whistle. Boyd felt the earth shake with the roar of the oncoming train. It missed him only by the inches his car had skidded backwards. He sat stunned and rigid until he could trust himself to proceed.

As terrifying as that experience had been, Boyd Packer would face even more soul-shaking experiences.

Chapter Eleven

Assistant to the Twelve

Shortly before October general conference in 1961 President Henry D. Moyle called William E. Berrett and said, "We don't wish to call Brother Packer as an Assistant to the Twelve without your approval, but I must say that we will call him whether you approve or not."[1]

About that same time Boyd's wife, Donna, fell as she walked up the Timpanogos Stake Center steps to a Primary preparation meeting. Her shin was badly injured and the wound would not heal. Her doctor said it was osteomyelitis, a bone disease. He prescribed daily multiple units of penicillin and warned that she must stay in bed for at least two weeks.

With eight children to care for, and Boyd preparing for Church education meetings during general conference, staying down required organization. Donna assigned tasks to each child and hired a young neighbor girl to help for an hour at supper time. A Primary co-worker came one day a week and helped the children clean the house. A neighbor nurse came twice daily to inject penicillin. Toward the last of Donna's enforced rest her mother came to help.

Meanwhile Boyd was attending his meetings on the upper floor of the old Presiding Bishop's building. A secretary interrupted with a phone call for him. He told her it could wait until after the meeting. She countered, "It is President Hugh B. Brown."

Picking up the phone, Boyd heard a rather gruff voice say, "Go to President McKay's office immediately." Boyd's first thought was, "What have I done?"

He hurriedly left, and entering the back door of the Administration Building was stopped by the security attendant, who ignored Boyd's request to see President McKay and motioned him to sit down and wait.

Soon Brother Brown approached the President's office and, seeing Boyd, asked him, "What are you waiting for?"

"I can't get in," Boyd answered.

President Brown said, "Well, we'll fix that."

In moments Boyd faced President McKay. It was nearing time for the Saturday morning session of conference to begin, so the interview was brief. The President then said: "The Twelve are waiting in the next room. I am going to present your name as an Assistant to the Quorum of the Twelve Apostles, and I think they are going to approve you."

Tears welled in Boyd's eyes as the President added, "Sister Packer will have to hear about it over the air."

On the way out, Elder Spencer W. Kimball spoke to Boyd. "Well, I have expected this, but not quite so soon."

It was a dazed Boyd that walked from the Church offices to the Tabernacle. One of his seminary men joined him, wanting to talk. Getting unintelligible responses he said, "You are not making much sense, you know," and then asked, "Are you all right?"

At their home in Lindon, Donna and her mother listened to the radio as they washed the dishes. Suddenly they heard President Moyle present the names of Thorpe B. Isaacson of the Presiding Bishopric and Boyd K. Packer to become Assistants to the Quorum of the Twelve. As President Moyle called for a sustaining vote, Donna sensed what this call would mean in their lives. She raised her hand. It was 30 September 1961. Boyd was thirty-seven years of age, the youngest among the General Authorities.

It was a sober Boyd who sat in conference pondering the years

The Packer family at the time of his call as a General Authority

since he and Donna, as a newly engaged couple, had watched Elder Henry D. Moyle take his place on the stand as an Apostle. As he now called Elder Packer to the stand, Boyd's early witness to this event was confirmed.

Sensing their need to be together, Roy Fugal drove Donna from Lindon to be with Boyd for the afternoon session of conference. Her mother stayed with the children, and from her they heard of their father's call.

The next day Donna went with Boyd to the Sunday sessions. That afternoon President Moyle told Boyd that after his trip to Europe he would have an assignment for him. The Packers drove home to Lindon feeling that his call was but a dream. They hoped the reality of it might come with his setting apart, scheduled for October 6.

Of that occasion Boyd said: "I will not forget that day when I stood before President McKay. He sat at the end of the table in the First Presidency's board room and said: 'We have explained to you what your obligation will be as an Assistant to the Quorum of the Twelve Apostles. This obligation includes standing with the members of the Quorum of the Twelve as a special witness of the Lord Jesus Christ. Before proceeding with this ordination and setting apart, I want to know if you have that witness. Bear your testimony to us.'"[2]

President Moyle was voice in setting Boyd apart. He left immediately for Europe. Arriving in Denver, however, he was notified that President J. Reuben Clark, Jr., had just died and that he was to return. It was still October 6. On October 10 Boyd attended the funeral, his first as a General Authority.

Elder Packer then began his apprenticeship to the Quorum of the Twelve Apostles—a training period that was to last nine years.

Elder Boyd K. Packer, new
Assistant to the Twelve

Twenty years earlier President Clark had explained the need for Assistants to the Twelve. He had then presented the names of five men called to that position.[3] Now, with Elder Packer's appointment, there were twelve Assistants.

These men served the First Presidency, already named, and the Quorum of the Twelve as follows: Joseph Fielding Smith, Harold B. Lee, Spencer W. Kimball, Ezra Taft Benson, Mark E. Petersen, Delbert L. Stapley, Marion G. Romney, LeGrand Richards, Richard L. Evans, George Q. Morris, Howard W. Hunter, and Gordon B. Hinckley, the latter having been ordained an Assistant to the Twelve on 6 April 1958 and an Apostle on 5 October 1961, the day before Elder Packer's ordination.

Not certain whether he should now complete his doctorate, Elder Packer sought counsel from President McKay. He told the President that after eight years he had completed his course work and had started his dissertation. "I want you to get your degree," the President said, "and when you have it, use it. It will be very helpful to you, especially among nonmembers."

Assistants to the Twelve in 1961

Following that counsel, Elder Packer worked on it every free moment from then until it was approved. He received his Doctor of Education degree from Brigham Young University on 25 May 1962. According to BYU President Ernest L. Wilkinson, Boyd was one of the first three candidates to earn doctoral degrees from that university.[4]

When President Moyle returned from Europe he assigned Elder Packer to the Church Missionary Committee as an assistant to Elder Gordon B. Hinckley. Elder Packer felt fortunate to have served with Brother Hinckley in this and other capacities. From Elder Hinckley's long service and wide experience he received valuable training and learned much.

The Missionary Department operated worldwide. It took day or night phone calls having to do with mission business, sick missionaries, and special problems. The scope of the work was staggering to

Elder Packer and greatly enlarged his vision and experience in Church government.

It was President Moyle's responsibility to assign missionaries to their fields of labor. Going home for lunch, he would call Boyd to bring the files to his study where it was quiet and free from interruption. Elder Packer would read missionary names and President Moyle would make the assignments, which Boyd would write down.

On the day he received his doctorate

One day he read the name of a young man who had completed six years of A-grade German. President Moyle thought for a few minutes and said, "Andes Mission." Elder Packer said, "President, that was German, not Spanish." Brother Moyle thought a little longer and said, "Andes Mission." Brother Packer never questioned an assignment again.

Being constantly associated with members of the Quorum of the Twelve, Elder Packer said, "was as if I were flying with a higher flock than I belonged to." Sensing how he felt, President Moyle took an interest in him. He invited him to luncheons with prominent people and was solicitous and encouraging.

In August 1963 he asked Elder Packer and his wife to tour the Alaska mission with him and Sister Moyle. For the Packers, the request seemed impossible. When Brother Packer became an Assistant to the Twelve his income decreased substantially. With their son Lawrence's birth on 7 July 1962 the Packers had nine children. Although Elder Packer's fare would be paid, they had no money for Sister Packer's plane ticket.

Accordingly Elder Packer asked if he could be excused from going. President Moyle responded, "President McKay has assigned you to go." Then with deep seriousness he said: "I will not be here

Elders Packer and Tuttle arriving in Montevideo, Uruguay

much longer. If the things I know are worth keeping, the only place I know to preserve them is with someone younger. I want you to come with me and I want you to stay with me and I want you to listen."[5]

And so they went to Alaska. For ten days Elder Packer listened and learned lessons from a leader who was keen to teach him. Of importance was one lesson he would use many times himself. The setting was a television interview at Elmendorf Air Force Base near Anchorage, in connection with a youth conference they attended. President Moyle faced a commentator who was openly antagonistic to the Church. With great skill the president took control of the interview, responding to the bitterly-phrased barbs with answers to questions his opponent, in fairness to his audience, should have asked.

Upon their return President Hugh B. Brown invited the Packers to dinner along with the Moyles, the N. Eldon Tanners, and the Victor L. Browns. As the guests were leaving, the Packers talked briefly with the Moyles, who were leaving for Florida that weekend. It was the last time they saw President Moyle alive. He died 18 September 1963 at Deer Park, Osceola County, Florida, just weeks after the Alaska trip.

On assignment from the Missionary Committee Elder Packer made his first trip to South America in November 1964, where, as General Authorities, he and Elder A. Theodore Tuttle toured the South American missions together. That tour enlarged Brother Packer's vision of the work to be done among the Lamanites. He saw that their numbers and potential in South America were far greater than those of the various tribes within the United States and Canada.

One experience in the city of Cuzco, high in the Andes of Peru, was unforgettable. He and Brother Tuttle were attending a sacrament meeting in the Cuzco Branch. They were seated at one end of the room facing the congregation, beyond which a door stood open to the street to let the cool night air into the crowded room. Against the wall to Elder Packer's left was a small sacrament table. Of this he recalled:

> While Brother Tuttle was speaking, a little boy appeared in the doorway. He was perhaps six or seven years old. His only clothing was a tattered shirt which almost reached his knees. He was dirty and undernourished, with all the characteristics of a street orphan. Perhaps he entered the room to get warm, but then he saw the bread on the sacrament table.
>
> He began to approach, carefully walking next to the wall. When he was just about to reach the sacrament table, one of the sisters saw him. Without saying a word, with only a movement of her head, she clearly communicated the message, "Out." He hesitated an instant, turned around, and disappeared into the night. My heart wept for him. Undoubtedly the sister felt justified because this was a special meeting, with General Authorities present, and this was a dirty little boy who wasn't going to learn anything, and after all, he wasn't even a member of the Church.
>
> In a short time he appeared in the doorway again, looking toward the bread. Again he began to quietly approach the table. He had almost reached the row where the woman was sitting when I got him to look at me. I held out my open arms. He came to me, and I picked him up to hold in my arms. . . .
>
> I felt that I had an entire people in my arms. . . . A voice from the dust, perhaps from the dust of those small feet, already rough, whispered to me that this was a child of the covenant, of the lineage of the prophets.
>
> I have looked for him [since then] . . . in Chile, Peru, Ecuador, Colombia, and Brazil. . . .
>
> I have been in Cuzco since that time, and now I see this people whom I held in my arms, coming to be baptized, to preach, to preside.[6]

Returning home, Elder Packer shared his experience with Elder Spencer W. Kimball, who saw great significance in it.

Another missionary-related assignment came to Brother Packer when Elder Marion G. Romney, supervisor of the work in Mexico, said: "You've been approved as my assistant supervisor of the work in Mexico. We are to get the literature of the Church into the Spanish language." Elder Packer said he did not speak Spanish, to which Brother Romney responded, "I don't want a linguist; I want an administrator."

The Book of Mormon was available in Spanish, but instructional materials were not. Shortly thereafter these were translated and distributed.

Another matter of concern was that of obtaining missionary visas into Mexico. Waiting for visas months after their calls shortened their two-and-a-half-year missions. They were further hampered by the time it took to learn basic Spanish after reaching their fields of labor.

Elder Romney asked Joseph T. Bentley, former president of the Northern Mexican Mission (1956–58), to check into the situation. He reported his findings on 20 September 1961, and the missionary committee foresaw a program wherein missionaries to Mexico could learn Spanish on BYU campus while waiting for their visas.

It was decided that under the influence of their calls missionaries were working for the Lord, and that the Spirit of the Holy Ghost could operate as well on the BYU campus as in the mission field.[7]

Elder Hinckley recognized similar difficulties in obtaining visas from Argentina and suggested that those missionaries be included in the new program. Approval was given.

Elder Packer was appointed to the Advisory Committee and worked closely with Elder Romney and with Ernest Wilkins of the BYU Language Department to establish a language training center. He made many trips to BYU to arrange housing and classroom facilities and helped set the program in motion.

Elder Packer was assigned to serve on the Indian Committee with Elder Spencer W. Kimball as chairman, Elder LeGrand Richards, member, and Dean L. Larsen, secretary. They were to champion the cause of Indian peoples in the United States. They visited reservations, the Southwest Indian Mission, the Indian Mission they had established in Rapid City, North Dakota, and the Cherokee Mission in South Carolina. They later worked with other minority groups, particularly the Spanish-American people in the United States.

Elder Packer was also called to serve on the LDS Servicemen's Committee, taking Elder Bruce R. McConkie's place when the latter was called to preside over a mission in Australia. Elder Harold B. Lee chaired the committee, with Elder Gordon B. Hinckley as the other member. While it fostered the welfare of LDS servicemen, most of its work had to do with the chaplaincy.

Elders Harold B. Lee, Gordon B. Hinckley, and Boyd K. Packer, Servicemen's Committee members, May 1965

As a committee member, Brother Packer was sent to Washington, D.C., on many occasions. There he met with chiefs of chaplains, who were all ministers of other churches. They had established a rule that no one could be commissioned as a chaplain unless he had ninety semester hours of graduate work in a theological seminary. Because the Church had no such seminaries, LDS men could not qualify. To have this rule waived was the purpose of the meetings, but thus far the Church had met nothing but opposition.

Elder Harold B. Lee served on the board of Equitable Life Insurance Company with Robert A. Lovett, a former Secretary of Defense. He asked Lovett to use his influence in the matter, but neither his influence nor appeals to the chiefs of chaplains was successful. The Brethren then sought, and were granted, audience with the President of the United States, Lyndon B. Johnson.

Elder Packer assumed that Elder Lee would handle the interview. Instead, he called Boyd out of a meeting and assigned him to fly out that afternoon and meet with President Johnson at ten o'clock the next morning. He said that Senators Ted Moss of Utah and Howard Cannon of Nevada would join him in the Oval Office at the White House.

While Sister Packer was bringing his travel things he sought counsel from Elder Lee, who said, "Just remember when you meet the president, that this is *not* 1830, and there aren't just *six* of us."

"That gave me a good deal more courage," Brother Packer recalls.

The next morning when he and the senators met in the Oval Office, President Johnson expressed great admiration for President David O. McKay, saying, "I think of him almost as my grandpa."

He then listened while Elder Packer explained the problem: "As a church we encourage our men to be good citizens. We do not support them in conscientious objection nor can they give the doctrine of the Church as a basis for it. Rather, we foster citizenship and patriotism. Yet we are being prevented from having our own chaplains serve our men in the military."

President Johnson picked up the telephone and called Cyrus R. Vance, Deputy Secretary of Defense, and told him that he was sending Dr. Packer and the senators over. Secretary Vance was to fix things up for them.

There was terse conversation between the two men, with Vance evidently arguing the point on seminary requirements. President Johnson's voice showed irritation as he shot back: "I know that, Cyrus. I know *all* of that. But these Mormons have their men praying and preaching from the minute they are out of their mothers' wombs. They're qualified ministers as much as anybody else."

For the first time the Church had a fair hearing. The desired waiver was granted, and it became possible for the Church to again have chaplains for its men in the military. Perhaps this was an example of his doctorate's being helpful in Elder Packer's calling, as President McKay had foreseen.

Elder Packer was appointed to the Church Board of Education, the board of trustees for Brigham Young University, and the executive committee of those boards.

And so it was that Elder Packer, who always hungered after learning, was personally tutored and trained by great souls, earlier watchmen on the tower—President Joseph Fielding Smith, Elders

Harold B. Lee, Spencer W. Kimball, and Gordon B. Hinckley, who would become Presidents of the Church, and Elders Henry D. Moyle and Marion G. Romney, who served in turn as counselors to Church Presidents. He also learned from the other members of the Twelve as well as from his fellow Assistants and the Seventies.

In his capacity as an adviser to the Relief Society for a number of years, Elder Packer became well acquainted with Sister Belle S. Spafford, general president. He considered her to be one of the great women of her time. He speaks of the mystery and power of her "ordinariness." She was, he says, "a wide-heeled, flat-shoe woman, who never tried to be other than herself. She could go into the highest circles as a Latter-day Saint woman and command the respect and admiration of those present." Perhaps her genuineness stemmed from heeding her mother's wise counsel: "Never speak or act out of the wealth of your ambition and ego, and the poverty of your knowledge and experience."[8]

Elder Packer also says of Sister Spafford: "She had a fierceness about sustaining the priesthood. She would say, 'The Brethren have said this, and sisters, this is our duty. We *will* do it.'"

Brother Packer shared her commitment to obedience and, in certain situations, spoke in her defense. And she, observing him hold his ground on difficult issues in the face of criticism, said, "He has the courage of a lion."

For many years Elder Lee had seen a need to correlate the organizations and programs of the Church under priesthood authority and direction, and he became the principal advocate of this cause. In this connection, and while still a seminary and institute supervisor, Brother Packer had been asked to prepare a report for the Church Education Committee, which was later restructured and named the Priesthood Correlation Committee.

For this report he drew a picture of a house being split in pieces with an ax. He compared it to the Church being splintered and parcelled out to the MIA, the Sunday School, the Relief Society, and the Primary. In a sense, he explained, each was a church within the Church, with its own lesson manuals, meetings, activities, boards, and magazines. Together they were a drain on parents' time and money for their own families.

Early in 1964 a seminar was held to discuss matters pertaining to correlation and to outline the duties and responsibilities of Church correlation committee members. Their assignments were: Elder Harold B. Lee, committee chairman; Elder Spencer W. Kimball, missionary; Elder Marion G. Romney, home teaching; Elder Howard W. Hunter, genealogy; and Bishop John H. Vandenberg, welfare. Each subcommittee head had his assistants. Elder Gordon B. Hinckley and Elder Packer became assistants to Elder Kimball in the missionary work. This began Elder Packer's long service as a member of the Priesthood Correlation Committee.

As with the other General Authorities, Elder Packer was assigned to dedicate chapels, to speak at general conferences, stake conferences, funerals, commemorative celebrations, seminary graduations, and baccalaureate exercises. Such requests involved virtually every evening and every weekend. Being under the impression that he had to do everything asked of him, he found little time left for home and family.

One winter he received a letter from a mission president in Denver asking him to come and speak to his missionaries on Christmas Eve. Elder Harold B. Lee received a copy of the letter, and, meeting Boyd in the hall, said, "Don't bother to answer it. I will."

In responding to the letter, Elder Lee wrote: "Elder Packer will not be able to come on Christmas Eve. He has a previous appointment with his own family." He then counseled Boyd not to walk or run faster than he was able. And he was to keep Donna's and the children's needs in their proper perspective. His direction was as valuable to the Packer family as Jethro's counsel was to Moses.

For his prepared talks, Elder Packer labors diligently. He rises early to study, ponder, and write. "If I am worried about a subject, thinking about a subject, going to talk about a subject, I have learned to have ten one-hour sessions as compared to a ten-hour session. A subject must mature in your mind."

His early general conference talks were focused upon the youth of the Church and the children. After 1964 he began to broaden the subject base of his talks, indicating the expanding scope of his ministry.

To prevent his commuting daily to Salt Lake City, the Packers decided to leave Lindon and relocate nearer Church headquarters. They hoped for a place where they could keep animals and birds and the children could continue to have the daily chores. Elder Packer also wanted to insulate them from the publicity of his position as a General Authority. Away from the city he could come home with no more fanfare than from work in any business office. Sister Packer's Lindon experience had given her confidence, in his absence, to manage their nine children, a home, and a large piece of property.

President Moyle had kindly assigned someone to help locate such a place. When it was found, the Packers fell in love with it. Elder Harold B. Lee looked over the house and property one day and counseled, "By all means, you are to proceed."

There was a problem, however. When they added up every asset they possessed, including a projected loan on their insurance, they could not see any way to get into the house.

Still Brother Lee insisted, "Go ahead; I know it is right."

"I was in deep turmoil," Elder Packer has written, "because I had been counseled to do something I had never done before—to sign a contract without the resources to meet the payments."

Sensing the turmoil, Brother Lee sent him to President David O. McKay, who listened very carefully, then said: "You do this. It is the right thing." But he extended no resources to make it possible.

Brother Packer recalled, "When I reported to Brother Lee he said, 'That confirms what I have told you.'

"I was still not at peace, and then came the lesson.

"Elder Lee said, 'Boyd, do you know what is wrong with you— you always want to see the end from the beginning.'

"I replied quietly that I wanted to see at least a few steps ahead.

The Packer home in Salt Lake City

He answered by quoting from the sixth verse of the twelfth chapter of Ether. 'Wherefore, dispute not because ye see not, for ye receive no witness until after the trial of your faith.'

"And then he added, 'My boy, you must learn to walk to the edge of the light, and perhaps a few steps into the darkness, and you will find that the light will appear and move ahead of you.'"9

For Elder Packer it was a great test of faith, but he moved ahead and step by step the way opened for him to acquire the property, move his family, make the payments, and begin to make it their home.

In the latter months of 1964 Elder Packer's mother, Emma Packer, was taken from Brigham City to St. Mark's Hospital in Salt Lake City. She had a dread of cancer, for which tests were now being run. The family had never dared speak the word in her presence.

Brother Packer was called to her bedside in the early morning hours. She said to him: "I want you to take me home right now. I'll not have more of these tests."

"But, Mother," he protested, "you must go through with them. The doctors have reason to believe that you have cancer, and if it is so, you have the worst kind."

After all the whispered conversations, he had spoken the dread word. Emma sat quietly on her bed for a long time. Then she spoke. "Well, if *that's* what it is, that's what it *is*, and I'll fight it."

During the period that followed she experienced some of the great spiritual experiences of her life. Twice in full daylight she saw her mother, who had been gone from her for some seventy years. She felt that this was to prepare her for the reunion she would soon have with her loved ones beyond the veil.

Through the last days of her illness Dr. Gordon Felt treated her as a loving son would do. Her own sons and the stake patriarch gave her a blessing and, in a marvelous way, she was released from pain and rested comfortably unless moved.

One Friday afternoon Boyd was impressed that he and Donna should go to Emma. They found her much as they had seen her last, but she whispered over and over the word *tomorrow*.

Elder Packer asked, "Is tomorrow the day?"

She smiled and said, "Yes."

"Mother, are you sure?"

"Oh, yes," she said, "I am sure."

That evening her other sons gathered about her, and Boyd, under inspiration, gave her a final blessing.

It was Friday and Boyd was reluctant to leave, but when the doctor told him there would be no immediate change he returned home and prepared for his conference assignment in Panguitch, Utah, the next day.

On Saturday he called Brigham City before leaving home and was told that there was no change. He called again from Panguitch and there was still no change. After the first meeting he placed another call, and this time his brother Lowell said: "Mother slept peacefully away. I heard her say, 'Ira, Ira, Ira,' so we know Father came to take her with him." It was 23 January 1965. She and Ira had been apart for six years.

On 9 June 1965 the *Church News* announced the enlarged world assignments of General Authorities. Under direction of the First Presidency and Joseph Fielding Smith, President of the Quorum of the Twelve, the world was sectioned into areas: five in the United States; the North American Spanish; the Orient and Hawaii; the South Pacific; South America; the British Isles; West European; East European. One Apostle and one Assistant to the Twelve were to preside over and direct the work for each area.

Elder and Sister Packer were called to preside over the New England Mission with headquarters in Cambridge, Massachusetts, succeeding President Truman G. Madsen on or about 15 August 1965.

For months they had felt impressed to *get ready*: for what, they did not know. But when the call came their home was in order and they were ready to leave. The A. Theodore Tuttles, just returning from their mission in South America, had agreed to live in and care for the Packer home while they were away. In preparation for their coming, Donna had left home-canned fruit in the pantry, and Elder Packer had replaced their own brass nameplate with one specially made for the Tuttles and attached to the side of the front door.

Elder Packer had not been a bishop or a stake president. Always, before this time, he had been an assistant: assistant stake clerk; assistant instructor to the high priests group in Lindon; assistant to William E. Berrett in the seminary and institute program of the Church; and Assistant to the Quorum of the Twelve. The Lord had been a long time in preparing him for this responsibility as mission president—one of the most independent offices in the Church. He now sensed his complete dependence upon the Spirit to guide and sustain him.

Chapter Twelve

President of the
New England Mission

Wilbur W. Cox, president of the Boston Stake in 1965, remembers seeing the Packers come off the plane at Logan International Airport and saying to himself: "Man! That is some organized family."

They had not been the first to deplane, but when they came down the steps onto the landing area it was Sister Packer first, then the president holding three-year-old Lawrence by the hand, and five more of their nine children following. All carried small cases containing items which had occupied them on this their first flight ever. The three older sons would join them after their summer's work at the Smith ranch in Wyoming. On their way to Boston they were to visit the New York World's Fair as the others had just done.

After greeting the family, President Cox and his wife, Nora, took them to the mission home at 15 Hawthorne Street in Cambridge. During the next three days Nora drove Sister Packer to schools, library, stores, market, and to the Massachusetts Transport Authority underground stops near the home.

Upon closer association with the Packers, President and Sister Cox were impressed not only with their organization but also with the pervading sense of order that was neither martial nor restrictive. Intelligence tempered by common sense created this climate.

The Coxes blended naturally into the role of adopted grandparents. They found the children strikingly different in looks, personality, and talents. "The children were full of spirit, and I liked that," Brother Cox says. "On one occasion we were preparing for a stake conference to which a General Authority had been assigned. After I had met the visitor at the airport, he asked me to drive him to the mission home to meet President Packer. As we pulled into the Packers' driveway and got out of the car, Russell and Spencer came running to me and we roughhoused for a minute or two."

"Boys, boys," the visitor reacted, "is this the way you treat your stake president?"

Brother Cox chuckles over the answer one gave: "That's the way we keep him humble."[1]

President Cox was drawn to the Packer boys and especially to Allan, who shared his interest in amateur radio and whom he helped obtain needed equipment for that hobby. Elder Packer encouraged their mutual interest by installing wires and a bulky antenna for the project. "The mission home was a three-story house, very high, and it was with breathless concern that we climbed onto the roof to get that aerial up so that Allan could have his hobby."

The parents gave the same encouragement to each of the children in pursuing their individual interests. They provided a room in the basement where the boys were free to paint, pound, and hammer. The girls liked to go down and see what was going on there, but they preferred playing school on the sun porch where their father's chalkboard was available when he was not teaching the missionaries. There they taught their dolls endless lessons or sewed for them—miniature models of clothes they would soon be making for themselves.

The transition to mission life was not easy for Allan, a senior in high school who had lettered in football and wrestling and was in line for a sports scholarship to college. But he had been obedient to the family's call, setting a good example for the others. His obedience was rewarded, however, when he again lettered in football, met the more rigorous scholastic requirements of his new school (Cambridge High and Latin), and met his future wife, Terri Bennett.

Each of the children acknowledges blessings that came from the experience: They became acquainted with the sites, history, crafts, and literature of their American heritage. They made friends among children of different ethnic groups and religious persuasions. They took piano and ballet lessons and were exposed to the cultural climate of the Boston area.

This family of eleven were, in a sense, on display for local Church leaders, missionaries, and visiting notables who came into the mission home. They fared very well by just being themselves.

When Elder Spencer W. Kimball had set Sister Packer apart for the mission, he had blessed her that she would have the "ability to handle not only [her] immediate family but the great family of the mission" and that she might be able to do so "in calm tranquility and without frustrations."[2]

Dinner with family and missionaries
in the mission home

At first she did not feel calm tranquility; she felt overwhelmed! Sensing this, Elder Kimball counseled her to put her family first, to support her husband, and to carry her part in the women's auxiliaries only as her time and strength would permit. Following his counsel, Sister Packer directed most of her auxiliary organization work from the home and traveled much less than many mission presidents' wives do.

When the family first settled into the mission home its exterior was badly in need of repair. President Packer obtained a building permit to cover the deteriorating wood with colonial-buff aluminum siding, selecting material that matched the width and character of the original clapboard of that historic-register home. Even so, a representative from the Historical Society harassed him, obtained a cease-and-desist order, and requested a hearing. When Elder Packer showed that he had a building permit and was indeed protecting the original character of the landmark house the matter was dropped.

At the back of the Cambridge chapel, just steps away from the mission home, there were rooms formerly designated for the mission office. However, they had since been used for other purposes. President Packer felt them to be more appropriate to present needs than the existing mission office at 1430 Massachusetts Avenue, which overlooked Harvard Square. It was crowded, and tobacco smoke seeped through adjoining walls. Accordingly he had the office moved to the Cambridge Ward chapel.

Elder Packer had always tried to be with the family as much as his ministry had allowed. Now, because he had more control over his schedule, the mission experience afforded additional opportunities. The older children recall that their father was at home more and that he occasionally took one of them with him when he traveled. Kenneth remembers when he and his father visited the Prophet Joseph Smith's birthplace at South Royalton, Vermont. It was there that this son gained a special witness of the Prophet's mission and the Restoration.

Later, President Packer oversaw the remodeling of the Joseph Smith Memorial, a project dear to his heart. Rather than being just a historic site as previously, it then became a gospel-teaching center offering displays, instructions, and literature which were designed for that purpose. In June 1967 it was opened to the public and given extensive media coverage. Missionaries from the Vermont zone were trained as tour guides for school, church, and club groups. As a result, the number of visitors increased tenfold.

As an assistant to the president, Steven Smith (who later became the family dentist) told what his mission president taught him about public speaking. After Elder Smith had given a rambling talk at a zone conference, President Packer asked if he would like to know how he could improve. "Oh, yes!" was the answer. "You're machine-gunning," Elder Packer said. "You've got to center on one idea, one theme, and give it in the first sentence or paragraph. Then let everything from there on support it. Let your audience know right up front what you are talking about and don't keep them guessing.' "3

Elder Don Butler, also an assistant, who later became a stake president, told how President Packer taught his missionaries the value of time. Promptly at 8:00 A.M. the president began a meeting for the leaders of six zones. After the opening song and prayer, one of his counselors began his presentation. Elders began slipping in late. After fifteen minutes, two zone leaders still had not arrived. When they finally entered, President Packer interrupted the speaker and announced, "We will now begin the meeting." The song and prayer were repeated, and the counselor once again began his talk. At its conclusion, President Packer told the group, "If you are not fifteen minutes early to a meeting, you are late." The word spread through the mission, and thereafter tardiness among the elders ended.

The president also taught three cardinal rules—work, obedience, and common sense. Linked to each was the concept of self-reliance in seeking inspiration to handle their own problems.

One evening his assistants arrived from Barton, Vermont, about a five-hour drive away. They reported that one of the elders had left his companion several times to visit with a girl who clerked at a grocery store. At the conclusion of their report, President Packer, remembering an earlier lesson taught him by President Joseph Fielding Smith, asked, "Well, what did you do about it?"

"We came right down to report," they said.

"That doesn't do much good, does it?" he responded.

Elder Packer commented: "After Sister Packer had given them a good meal they headed for Barton. Late the next day they reported having corrected the problem. They had handled it more effectively and much more wisely than I could have done, for they understood just what that elder needed most and supplied it."[4]

Another time he taught that calls come through inspiration and not by rational, arbitrary choice. He was to appoint a new assistant. He had prayed about the matter. He called a zone conference and, as he interviewed each missionary, thought, "Is this the man?" Finally the answer came, "This is the man." He was appointed. Elder Packer recalled, "He had been permitted to come on a mission only after some considerable shaping up to become eligible."

After the announcement, one of the zone leaders came to see me privately. He came from the same community in the West as did the new assistant. He was obviously disturbed. His first question was, "Do you really know the elder you have appointed as your assistant?"

"Yes, Elder. I know all that you know about him, and a good deal more," was my answer.

"Why, then, was *he* appointed your assistant?"

I pondered for a moment and then said, "Elder, why don't you ask the question that you came to ask?"

"What do you mean?"

"Ask the question that is really on your mind," I encouraged.

"But I did," he said.

"No," I said, "There is another question. The thing that is on your mind is not 'Why did you appoint him as your assistant?' It is 'Why did you not appoint me?'"

Elder Packer explained:

Now, please understand. I thought his unexpressed question to be a very logical and a sensible one. For it included this thought: "Here I am. I have worked as hard as I know how to work. All my life I have been a straight arrow. I have not rebelled nor been disobedient. I have prepared myself for a mission in every way I knew how to prepare. I have been trained, and I have studied. I have respected my parents and my bishop, and I have presided over my quorums. And here I am a missionary.

"Now another, whose path has been crooked, who has skipped meetings and dabbled in mischief, who winked at restriction and snickered at obedience, has been elevated above me."

I had sympathy for this young man and admired him greatly for his courage to speak. "If you should ask why you were not chosen," I said, "I would have to answer, 'I do not know, Elder.' I only know that he was chosen. Perhaps he may fail. But at least I know he is the one with the combination of talents and ability and qualities best calculated to get done what the office needs at the moment.

"This is no reflection upon you. You may yet preside over him and many above him. You may be his bishop or his stake president. You may preside over the Church. I do not know. But his call is no reflection upon you. Do not be injured by it.

"Go back to work and serve the Lord. Sustain him," I counseled, "Your contest is not with him, but with yourself."

And then I gently added, "You may have a bit of repenting to do."

Some weeks later I saw him again. This time he said with simple assurance: "I know one reason why he was appointed your assistant. So that I could learn the greatest lesson that I have ever learned in my life."[5]

At one point President Packer felt that something significant was lacking in the mission. "The missionaries were well groomed. They were following mission rules. They were up early; they studied, learned the discussions, and went to their areas of work prepared. On the surface, everything was excellent."

But something was missing. We were having baptisms, but not what we should expect. I prayed about it and did every obvious thing. What was I doing wrong?

Sister Packer suggested that we prayerfully study the missionaries during the next series of zone conferences. She was sure that this would provide the answer.

We had seven zones. During the first six conferences we heard each missionary bear testimony. It was in the last zone that the answer came.

We met in the chapel at the Joseph Smith birthplace. We were nearing the end of the testimonies. Then one frightened young elder with hair that never would stay combed stood to bear his testimony. He blurted out one sentence only: "I know that the gospel is true, that Jesus is the Christ, and that Joseph Smith was a prophet of God. In the name of Jesus Christ, amen." And he sat down.

The instant he sat down I knew what was wrong in the mission. At last we had isolated the missing ingredient. It had to do with testimony. All of the other missionaries had expressed gratitude for their parents and for being on a mission. They were grateful for the Church. They had related some very faith-promoting experiences. They said how thankful they were to have a testimony. They usually concluded, "I have a testimony of the gospel." But they had not borne it.

President Packer then knew what to teach. He told them that when conversion takes place it is done through the power of the Spirit, and that the missionaries must acquire greater power in their lives so that they might bring that power into the lives of all who investigate the gospel under their guidance.

He taught them that it was for this purpose that Alma gave up the judgment seat and went among the people preaching, "seeing no

President Packer of the New England Mission in his office in
Cambridge, Massachusetts

way that he might reclaim them save it were in bearing down in pure testimony against them" (Alma 4:19).

The missionaries were both to *bear* (or carry) their testimonies with them at all times and to *bare* (or make known) the things they actually knew, as Alma knew and bore witness of: "Behold, I say unto you they are made known unto me by the Holy Spirit of God. Behold, I have fasted and prayed many days that I might know these things of myself. And now I do know of myself that they are true; for the Lord God hath made them manifest unto me by his Holy Spirit; and this is the spirit of revelation which is in me." (Alma 5:46.)[6]

These teachings created a turning point in the lives both of missionaries and of investigators who were receptive to the witness of the Holy Spirit.

Loren C. Dunn, Communications Director for the New England Council for Economic Development, was called as a counselor to President Packer. He had served as a counselor to the former mission president, a man whose capacity to concern himself with every aspect of missionary work had been a positive influence in the lives of many.

"By contrast," Elder Dunn recalls, "President Packer stood back and put things together in priesthood order, inspired people from where he was, and caused things to happen without his being present."

> I learned more from him about how the priesthood should operate than from any other person. He had the capacity to put things together in such a way that people would function in their callings, and as they did so growth came to them personally. He brought a vision of the Church and how it should operate and what it should do.
>
> The New England Mission at that time included Connecticut, Rhode Island, Massachusetts, New Hampshire, Vermont, Maine, and the Canadian Maritime Provinces—New Brunswick, Nova Scotia, Prince Edward Island, Newfoundland, and Labrador. At its far points, missionaries and members were farther from the mission home than the home was from Church headquarters in Salt Lake City. There were in this whole area only one stake—Boston; seven districts; and forty-five

branches. The membership was holding its own, but it was not growing to where it could qualify for stakes and wards, and things had been that way for some time. Because of the geography, the previous president had divided the mission into three parts, with each of us supervising two or three districts and the mission president directing the whole.

President Packer changed that. He said, "Now, that is good, but there is strength and power in presidency," and so he and I with the other counselor, an able older man who had served with several mission presidents, began to do things as a presidency. I could immediately feel the difference. As we counseled together, we received direction and inspiration. I learned that the principle of presidency goes way beyond three people just being together. There is a power present because it is what the Lord has ordained as part of Church government. When the presidency acted as a presidency, the district and branch presidencies began to do so, just as the Lord would have them do.

Elder Dunn recalls that traditionally the mission presidency had handled all emergencies.

President Packer would not do that. Instead, he called in our district and branch presidents and held a meeting. He then taught them to act in their offices as the Lord expected them to do, because the mission presidency was not going to do that for them.

Suddenly we were out of the brush-fire business, and the districts and branches began to grow because we did not resolve their problems for them.[7]

Thus things were set in priesthood order. Branch and district presidents began to wrestle with member problems and taught their auxiliary leaders the same principles. President Packer further determined to fill all key positions with local brethren as opposed to those who had moved into the area from the West. Priesthood leaders began to blossom from that point on.

It was during the early stages of setting things in priesthood order that Elder Packer met a severe challenge. His older counselor was set in traditional ways. He knew the area, the members, and what could and could not be expected of them. He was a walking catalog of mission history and all matters relating to it.

Elder Packer recalled: "We wanted to adjust district conferences away from their usual scheduled Saturday activity programs and dances, followed by a Sunday conference session. We desired to conduct them like stake conferences, with a priesthood meeting Saturday afternoon, a general evening meeting, and of course the Sunday general session."

Accordingly President Packer recommended that they call a mission district conference at South Royalton, Vermont, and have a priesthood meeting Saturday afternoon. The older counselor said: "Well, they won't come. The Vermonters are used to handling it in a different way."

Feeling sure that they would respond to the call, the President sent out letters announcing the meeting.

On the appointed afternoon the mission presidency went to South Royalton, and there the three of them faced only two others. "Well, my counselor was right and I was wrong," Elder Packer said.

Despite the lack of priesthood support, he knew what he had tried to do what was right. He was prompted that he must not allow himself to be persuaded by his counselor's estimate of what could or could not be done. He must be free to set things in order as the Lord would have him do.

> I learned a sobering lesson. . . . I had been prompted several times, for the good of the work, to release my older counselor. Besides praying about it, I had reasoned that it was the right thing to do. But I did not do it. I feared that it would injure a man who had given long service to the Church.
>
> The Spirit withdrew from me. I could get no promptings on who should be called as a counselor should I release him. It lasted for several weeks. My prayers seemed to be contained within the room where I offered them. I tried a number of alternate ways to arrange the work, but to no avail. Finally, I did as I was bidden to do by the Spirit. Immediately, the gift returned! Oh, the exquisite sweetness to have that gift again. You know it, for you have it, the gift of the Holy Ghost. And the brother was not injured, indeed he was greatly blessed and immediately thereafter the work prospered.[8]

The blessing upon the brother was realized when Elder Harold B. Lee visited the mission and helped organize the Connecticut Hartford Stake. As he and Elder Packer were interviewing brethren for that purpose, Elder Lee looked at the president and said of the released counselor, "Here we have our patriarch," and the man was ordained to that calling.

The release of another counselor, Major Grant Claybourne of the Strategic Air Command Base in Bangor, Maine, caused Elder Packer concern; but this time he followed the promptings of the Spirit. The presidency had determined to put the two Maine districts together, and President Packer was strongly impressed that Grant Claybourne should be president of the new combined district. He was concerned lest Brother Claybourne feel that he was being demoted. When he discussed the change with him, however, the counselor answered, "I've already had the inspiration that this is what you are going to do."

When the presidency went to Maine to organize the district and hold the conference meetings, Brother Claybourne told President Packer that his name had been on the list for command school for a long time and suddenly he had his orders; hence he would be in the area for only two or three more weeks. Elder Packer was puzzled about what to do. After praying he decided that the inspiration to install the major was very definite, so he said: "Well, we'll organize the district and we'll install you as district president. You may only be president for a couple of weeks, but district president you will be."

He then added: "Now, you think the generals are in charge of your destiny, but they are not. They cannot do one thing with you that is contrary to the will of the Lord. You're living the gospel and trying to do what you ought to do and the Lord will have His way."

The next week a telephone call came from the new district president, who was chuckling because he had been bumped from the roster of those to go to command school. A general had knocked his name off in favor of somebody he was fostering.

After a year, when the district had been set in order under his leadership and was ready to be organized into the third New England stake, Major Claybourne had his opportunity to go to command school.

During President Packer's administration, prejudice and antagonism toward the Church were evident. At one point a newspaper in the area published a scurrilous article about the Church. "It was filthy; it was evil; it was entirely wrong," he recalled.

> The missionaries got all excited about it. Some of them drove a hundred miles to bring that paper for me to see what had happened. I read it and said, "Well, thanks; go on back and preach the gospel." They couldn't understand why I wasn't excited about it. . . . They said, "What shall we do?" And I said, "Go about your work; preach the gospel."
>
> "But aren't you going to call the editor, and aren't you going to demand equal space and answer this?" And the answer was no. . . . [they were] to stay on course, to stand steady, to be secure, to have faith, to be an anchor, and all [would] be well. And it was.[9]

Later, representatives of one of the churches hired the high school auditorium and announced a series of lectures, an exposé on Mormonism. A stake mission leader was greatly concerned and asked how to counteract them. "It is too bad you can't put them on your payroll," President Packer answered. "They will do you more good than ever they will do you harm. Ignore them. Go back to work. Teach the gospel."

The lectures misrepresented the Church so outrageously that the honest in heart became curious about the Church and, through sincere investigation, some became members.

President Packer's ability to gain the support of civic and government leaders and the media minimized the prejudice and antagonism toward the Church. Illustrating this was the *Boston Globe Magazine* article by George M. Collins, its religion editor. Titled "The Mormons," it was subtitled, "From National Pariahs to Presidential Possibilities, a Happy, Expanding, Prosperous, Controversial American-born Faith." By permission, the article was reprinted in pamphlet form on 22 January 1967 and then distributed worldwide by the Church.

A landmark in gaining respect for the Church was the Mormon Tabernacle Choir visit in 1967. Singing at the World's Fair in

Montreal, the choir had one unscheduled day, so a concert in New England was arranged. C. Robert Yeager, president of the Balfour Jewelry Manufacturing Company, asked that his company have the privilege of sponsoring the concert. His request was granted. Twelve hundred formal invitations were sent to leaders in government, business, education, and music over the signature of the President of the New England Mission, The Church of Jesus Christ of Latter-day Saints.

The media reported that few events in New England had attracted such a gathering of leaders and music lovers as did that out-of-doors concert at Narragansett Park, Rhode Island, 24 August 1967. Choir members heard Governor John A. Volpe of Massachusetts give a gracious introduction, saying among other things, "I have never known a finer man or a better man in my entire life than President Boyd K. Packer of the LDS New England Mission." His words, reported in the *Church News*, were picked up and printed by the *Box Elder Journal* on 7 September 1967 in the Packers' hometown of Brigham City, Utah.

Reporting the event to Elder Harold B. Lee, President Packer wrote: "This concert was the single most significant event to allay prejudice that has ever happened in New England. It was attended by over 27,000 people, was heard by radio locally, and was the means of obtaining extensive newspaper, television, and radio attention. The names and addresses of those who attended were taken and cataloged for missionary follow-up."

One employee of the Balfour Company who attended the concert contrasted the beauty of the night at Narragansett Park and the Choir's singing of "All is well, all is well" with her thoughts about our "boys fighting and dying in the [Vietnam] war."[10]

The effects of the Vietnam war caused much concern during the Packers' time in New England. With some ninety colleges and universities in the general area, the unrest was particularly vigorous. With the unrest came a high number of conscientious objectors who determined that they would fight authority at home or seek sanctuary out of the country, specifically in Canada. Dissenters vandalized time-honored buildings and monuments and spoke radically against leaders of schools and of the United States government.

At April 1968 general conference Elder Packer addressed the issue of a young man's military duty in time of war. He maintained that groups who challenged military service were unrighteous. He had counseled a confused and worried young Church member when fellow students and faculty members were pressuring him to refuse induction and to leave the country. With the issues as confusing as they were during the Vietnam war, what was he to do?

President Packer answered with words from the First Presidency given 6 April 1942, just before the time of his own years of service during World War II:

> The Church is and must be against war. . . . It cannot regard war as a righteous means of settling international disputes; these should and could be settled—the nations agreeing—by peaceful negotiations and adjustments.
>
> But the Church membership are citizens or subjects of sovereignties over which the Church has no control. The Lord himself has told us to "befriend that law which is the constitutional law of the land": . . .
>
> When, therefore, constitutional law, obedient to these principles, calls the manhood of the Church into the armed service of any country to which they owe allegiance, their highest civic duty requires that they meet that call. If, hearkening to that call and obeying those in command over them, they shall take the lives of those who fight against them, that will not make of them murderers, nor subject them to the penalty that God has prescribed for those who kill.

President Packer then spoke from his own experience: "While war permits stomping out of a man's heart the reverent and tender virtues that exemplify true manhood, military service does not require it. You can serve and yet be exemplars of righteousness."[11]

Closely related to the student demonstrations and rebellion against authority was the bolting of young people from the traditional moorings of their various churches. They were not finding answers or receiving what they needed to see them through the challenges they faced. The clergy was attempting to draw them back by innovative worship services that included jazz combos, poetry reading, interpretive dancing.

Having seen the opposite among the youth of the Church in the mission field, President Packer addressed "his brethren" of the Christian clergy in his general conference talk of 9 April 1967.

He gently persuaded, "Is it unreasonable to ask you—you who are by disposition such seekers after truth that you have chosen the ministry—to set aside for a moment self-interest, prejudice, even concern over the source of your livelihood, and to openly and honestly and prayerfully consider that there may be an answer provided by the Lord that cannot be arrived at in ecumenical councils."

He then bore witness of the Prophet Joseph Smith, of the Book of Mormon, and of the restoration of priesthood keys and authority from the Lord himself, before quoting President J. Reuben Clark, Jr., as follows: "What today's world must have, if humanity is to go on climbing upward, is men—those wearing the cloth as well as the laity—who know that God lives and that Jesus is the Christ; men who, having this knowledge, have also the intellectual honesty not only to *admit* but to *proclaim* it; who have further the moral courage and the sterling character to live the righteous lives this knowledge demands."[12]

During Elder Packer's mission tenure, President David O. McKay assigned him to teach institute classes for Latter-day Saint young people and their friends from Harvard, MIT, Boston University, and other schools, which were held in the Cambridge Ward chapel. He related an experience from that period:

> Professors from Harvard University who were members of the Church invited me to lunch over at the Harvard Business School faculty dining room. They wanted to know if I would join them in participating in a new publication; they wanted me to contribute to it.
>
> They were generous in their compliments, saying that because I had a doctorate a number of people in the Church would listen to me, and being a General Authority, . . . I could have some very useful influence.
>
> I listened to them very attentively but indicated at the close of the conversation that I would not join them. I asked to be excused from responding to their request. When they asked why, I told them this: "When your associates announced the project, they described how useful it would be to the Church—a niche that needed to be filled. And then the spokesman said, 'We are all active and faithful members of the Church; however, . . .'"

I told my two hosts that if the announcement had read, "We are all active and faithful members of the Church; therefore, . . ." I would have joined their organization. I had serious questions about a "however" organization. I have little worry over a "therefore" organization.[13]

Under Elder Packer's leadership much growth was experienced in New England Mission branches and districts. The foundation had been laid. Priesthood ordinations had increased; branches were growing into wards; two districts had reached stakehood, with many more to follow; and both member and missionary lives had been changed.

President Packer was not free of disappointment, however. He agonized as he dealt with an excommunication, effected some early missionary releases, and experienced in the mission a slower rate of convert baptisms than he had hoped for. About to leave the mission field and return to other assignments from the Brethren, he gave his last mission address at a Boston Stake fireside on 5 May 1968. He prayed for courage to talk about what those young people needed to hear—the "disease of impenitence."

He spoke of the evils in their world—intemperance, immorality, perversion—and counseled: "We must look at ourselves. The Lord has set rules and standards and will hold us accountable unless we ask forgiveness. If we ask for forgiveness, we will receive it. Get your lives in order. I need to do it also. . . . I don't know of anyone who does not."

He continued: "Some among us would rather criticize the Lord and His church than concentrate on the problems. That is a symptom of impenitence.

"Follow the Brethren. . . . If you don't understand a problem or a position of the Church, restrain your tongue. Check the mote in your own eye before you criticize. . . . There is nothing in your lives that will destroy you if you will follow the Brethren. Enough evil doesn't exist in the world, even if it were brought together and focused on you, to destroy you except you consent to it."[14]

On 16 May 1968 the First Presidency wrote: "In extending your

release, it affords us much pleasure indeed to say that you retire from your present position with our utmost confidence, goodwill, and appreciation."

Elder Paul H. Dunn and his wife, Jeanne, were called to succeed the Packers in the New England Mission.

Shortly before leaving for home the Packers were honored at a luncheon held at Boston's Union Club attended by civic and business leaders. Governor John A. Volpe presented President Packer with a large, silver Revere bowl bearing the State of Massachusetts coat of arms and the inscription dated 19 June 1968, "To Dr. Boyd K. Packer with best wishes from his friends, John A. Volpe, Governor." C. Robert Yeager presented him with a Certificate of Appreciation from Associated Industries of Massachusetts inscribed, "To Our Friend and Brother."

The family returned to their Salt Lake home in late June 1968. Elder Packer was given a month's leave from Church assignments in

*President Packer receiving an engraved silver Revere bowl from
Governor John A. Volpe of Massachusetts and
C. Robert Yeager, president of the Balfour Jewelry Manufacturing Company*

order to get his family settled. Meanwhile the A. Theodore Tuttles, who had lived in the Packer home during their three-year absence, moved to a temporary home nearby while they built a new one. Thus the close association of Elders Tuttle and Packer was renewed to their mutual satisfaction.

Chapter Thirteen

Call to the
Quorum of the Twelve

 As enriching as the mission years in New England had been for the Packer family, coming home was a time of renewal. The Brethren had given Elder Packer a month free from Church assignments. No longer in the spotlight, the family put on old clothes and went to work. They weeded and watered the garden the Tuttles had planted. They cleared brush and fallen trees from the woods. They also refurbished the home.

As Elder Packer bent his efforts to physical tasks the old pains from polio flared again in his hip, reminding him that pain was with him to stay.

When yard and home improvements were complete, the Packers settled into their normal pattern of home management, Church service, and individual interests. Sister Packer became Primary president to the 280 children in the Union Twelfth Ward. She also pursued her lifelong interest in family history. Lillian Millett, an elderly Packer relative from Arizona, was especially helpful to Sister Packer in research and history writing. She often visited in their home and later accompanied them to England, where she introduced them to Groombridge Place, a Packer ancestral home.

Before their mission, Elder Packer's sister Verna had been wasting away after twenty years of rheumatoid arthritis. With brotherly candor he had forbidden her to die while they were gone. She survived until they returned and visited with her several times. Then on 15 February 1969 she passed away at age sixty.

Also before the mission, Sister Packer's brother Robert had been killed in a farm-tractor accident. Donna's mother, Nellie Smith, had grieved inconsolably. Her grief had changed her sparkling, optimistic personality to one of tearful brooding.

One day when the Smiths came to visit, Elder Packer (at some risk, he says) talked to Nellie very pointedly. He said, "Mother, evidently you don't believe the gospel is true."

She was greatly hurt and said, "How could you say such a thing!"

Elder Packer answered, "Mother, Bob is gone, but there is the resurrection." Tenderly, he then affirmed gospel truths which she knew but had allowed grief to obscure. He reminded her that while we are confined in mortal flesh we have a beginning and an end. "We like beginnings," he continued, "but with good things, we do not like ends; nevertheless, the resurrection *is* a reality, and eternity always was and ever will be."

Despite Elder Packer's first painful thrust, their talk brought peace and comfort to Nellie's soul. Color came back into her life and sparkle into her voice, and she became herself again.

Elder Packer's direct thrust to the heart of an issue is one of his most characteristic traits, and it causes his brethren to acknowledge, with him, that he is not always a diplomat. He focuses on issues and is concerned about where they eventually will lead.

In his early ministry his intensity over issues prompted him to approach problems with a directness that sometimes offended people. Through the years he has developed a quiet restraint that has tempered him. Of this Elder Neal A. Maxwell says:

> Whereas Boyd formerly might have been agitated and lashed out against something that wasn't right, he has grown. With his increased spiritual composure his influence and impact are quiet, steady, and deep. He does not simply point out problems; he reconnoiters them perceptively, then in a prophetic, apostolic way he becomes a clarifier, a mover,

and a resolver. In patience and meekness he uses his insights and influence to bring about what needs to be done.

Boyd possesses another attribute that relates to the one just mentioned. He is quite unconcerned with self. He is anxiously engaged in good causes, and if issues require him to stand alone until others catch the vision, he'll pay the price and doesn't worry about the consequences for him. He takes the eternal view that if what you have done is right, the fact that you got bruised a bit in the process doesn't matter much; the bruises will heal and the progress will have been made.[1]

The years of Elder Packer's mission gave him experience in public relations and proved his sound understanding of Church government. The post-mission years refined his powers of seeing both people and issues in their eternal perspective.

The post-mission years also brought challenging assignments from the Brethren, whose charge it was to watch over the worldwide Church. One of these came at a critical time for his family. Sister Packer was expecting her tenth child. Their next youngest, Lawrence, was nearly seven years old. Elder Marion G. Romney assigned Elder Packer to tour the missions of Western Europe just when the baby was due. Concerned about Donna, Elder Packer was relieved when she delivered a son on 5 May 1969, the day before he was to leave.

At the hospital, however, the doctor told him, "I think you may not be able to keep this one." The baby had hyaline membrane disease, and for seventy-two hours his life was uncertain. Brother Packer blessed the child in the hospital and gave him the name Eldon Theodore. He delayed his trip and stayed with Donna. They prayed fervently for the child. The crisis passed. Eldon took on color and began to breathe normally. The doctor then assured Elder Packer that it would be safe for him to leave.

The mission tour took him to Holland, Belgium, Luxembourg, Switzerland, and France. The French East Mission encompassed cities in lower France, including Nice, Marseilles, and Toulon, as well as León in Spain. The mission had been in León for 120 years, but baptisms were low and tithing receipts still were not enough to operate the mission. All of its nineteen branches were presided over by missionary elders, and there were twelve missionaries on the office staff.

Brother Packer traveled each day with the mission president, who asked a steady stream of questions. Elder Packer answered them in the same way, yet he never seemed able to communicate effectively. At last the president began to comprehend. He asked for counsel.

Elder Packer had studied and analyzed everything he could find in the scriptures and in the words of the prophets of this dispensation on what the Lord had revealed about priesthood and Church government. Further, his understanding of these had been tried and tested during his own mission experience.

"First of all," he said, "you must cut your office force in half. Second, you must release all missionaries as branch presidents and put native priesthood holders in their places."

"But we don't have any natives who are worthy," the president countered.

Brother Packer answered with a story. He had toured a mission with Elder Spencer W. Kimball when a district president reported that he had released the branch president for immorality and had dissolved the branch.

"Well, you can't just dissolve a branch," Brother Kimball said. "You've got to install another man."

"We don't have another man," he answered.

"Surely with as many members as are in the branch you must have somebody," Brother Kimball said.

"Well, we don't," responded the district leader.

Irritated, Elder Kimball said, "President, do you think there is a twelve-year-old boy in this branch that hasn't committed adultery?"

The man was shocked but said, "Well, yes."

"Then install him as branch president."

"You've got to be kidding!"

"I'm not kidding! We can't dissolve a branch."

With that the man allowed that he might find somebody worthy to get the branch organized and going again.

Elder Packer said to the mission president, "I am sure that you, too, can find men worthy to replace your missionaries as branch presidents."

The president followed Elder Packer's counsel. Within eighteen months his office staff numbered six, and local leaders presided in all of the branches. Baptisms increased and tithing receipts grew till they more than covered the mission's operating expenses.

When Eldon was five months old Elder and Sister Packer were assigned to tour the South African Mission and to dedicate eight chapels. As they prepared to leave, President Joseph Fielding Smith told them that flights from Australia to Africa had recently been introduced. He wondered if, on their way to Africa, they would mind going through Australia to hold a stake conference. They were delighted.

They left Eldon with a sister-in-law, and the other children with another family member. They flew first to Adelaide and Melbourne, then to Perth, where their son Kenneth was serving a mission. Having received permission from his mission president, Kenneth met their flight and had a brief visit alone with them the next day. They learned that their son had known of their coming just days before, and that his greatest desire had been to have a baptism while they were there. Kenneth and his companion had fasted, prayed, and worked diligently. They had tracted an apartment building and there met a young couple who had been taught the gospel by missionaries in Sydney. The couple had accepted the challenge to be baptized the Saturday of conference. Kenneth's joy was great when Elder Packer left the stake presidency meeting long enough to be present for the event.

After conference on Sunday the Packers flew to South Africa. At Johannesburg they were greeted by a large crowd of Saints singing and holding armloads of flowers. It was still Sunday. With no time to freshen up or to rest from their long flight, they went directly into meetings.

Howard Badger was the mission president, and his wife, Eleanor, was a sister of Elder Marvin J. Ashton. "They were wonderful to us," Elder Packer says. "Our schedule was very full. We dedicated chapels at East London, Benoni, Carletonville, Pietermaritzburg, Vereeniging, Germiston, Pretoria, and Durban."

On 9 September 1969 they went to Salisbury in Rhodesia (now Zimbabwe), where they held meetings. Then to Elder Packer's surprise President Badger had scheduled nothing for September 10. Pressed for a reason, President Badger had told him that, knowing it was Elder Packer's birthday, and also knowing of his great interest in animals and birds, he had arranged a side trip by way of Victoria Falls to the Wankie Game Preserve. He had arranged for a rented car and for a park-compound cabin for the night. Brother Packer recalled:

> We arrived in the park in the late afternoon. By some mistake, there were not enough cabins for all the visitors, and they were all taken when we arrived. The head ranger indicated that they had a cabin in an isolated area about eight miles from the compound and we could spend the night there.
>
> Because of a delay in getting our evening meal, it was long after dark when we left the compound. We found the turnoff and had gone up the narrow road just a short distance when the engine stalled. We found a flashlight and I stepped out to check under the hood, thinking that there might be a loose connection or something. As the light flashed on the dusty road, the first thing I saw was lion tracks!
>
> Back in the car, we determined to content ourselves with spending the night there. Fortunately, however, an hour or two later we were rescued by the driver of a gas truck who had left the compound late because of a problem. We awakened the head ranger and in due time we were settled in our cabin.[2]

The next morning Elder and Sister Packer stood on the overlook near the cabin waiting for the car to take them back to the compound. Suddenly a huge eagle owl dropped from the sky at full speed and flew toward him as if to attack. Instinctively he raised his arm to protect his face. To his amazement the bird stretched forth its talons and landed on his arm as if it knew him.

When the ranger arrived and learned of the incident he told the Packers that he had raised the eagle owl. Surprised at Brother Packer's knowledge of African birds and animals, he took them to a partly finished lookout that offered a full view of the water hole below. There they could spend the day waiting for a replacement car. Doing so, they saw more game than ever they could have done by touring with the group. Birds, elephants, zebras, and all kinds of antelope were there. The ranger pointed out treacherous crocodiles hidden in the mud. From this experience Elder Packer drew inspiration for his April 1976 general conference talk "Spiritual Crocodiles."

When their Church assignments were completed the Packers flew to Rio de Janeiro, then to Caracas, Venezuela. Arriving there on the last day of Allan's mission, they were able to travel home with him. They had been gone a month.

Elder Packer began to sense that there is a basic core of truth and doctrine within the Church that must be protected against the encroachment of proliferating programs and activities if it is to survive. One area of concern was the direction in which the family home evening program was tending. The average lesson outline in the manual was thirteen pages long as compared to six and a half pages for Gospel Doctrine classes. This meant that parents in the Church were expected to cover more material than were Gospel Doctrine teachers.

Elder Packer pointed out the problem to the family home evening committee, whose members were all professors. They were attempting to improve the doctrinal strength of the program but at the same time to raise the literary and cultural level of families in a college-type way.

Discussing the situation with Brother Romney, Elder Packer said, "What we need on that committee is a 'people.' There is not a 'people' on it."

"What do you mean?" Elder Romney asked.

"We need to balance the professionalism of the committee by calling a wife and mother to serve on it who is raising a family. She will know the importance of reducing the lesson material to meet the requirements of her family."

Accordingly a woman was called who understood the stated purpose of family home evening: "To draw families together in love, to open the doors of communication between parents and children, to make them happy they live together and belong to one another—eternally."[3] In time, and with other appointments to it, the orientation of the committee turned to simplifying lessons, to basing them on the scriptures, and to meeting the needs of ordinary families more effectively.

Also under Brother Romney, Elder Packer served as managing director of the Priesthood Home Teaching Committee. He had observed the terminology change from *ward* teaching to *home* teaching by the Correlation Committee. Elder Romney asked Brother Packer to instruct the Regional Representatives about the responsibility of bishops and home teachers in implementing the program more effectively.

In doing so Brother Packer quoted Elder Gordon B. Hinckley: "We won't get the home teachers moving and doing what they ought to do until they have something to take into the homes." Then Elder Packer said, "Priesthood home teaching is the vehicle by which any or all of the programs of the Church or the messages of the Church are delivered into the home."[4] Through his, Elder Hinckley's, and others' work, the home teaching program became much more effective.

Between his travel and committee assignments Elder Packer accepted others. With Sister Packer he had represented the Church

The Packer family at the time of his
call to the Twelve
Inset: Kenneth Packer serving as a
missionary in Australia

at President Richard M. Nixon's second inauguration on 20 January 1969. He attended mission presidents seminars, dedicated chapels, spoke at graduation exercises, and represented the Church at special award ceremonies.

At one award event he received, for the Church, a plaque from the national Jaycees. They had adopted a family unity program based on President David O. McKay's statement, "No other success can compensate for failure in the home." Their program was designed "to build spirituality, American idealism, and good moral principles in the younger generation."[5]

It was timely that the Jaycees should so honor David O. McKay, President of the Church since 1951. Throughout his ninety-six years he had lived by the simple, profound gospel principles for which he was honored. Loved and revered as a prophet by his own people and admired and respected by countless nonmembers who felt that, "indeed he looked like a prophet," he died on 18 January 1970.

A few days later Elder Packer had a singular experience. "I was alone in the lower corridor of the Administration Building, waiting for the elevator. When it arrived, the door opened and there President Joseph Fielding Smith stood.

"I was struck with a marvelous infusion of spiritual power. It impressed this witness: Here stands the prophet of God!

"We shook hands cordially. I went up on the elevator alone. I was unsteady, nearly overcome by the impression I had been given."[6]

Five days after President McKay's death, on 23 January 1970, Joseph Fielding Smith became President of the Church, with Harold B. Lee as first counselor and N. Eldon Tanner second.

At the next general conference President Lee spoke of the transfer of presidency: "The transition . . . is by a procedure unique and by an ordained plan that avoids . . . the possibility of using political devices or revolutionary methods that could cause much confusion and frustration in the work of the Lord."[7]

When Joseph Fielding Smith became President of the Church his counselors kept nudging him to consider faithful men who might fill the vacancy in the Quorum of the Twelve Apostles left with the death of President McKay. They seemed unable, however, either to persuade him to look at name lists or to move on the matter. As general conference drew near, they pressed him further.

In connection with the conference, Elder Romney and Elder Packer were attending a seminar for the Regional Representatives in the Seventeenth Ward chapel. They were in a classroom alone when President Lee entered the room. "You are looking well," Brother Romney said to President Lee. "Then looks are deceiving," Brother Lee responded. He was weighed down with a critically serious Church matter.

As the two older men talked, Brother Packer saw Elder Romney put his arms around President Lee and assure him, "You are going to be all right." It was then that President Lee reached out to Elder Packer and drew him into that embrace. At that moment, Boyd's heart flooded with sure knowledge that he was to become one of their number.

Through all the sessions of the three-day conference he fought that knowledge. Soberly he recalled: "All this time, while I knew what the Lord had told me, I was in an agony of self-recrimination

Elder and Sister Packer on the day of his call to the Twelve

for even having the thought. I just hoped that conference would soon be over and I could crawl back into my shell and repent of the thoughts that I had had and could not seem to get rid of. Then I reasoned: 'Well, at least I have one shred of decency left. I haven't suggested to *anyone* that such a call was a possibility.'"

Finally the Sunday afternoon session ended and Boyd had yet to speak to the LDS chaplains. He was doing so when Brother D. Arthur Haycock interrupted the meeting and asked if he could come in with the First Presidency, who were then meeting with a delegation of Japanese people. Brother Packer thought this a natural request because of his experience in Japan, so he turned the chaplains meeting over to another.

Sister Smith was with the First Presidency to receive the delegations' presentation to them. When the guests were excused and Sister Smith left, Elder Packer also prepared to leave.

"I think the President wants you to stay," President Tanner said. It was then that President Joseph Fielding Smith delivered to Brother Packer his call to the Quorum of the Twelve Apostles and told him he would be sustained in a solemn assembly the next morning.

Elder Packer in a meditative mood at the solemn assembly when he was sustained a member of the Twelve

It was a very solemn Boyd K. Packer who left the room, only to meet the equally solemn David B. Haight going in to receive his call as an Assistant to the Twelve.

Elder Packer now was free, *obediently free*, to accept the mantle of the apostolic ministry, a burden that would prove to be heavier than the one just lifted from him. Yet, shared by the others, called to testify of Jesus the Christ, and to watch over His Church worldwide, the burden, he knew, would be bearable. With these soul-subduing reflections Elder Packer went home to Donna and their family.

*Elder Packer in the solemn assembly being sustained as a member of the
Quorum of the Twelve Apostles*

He remembers: "About nine-thirty that night President Tanner
called and said that he had reserved seats for our large family on the
north side of the balcony just above the pulpit area so they could
attend the solemn assembly the next morning. We have always been
grateful for President Tanner's thoughtfulness; otherwise we could
not have had our family there."

Sister Packer again prepared the children's Sunday clothes. Since
she would need to be with the General Authorities' wives, she told
the children what would be expected of them. Only their missionary,
Kenneth, would be absent.

On Monday morning, 6 April 1970, they took their places at the
Tabernacle. They listened as priesthood quorums and the general
membership of the Church unanimously sustained Joseph Fielding
Smith as President of the Church, and with him his counselors, Presidents Harold B. Lee and N. Eldon Tanner.

When President Lee, then conducting, called for the Quorum of
the Twelve to stand, Elder Packer, a little dazed, remained seated
with the Assistants until he heard President Lee say, "You, too,
Brother Packer."

Then he stood. In his heart was the thought, "I suppose there must be *one* qualification I have for this calling; the certainty of my witness."

From the corner of his eye the new Apostle saw his children in the north balcony raising their arms to the square. One son, the tease, however, smiled at his dad and brought his arm up just one step at a time until it came to the full square.

Chapter Fourteen

The New Apostle

 Sustained as a prophet, seer, and revelator, and now ordained an Apostle, forty-five-year-old Boyd K. Packer began that ministry with a nine-year apprenticeship to the Quorum of the Twelve behind him. Their tutoring had helped to season him.

During that period Elder Packer had learned that, because of its rapid growth and administrative complexities, the Church relies on committees to lighten the work load carried by the General Authorities.

He had also learned that the Church functions through quorums and councils, the highest being the First Presidency. The First Presidency and the Quorum of the Twelve together form a council. Each quorum member works, travels, and fulfils speaking appointments under assignment. Thus no accomplishment of any General Authority is credited to him alone, but is shared by his council members.

As a member of the Twelve, this truth became even clearer to Elder Packer. Thus, in reviewing his ministry it must be remembered that even though his name may be prominently listed with an achievement, credit is also due his brethren of the Quorum of the

Twelve who in unity worked, counseled, and aided him. They share in a brotherhood that is unique in all the world. Not only do they share the burden of being watchmen over the kingdom, but they watch over one another. If one temporarily goes down because of illness, surgery, or sorrow, his work load is borne willingly by the others.

With a sure witness that Apostles are men of God, Elder Packer had consistently and obediently followed their counsel and teachings. Consistency is never burdensome to him; rather, it is the orderly way in which he thinks and works. And obedience to God and His appointed servants is never restrictive to him; instead, it is the highest expression of his independence.

"Just think," he said, "of giving Him that one thing that He would never wrest from you. . . . Obedience—that which God will never take by force—He will accept when freely given. And He will then return to you freedom that you can hardly dream of—the freedom to feel and to know, the freedom to do, and the freedom to *be*, at least a thousandfold more than we offer Him. Strangely enough, the key to freedom is obedience."[1]

Through the years these character traits had been strengthened by study and prayer. And it had been study and prayer that had brought about his early, sure witness that Jesus is the Christ, that the scriptures are the word of God to His children, that His Church has been restored in its purity and is led by a prophet of God. He also came to know that additional knowledge comes by following the simple procedure that men of God through the ages had followed.

Shortly after receiving his call he said: "It seems to me that there is a great power in the Church—in all of us—that is untapped because we are always setting about to do things in our way, when the Lord's way would accomplish much greater returns. And then, when we don't know what to do or think, or what would be the Lord's way or will, we don't ask. Why don't we talk to our Father? In specifics? About real problems? As often as we would with our earthly father if he were nearby?"[2]

Boyd K. Packer was ordained an Apostle on 9 April 1970 by Joseph Fielding Smith, who was ordained an Apostle on 7 April 1910 by Joseph F. Smith, who was ordained an Apostle on 1 July 1866 by Brigham Young, who was ordained an Apostle on 14 February 1835 under the hands of the Three Witnesses—Oliver Cowdery, David Whitmer, and Martin Harris.

The Three Witnesses were called by revelation to choose the Twelve Apostles, and on 14 February 1835 were "blessed by the laying on of the hands of the Presidency"—Joseph Smith, Sidney Rigdon, and Frederick G. Williams—prior to their choosing and ordaining the Twelve Apostles.[3]

Joseph Smith and Oliver Cowdery received the Melchizedek Priesthood in 1829 under the hands of Peter, James, and John, who were ordained Apostles by the Lord Jesus Christ (see John 15:16).

Several brethren have been mentioned as teachers and mentors of Elder Packer: President Kimball, President Lee, President Romney, President Moyle. None of them, however, had greater influence upon him than did President Joseph Fielding Smith. The training he received from the others centered on administration and principles of priesthood government. The influence of President Smith centered on doctrine and example. Elder Packer revered him as something of a prophets' prophet.

The Quorum of the Twelve in 1970

President Smith was regarded by some as being austere, perhaps in the image of the Old Testament prophet; a keeper of the rules; an orthodox preacher of pure doctrine. He was all of that; but further, he was an example of compassion and courage. From the day he was called as a General Authority, Elder Packer found President Smith to be the most approachable of all of the Brethren.

Invariably pleasant, with a quick wit that seldom showed at the pulpit, he readily responded to the humor in a situation. It was easy to seek counsel from him, to be open and comfortable in his presence. Few people really understood President Smith as did Elder Packer, who knew him as a friend, loved him, and took much courage from his example.

On one occasion when President Smith was chairman of the Missionary Committee, a report was presented concerning an accident involving two missionary elders in a Church-owned automobile. An elderly vegetable vendor had run a stop sign with his truck. The missionary car was struck broadside and totally wrecked. The driver of the truck was cited by the police. He had no insurance. Fortunately, neither missionary was seriously injured.

President Smith sat silent as the members of the committee considered the matter. After some discussion they instructed the managing director of the Missionary Department to retain an attorney and press the matter in court.

Only then was President Smith asked if he agreed with that course of action. Quietly he said: "Yes, we could do that. And if we press with all vigor, we might even succeed in taking the truck away from the poor man; then how would he make a living?"

"We looked at one another, a little ashamed," Elder Packer said. "Then we allowed that the Church could buy another missionary car, go about its work, and leave the matter alone."

A few days after his ordination Elder Packer fulfilled an assignment to speak at Brigham Young University. There he said, "I want to affirm to you that whatever other qualifications I may not have (perhaps they are numerous) for the calling that has come to me, the one I do have is the witness. I know for sure that Jesus is the Christ, that this is His Church, that we are led by a prophet, and that the Church is on the right course."[4]

In general conference on 6 April 1971 he said: "I have that witness. I declare to you that I know that Jesus is the Christ. I know that He lives. He was born in the meridian of time. He taught His gospel, was tried, was crucified. He rose on the third day. He was the first fruits of the resurrection. He has a body of flesh and bone. Of this I bear testimony. Of Him I am a witness."

While on assignment in New Zealand, Elder Packer had failed to *bear* that witness. He had been in Wellington with Sister Packer, where a television interview with him had been arranged. The interviewer had asked a simple question: "What are you doing in New Zealand?"

Elder Packer had responded, "We are here to hold a Church conference and to attend to some business for the Church."

At the close of the session the interviewer had been complimentary. Elder Packer, however, knew that he had *not* done well. For a day and a night he had worried and fretted. Finally, Sister Packer had said, "Boyd, you did your best, now put it behind you." But the sense of his failure to testify had weighed upon him.

The next morning he received a call from the television station. They had not aired the interview; and they asked if they might attend the conference, visit the mission home, and put together a brief documentary on the Church. Sensing their genuine interest, he told them they would be welcome. This became his second chance.

Upon his return, he reported to his brethren of the Twelve: "I told them what I should have said in the interview: that the reason I was in New Zealand was because I was one of the Council of the Twelve Apostles. That I had been commissioned by the chief Apostle to visit New Zealand. That we had the same organization and the same authority that had existed at the meridian of time when the Lord was upon the face of the earth. Where there had been Peter, James, and John, Andrew, Philip, Bartholomew, Matthew, and the others, there were now Joseph, Nathan, Harold, Spencer, Howard, Gordon, Thomas, and others."[5]

Hearing this experience, Elder Marion G. Romney affirmed to his young friend, "You *are* an Apostle!"

As one of their number, Elder Packer joined them in bearing witness to one another, saying: "I love the Lord and marvel that He
called me to this position. I know He did; I have that witness, and I
want to serve Him. I am grateful for His teachings and how He
taught. I remember the day when I was finally willing to yield to Him
in all things. I have no desire other than to please Him."[6]

With continuing growth Elder Packer testified concerning the
restoration of the Church upon the earth. In answer to those who
claim that all churches are right and who are offended by the asser-
tion that the exclusive delegation of priesthood authority rests with
The Church of Jesus Christ of Latter-day Saints, he said:

> Now we do not say that they are wrong so much as we say they are
> incomplete. . . . They become attracted by a single key, a doctrine, often
> one to which they take immediate exception and object to. They inves-
> tigate it by itself alone. . . . They want to hear that key played over and
> over again. It will give them little knowledge unless they see that there
> is a fullness. . . .
>
> Any soul has the right, indeed the obligation, to make an appeal
> through prayer for the answer to this question: Is there a true church?
> That is how it all began, you know, with a fourteen-year-old boy who
> went into a grove. Two questions: Which of all the churches is true? and
> Which should he join? There he experienced a marvelous vision of the
> Father and the Son, and the dispensation of the fullness of times was
> ushered in. Subsequently the authority to act for Him was restored and
> rests yet with this Church. We heard in this meeting a prophet of God,
> Joseph Fielding Smith.
>
> I bear witness that he is a prophet of God. I have a witness that
> Jesus is the Christ. He lives. The Church of Jesus Christ of Latter-day
> Saints is the only true and living church upon the face of this earth, of
> which I bear witness in the name of Jesus Christ.[7]

As people heard him bear witness of the Savior, there were those
who wondered, even asked, "Have you seen Him?" To these and all
others he gave public answer, as his friend Elder Marion G. Romney
had once given private answer in Boyd Packer's hearing: "I do not
tell all I know. If I did, the Lord could not trust me."

Elder Packer's public answer was given to the Church at large in
general conference:

"Have you seen Him?" That is a question that I have never asked of another. I have not asked that question of my brethren in the Quorum, thinking that it would be so sacred and so personal that one would have to have some special inspiration, indeed, some authorization, even to ask it. . . . I have come to know what the Prophet Alma meant:

"It is given unto many to know the mysteries of God; nevertheless they are laid under a strict command that they shall not impart only according to the portion of his word which he doth grant unto the children of men, according to the heed and diligence which they give unto him.

"And therefore, he that will harden his heart, the same receiveth the lesser portion of the word; and he that will not harden his heart, to him is given the greater portion of the word, until it is given unto him to know the mysteries of God until he know them in full." (Alma 12:9–10.)

There are those who hear testimonies borne in the Church, by those in high station and by members in the wards and branches, all using the same words—"I know that God lives; I know that Jesus is the Christ," and come to question, "Why cannot it be said in plainer words? Why aren't they more explicit and more descriptive. Cannot the Apostles say more?" . . .

Some seek for a witness to be given in some new and dramatic and different way. . . . To one who is honestly seeking, the testimony borne in these simple phrases is enough; for it is the Spirit that beareth record, not the words.[8]

With an ever-deepening awareness of both the sanctity and the responsibility of his call, Elder Packer studied deeply and gave intense consideration to the orderly nature and correct function of the Melchizedek Priesthood in governing the Church as the Lord would have it done. He came to understand with ever greater clarity that it is the responsibility of each of the Twelve to act as a "watchman on the tower."

A number of his brethren recognize in Elder Packer the gift of sensing drifts, trends, and directions that would alter or endanger the course of the unseen, or spiritual, core of the Church. To its leadership, the Church is a sanctuary in which are kept the pure gospel of Jesus Christ and the crucial ordinances which have the power to bless the Father's children and bring them back to Him.

Always concerned about families and their eternal welfare, President Lee said: "It seems clear that the Church has no choice, and never had, but to do more to assist the family in carrying out its divine mission. Not only because that is the order of heaven, but also because that is the most practical contribution we can make to our youth—to help improve the quality of life in the Latter-day Saint homes." In part he desired to safeguard families against proliferating Church programs.

Sharing with Donna the responsibility of a large family, Elder Packer was in total agreement with the President. Speaking under assignment, he said:

> With great effort we are trying to get each father to assume his responsibility as the head of his home. That is not an easy task. We have come to know that if we are going to deliver [priesthood] power to the individual, particularly to the youth, it must come through the parents, through the father.
>
> One reason we are having difficulty now is because for a generation or two we have wired around [fathers]. In all generations there are some fathers who are unwilling, some unworthy, and perhaps a few unable to manage their families. . . . In these cases we've stepped in to help them. . . . If we couldn't get the power through, we'd just change the diagram and wire past him.
>
> Perhaps with a little more patience, a little more long-suffering, perhaps by waiting it out for a while, or perhaps by increasing the power from above, we might have had the circuit opened.
>
> But it has always been so easy just to run another line, an auxiliary program.[9]

As he traveled worldwide Elder Packer taught leaders and families alike to encourage and honor fathers in their priesthood responsibilities.

He tells of going, as an Assistant to the Twelve, with Elder Spencer W. Kimball to reorganize a district in the Southwest Indian Mission. They called as district president a government worker, and he selected as a counselor a Navajo brother who had been an elder for twelve years. They were setting a member apart to a calling and Elder Packer tried to get this Navajo brother to assist, but he held back. Finally the only one yet to be set apart was the assistant to the secretary of the branch Sunday School.

Elder Packer recalls: "I then insisted that the Navajo counselor set the young woman apart. Reluctantly he put his hands on her head and rather clumsily set her apart. I put my arm around him and said, 'You did very well. She is as set apart as if the prophet were here.' Then I asked, 'Is this new to you?' He said that in the twelve years he'd been an elder and a faithful tithe payer this was the first time he had ever been called upon to use his priesthood to set apart, ordain, or bless anyone."

Since it was not uncommon at the time for members to seek blessings from Apostles or even from the prophet, many did not recognize or accept the truth that the same authority to bless is vested in all Melchizedek Priesthood holders. So it was a difficult principle to teach. On one occasion Elder Packer was called into the home of a sick young man. The boy's father was present, but being of a quiet nature he remained in the background. Elder Packer asked if the boy's father held the priesthood. Yes, he was an elder. It was then that Elder Packer pointed out to the alert young man that, as a priesthood holder, the father had the authority to bless him.

To the young man he said: "Figuratively speaking I have a key, a priesthood key, which authorizes me to give blessings to the sick. Your father has the same key. If I took my key off its ring and put it by his key you would not see any difference except that mine is shiny and his might be a little rusty."

Comprehending, the boy said, "That would be because you use yours more often than my father uses his."

Elder Packer asked the father to join him and said to the boy, "All the authority we have will be present as your father administers to you." The man gave his son a heartfelt blessing.

In April 1972 Elder Packer was assigned to tour the mission in Japan. It was his first trip back since he had served with the occupation forces at the close of World War II. His appointments took him to all the areas in which he had been stationed, and he saw the remarkable rebuilding and prosperity of a nation that had been beaten and gutted by war.

In Japan, as always, he taught the missionaries "to discontinue teaching families unless or until, one—you have every father present, or two—you've made every reasonable effort to get him. Why? Because this is the church that puts families together, not the one that pulls them apart."[10]

Fathers and husbands, however, could not fulfil their priesthood roles without the aid and support of faithful wives and mothers, so the sisters too came under the influence of his teaching. He told a large assembly of British women: "Never say, 'My husband is not a member.' Instead say, 'My husband is not *yet* a member.' . . . Be tolerant and faithful and patient with him. . . . Treat him just as though he were active and faithful and honoring his priesthood and live in expectation."[11]

The call to be a General Authority is a call to travel. Perhaps no group of men move out across the world and back again as do the Twelve and the Seventy. They do not go as tourists but as caring watchmen over the Church. Only those who travel worldwide can know how demanding it is.

During the thirty-plus years of his ministry, Elder Packer has been to each of the United States, to Canadian provinces, to Mexico, to countries in Central and South America, to Scandinavia and the countries of Europe, to Israel, the Middle East, Egypt, African countries, Pakistan, India, Thailand, Japan, Korea, the Philippines and the Islands of the Pacific, and to New Zealand and Australia. In so traveling he and his brethren have had their share of experiences. A few of Elder Packer's will serve as examples that could be matched by the others.

In 1971 he was in England to arrange for the first Area Conference. He left London for home on September 7 and was assigned, at once, to fly to South America, then to Johannesburg, South Africa. On 21 September he was back in London. He finally arrived home, having crossed the Atlantic four times. Jet lag, the enemy of world travelers, kept him sleepless at night until well into the Christmas holidays.

On one occasion he was taken to the NATO Hospital in Brussels, Belgium, and treated for severe food poisoning resulting from an airline meal.

Another time the pilot of a small commuter plane flying from Tonga to Samoa stopped to pick up a passenger and left the motor running and the cabin door open. Exhaust fumes filled the cabin. While he was continuing on a Pan American night-flight from Pango Pango to Hawaii, the heating system malfunctioned. With too few blankets on board, passengers were cold. When Elder Packer returned home and checked with his doctor, he had double pneumonia.

Perhaps his most dramatic travel experience came when he was assigned to conduct stake conferences in Western Samoa and then to organize the Upolu West Stake. With him were John H. Groberg, a Regional Representative; President Wayne Shute of the Samoan Mission; Mark Littleford, superintendent of Church schools in Samoa; and Brother Laeausa, a Samoan-speaking chief who would represent them in some ceremonies.

After the necessary interviews on Upolu Island, a chartered plane took them to the Island of Savaii for a midweek stake conference. The plane, which landed on a grassy field at Faala, was to return the next afternoon to take them back to Apia on Upolu Island.

The next afternoon, however, it rained hard. Knowing the plane would not land on the grassy field, they drove to the west end of Savaii, where there was a runway of sorts atop a coral water-break. They waited until dark; no plane arrived. By radiophone they learned that it was storming on Upolu Island and the plane could not take off. They then said they would come by boat, but that someone must meet them at Mulisanua.

After another three-hour drive back around the island to Salelologa, President Tuioti, a counselor in the Savaii Stake presidency, arranged for a boat and obtained the necessary police permit to make the night crossing. Elder Packer tells of the harrowing passage:

> As we pulled out of port, the captain of the 40-foot boat, the Tori Tula, asked President Shute if he happened to have a flashlight. Fortunately he did and made a present of it to the captain. We made the 13-mile crossing to Mulisanua on Upolu Island on very rough seas. None of us realized that a ferocious tropical storm had hit Upolu Island.
>
> At Mulisanua, there is one narrow passage through the reef. A light on the hill above the beach marked that narrow passage. There was a

second lower light on the beach. When a boat was maneuvered so that the two lights were one above the other, it was lined up properly to pass through the reef.

But that night, there was only one light. Someone was on the landing waiting to meet us, but the crossing took much longer than usual. After waiting for hours, watching for signs of our boat, they tired and fell asleep in the car, neglecting to turn on the lower light.

The captain maneuvered the boat toward the single light on shore while a crewman held a flashlight off the bow. It seemed like the boat would struggle up a mountainous wave and then pause in exhaustion at the crest of it with the propellers out of the water. The vibration of the propellers would shake the boat nearly to pieces before it slid down the other side.

We could hear the breakers crashing over the reef. When we were close enough to see them with the flashlight, the captain frantically shouted reverse and backed away to try again to locate the passage through the reef. After many attempts, he knew it would be impossible to find the opening. All we could do was try to reach the harbor in Apia, 20 miles away. We were helpless against the ferocious power of the elements. I do not remember ever being where it was so dark.

We were lying spread-eagled on the cover of the cargo hold, holding on with our hands on one side, with our toes locked on the other to keep from being washed overboard.

Mark Littleford lost hold and was thrown against the low iron rail. His head was cut front and back, but the rail kept him from being washed away. . . .

. . . We made no progress for the first hour even though the engine was full throttle. Eventually we moved ahead and near daylight pulled into Apia Harbor. Boats were lashed to boats several deep at the pier. We crawled across several of them, trying not to disturb those sleeping on deck. We made our way to Pesanga, dried our clothing, and headed for Vailuutai to organize the new stake.

I do not know who had been waiting for us at Mulisanua. I refused to let them tell me. Nor do I care now. But, it is true that without that light, the lower light—the light that failed—we all might have been lost.[12]

Because of this experience, the old hymn "Let the Lower Lights Be Burning" came to have very special meaning for Elder Packer.

Elder Packer's life was also preserved on 2 July 1972, a fast Sunday, when he and his brothers and sisters had gathered with their families at the Packer summer camp in Box Elder Canyon to celebrate the Fourth of July weekend. They had attended sacrament meeting in Brigham City.

Everyone had been fasting, and the women were preparing the afternoon meal, to be followed by a family meeting. Interested in the preparations, Elder Packer had been carrying his grandson Jonathan about the camp and Donna was with him.

One of the Coleman stoves had not been adjusted properly, and black smoke was pouring out around the kettle resting on its burner. Elder Packer handed Jonathan to Donna and began adjusting the valve to get the flame going.

When it would not adjust, he reached over to touch the end of the pressure pump. It was slightly tipped, and the minute he touched it, it broke and sprayed him with gas, first his eyes and face, then his body. Donna screamed. Others looked on, heard a loud "whoof," and saw him set aflame from head to knees.

In one sweeping motion he swung his arms down his face and burning clothes. Suddenly the fire was out.

His eyebrows, the hair of his forearms, and his clothes were singed. He could not see for the gas in his eyes. A nephew handed him a clean cloth and he bathed his eyes and face over and over again with water from a nearby tap until the burning was soothed and his sight was restored.

That same day, 2 July 1972, Elder Packer received word that President Joseph Fielding Smith had died. He was ninety-five years of age.

On 7 July President Smith's first counselor, Harold B. Lee, was set apart as President of the Church, with N. Eldon Tanner as first counselor and Marion G. Romney as second counselor. To fill the vacancy in the Quorum, Elder Bruce R. McConkie of the First Council of the Seventy was sustained as an Apostle on 6 October 1972.

Then just eighteen months after President Lee had been sustained, he died on 26 December 1973 at age seventy-four. Through his diligent efforts priesthood correlation, a major course change, would guide the Church through the troubled years ahead. On 30 December 1973 its principal architect was laid to rest.

On that same day Spencer W. Kimball, President of the Quorum of the Twelve, was sustained as President of the Church. He was seventy-eight years of age. How fervently he had prayed that President Lee would be preserved! Said he at the funeral services, "A giant redwood has fallen and left a great space in the forest. . . . Yes, among our generation has walked one of God's most noble, powerful, committed, and foreordained giant redwoods—President Harold B. Lee."[13]

Incredible as it was to President Kimball, the responsibility of watching over and guiding the affairs of the kingdom now rested upon *him*. Soon after he had moved into the office of the President of the Church, Elder Packer took for his approval the article he had been asked to write about President Kimball for the March 1974 *Ensign*. He found the President seated at his desk weeping. Concerned, he asked, "President Kimball, what is the matter?"

"I am such a little man for such a big responsibility!" was the quiet response.

Chapter Fifteen

The Eternal Family

With the deaths of Elder Packer's parents in 1958 and 1965, and the death of Sister Packer's mother in 1972, only one of the family's grandparent generation was alive in 1977—Donna's father, William W. Smith.

In January of that year Sister Packer visited him in Brigham City. William was ill at the time and she urged him to see a doctor. Although reluctant, he went for a thorough examination. It revealed a brain tumor. He was immediately admitted to the hospital.

After a series of treatments he was released to return to his home. His sister Millicent was there; she had lived with the family for many years, and being in poor health herself she was unable to provide the twenty-four-hour-a-day nursing care William required. Elder and Sister Packer welcomed him into their home, adjusted their heavy schedules, and prepared for what the doctors said would likely be long-term care. They tended him with the same reverence and affection that had been given to Elder Packer's grandfather, his parents, and Sister Packer's mother as each had lingered in discomfort, pain, and helplessness before being released from mortality.

William did not linger, however; he died in the Packer home on 10 May 1977, just three weeks after the Packers had brought him home. With William's passing, Elder and Sister Packer became the grandparent generation within their family. By then their four eldest children had married and there were ten grandchildren.

Thirteen years later there were forty-six grandchildren, and all the children were married except Eldon, who returned that year from his mission in Uruguay. His eldest brother, Allan, then the Packers' bishop, conducted Eldon's homecoming service on 8 July 1990 with other family members participating. Afterwards the family gathered at the Packer home for supper. Only two of them were absent: Laurel's husband, Carter, who was attending a Dillman family function, and Allan's son Jonathan, who had just left for his mission to East Germany. Jonathan was the first grandchild in what would be a long line of future missionaries to represent the family in the nations of the world.

Elder Packer spoke of these future missionaries to Yuri Dubinin, the Russian Ambassador to the United States, and his wife, Liana, who were attending a stake conference in Salt Lake City at the invitation of stake president Jon Huntsman: "We have seven sons and three sons-in-law who have been on missions. Three of them speak Spanish, one Japanese, one Portuguese, one Swedish. Others have served missions in England, Australia, Alaska, Tennessee. You notice that Russian is missing from that list of languages; but not to worry. We have 31 grandsons."[1] Four years later, one of these would serve in St. Petersburg.

Just as missions have been a part of the Packer tradition, so have temple marriages, followed by home receptions. Sister Packer has helped her daughters with their trousseaus and wedding dresses; flowers have come from the garden; and food has been prepared in the kitchen.

Elder and Sister Packer's philosophy of family life and child rearing had served them well during the years the children had lived at home. As their children chose companions, the Packers encouraged each couple to establish its own pattern of family life and tradition without interference from them. Meanwhile the Packers' own lives followed the same consistent pattern as before. Elder Packer presided with patience and kindliness; they counseled together; and Sister Packer was his constant strength and support while pursuing her own work at home and in family history and research.

Son-in-law David Kezerian observes: "I did not appreciate the value of true patriarchal order within a home until I saw it practiced by Dad and Mother Packer. It is straight-line, based upon living the gospel and keeping the commandments. The evidence of its practicality is there as it is lived day by day. As with my own parents, the Packers are an example upon which we are trying to pattern our lives. There is no yielding on principle, yet there is no compulsion. The children and the grandchildren know without reservation that Dad and Mom love them. This creates a natural flow of cooperation that extends beyond their own children to include those of us who have come into the family through marriage."

Continuing, David says: "Dad Packer has a deep desire to let his children work out their own salvation, yet if we ask for counsel he will drop whatever he is doing to listen and to respond. And his calm manner is most reassuring."[2]

Another observer is son Allan's wife, Terri Anne Bennett. Her association with the Packers began during the years of their New England Mission (1965–1968). She has seen the children mature from high-spirited, teasing, and sometimes boisterous stages to become close, supportive adults who are each other's best friends. She and Allan are trying to instill the same closeness and support within their family of eight children.

Terri attributes the Packers' success in child rearing partly to "their blessing of being given choice spirits to raise, perhaps so that Dad would be able to carry the responsibilities of his high callings." But she is quick to add that the children were likewise blessed. "They have always had an attentive mother in the home to guide and mold them, and a caring teacher-father to lead and counsel them."[3]

Several years before the death of Sister Packer's father, William Smith, President Spencer W. Kimball suggested that Brother Packer seriously consider writing a book. Beyond the writing of his master's thesis and his doctoral dissertation the idea had never occurred to him. He pondered the President's counsel and asked himself, "What would I write about?" His friend A. Theodore Tuttle suggested that he expand his master's thesis, "An Evaluation of the Teaching of Jesus in Terms of Selected Principles of Education."

He followed that advice, and *Teach Ye Diligently* was published in 1975. The book gives practical instruction in teaching as the Savior taught. For the jacket cover Elder Packer painted a picture of his children and their companions; and he illustrated the book. Elder Tuttle wrote the foreword. President J. Reuben Clark, Jr.'s address "The Charted Course of the Church in Education," which had had such a profound influence on Elder Packer, provided the appendix. The book has been translated into Spanish and has proved to be a successful teaching tool throughout the Church. The teaching methods set forth in the book are simply those that Elder and Sister Packer have practiced in their home.

Between the time of President Kimball's suggestion and the publication of his first book, Elder Packer had faced major surgery. He had developed trouble in swallowing during the New England Mission nearly ten years before. It had been diagnosed as achalasia, a disorder of the muscles of the esophagus. This caused severe spasms and pain.

Encouraged by his physician, he agreed to an operation. He received a priesthood blessing; and Dr. Russell M. Nelson, using a procedure he had helped perfect at Harvard University, repaired the affected area. All would have been well but for an incident that happened while Brother Packer was still weak and the incision from the surgery had not healed.

Seated in a chair on the front lawn, he heard Eldon screaming down by the pond. "I knew he was in desperate trouble," his father says. "I shouldn't have, but I started to run, and as I turned the corner of the house Eldon came toward me enveloped in a swarm of yellow wasps. He had pulled a stick out of a pile of debris down by the pond and had pulled their nest all to pieces.

"I rushed to him and began brushing them off with my hands. They were swarming around us both, but didn't sting me. Coming out from the house, Donna saw what was happening and ran for the insect spray. Together we fought off the wasps. She hurried Eldon to the doctor, who treated him for a serious allergic reaction to the multiple stings." Their son recovered, but the exertion of the incident damaged Elder Packer's incision and eventually it had to be repaired.

Eldon's mishap had begun at the pond, which had not existed when the Packers moved into the home. The original acreage upon which their house stood was smaller, but through the years they had purchased additional land. Then Brother Packer and his boys had cleared a path through the woods, cleaned out the poison ivy, and made a pond.

Surrounding the pond grows a dense thicket of river birch and alder, dogwood and hawberry, pussy willow and wild apple, and box elder. Swimming in the pond are geese and ducks both tame and wild. They eat the seeds and berries, which Elder Packer supplements with a daily grain ration. Quail, pheasant, oriole, pine siskin, Bohemian waxwing, redpoll, evening grosbeak, goldfinch, and flicker are visitors in all seasons and are certain of food when it is scarce in winter. He knows them all.

With the children grown and needing less of his time, and with the stress of constant travel upon him, his birds have provided inspiration for his wood carvings. Picked up at odd moments, working these with his hands has helped to counteract jet lag and to relax him.

Boyd's hands finish a carving

The peace of pond, woods, and wildlife blend harmoniously with the interior of the home, where in cold weather fires burn on the hearths and where family heirlooms combine to create a tangible warmth. No matter the stress and strain of travel or office, he truly can come *home* to that warmth and peace.

There is in their home setting something quite British, and rightly so, for both he and Sister Packer have deep roots in England. Her mother was born in London, and his ancestral home, Groombridge Place, is in Kent.

They first visited Groombridge in company with Elder Packer's relative Lillian Millett on 11 September 1970. Driving sixty miles southeast of London, they entered the small village of Groombridge. From there they turned left along a tree-lined lane bordering a pond where wild ducks swam, and continued about a quarter of a mile from the main gate to the manor house. Elder Packer had an immediate feeling of belonging. Although the genealogical link to its original owner, John Packer, was not yet in place, later research fully established the linkage.

Its owner at the time of their visit was an elderly bachelor, Mr. S. Walton Mountain. He welcomed the Packers and Lillian, guided them about the formally landscaped grounds and the manor house, then invited them to stay for lunch.

Seeing the Packer portraits, which had hung in place nearly three hundred years, Elder Packer was deeply touched, especially by the one of his direct ancestor, Philip Packer, son of John Packer and Philippa Mylles.[4]

Philip was born on 24 June 1618, the same year that his father had purchased Groombridge Place from Richard Sackville, third earl of Dorset. After John's death the estate was left to Philip, who rebuilt the manor house to be substantially what it was when the Packers first saw it.

John Packer, Philip's father, had built a chapel on the estate, and that also stands much as it did in the sixteen hundreds. Its story reflects something of its builder's religious life. While John served the

Groombridge Place in England, home of John Packer

doctrinally Presbyterian but politically Anglican King James I as Clerk of the Privy Seal and in court assignments, he remained a Puritan in his sympathies and was openly on the side of Parliament. When the king came under Spanish influence, John used what powers of persuasion he had at court to thwart King James and Prince Charles's intentions of making a Spanish alliance through the prince's marriage to a Catholic princess.

When Prince Charles returned unwed from his visit to Spain, John Packer expressed his gratitude to God by building the chapel at Groombridge Place in 1625, installing its stained-glass window depicting the Packer coat of arms, and naming the edifice St. Charles. When first at Groombridge, the Packers visited the beautiful chapel.

Were it not for Sister Packer's twenty years of meticulous British research the family would know John Packer only from the brief account found in the *Dictionary of National Biography*. Her research yielded extensive information:

She notes that "in the writings of Sir Francis Bacon, John Packer is mentioned a number of times as 'my ancient friend.' When Bacon incurred the anger of the king and faced the most desperate time in his life, he sent his appeal through the Duke of Buckingham by the hand of John Packer. Bacon's appeal was kindly received by the king and he lived to die of natural causes."[5]

A tribute to John Packer, written about 1650, just after his death, is included in the British Library's Harleian collection. Sister Packer found it to be a summary of John's public and private life written by his son-in-law, John Brown, Esq., clerk of Parliament. (Original spelling and punctuation are retained.)

> John Packer Esqr. born at Twickenham in the County of Middlesex November 12th 1572 of good Parents his Father being a Clerke of the Privy Seal to Queen Elizabeth had his first Education in Westminster Schoole and from thence being sent to the University of Oxford, where he spent 4 years in Trinity College and afterwards 4 years more in Trinity College in Cambridge where he was very well Reputed of, for his sufficiency in Learning and Civill behaviour.[6]

More precious to his descendants is the account of his personal allegiance to Christ and his teachings:

> In all this Time he was never charged, or Justly suspected of any crime, corruption, or miscarriage which might staine his Reputation of an Honest man . . . but held it his Duty, and oftentimes made bold to offer his opinion to the King, or the Duke, for hindring such things as were prejudiciall, and if they refused to hear him, he would desire to be excused from having any hand therein.

Of his religious life, the document reads:

> For the Discharge of his Duty in the Service of God, he was knowne to be from his very Childhood one that delighted in the Holy Scriptures more than in any worldly thing, and was seen by his daily reading of the same, and hearing ye same Read, by Learning the same by Heart, to the End he might meditate therein both day and night, as he usually did most Times when he was alone, either Riding or Walking in one Lan-

guage or another, having gotten by Memory the most Part of the New Testamt. ye Psalms and Proverbs and ye Booke of Canticles. He was frequent in Prayer both publick & private omitting no occasion that was offered for the discharge of that Duty either in Publick Congregations or in his Private Devotion.[7]

It was also John's commitment to tithe half of his means for charitable works, a fact that came to light from his accounts and his will and from the writings of his son-in-law. A listing of his known gifts to charity fills several pages.

As his compassion and care for the poor increased, the Lord blessed him with increased property and means so that his income expanded to match his desire to alleviate the poverty and suffering of those less fortunate, particularly the poorly paid clergymen. Not only did he buy Groombridge but also owned Shellingford Manor in Berkshire; Donnington Castle at Shaw, Berkshire; and a manor at Chilton Foliatt, Wiltshire. Donnington Castle had been a grant to John Packer from King Charles I upon his coronation in 1625.[8]

John Packer was but one of the Packers' ancestors whom, through Donna's research, they came to respect and love. Their feelings were intensified by successive visits to Groombridge Place, which Mr. Mountain later deeded to his niece, Rosemary Newton. On occasion they were overnight guests there, and Mrs. Newton later visited the Packer home in Salt Lake City.

Sister Packer's British research on Packer and related lines prompted her, with her husband's encouragement and support, to write a book of family history, *On Footings from the Past*. Of it, the director of the Society of Genealogists in London, Anthony J. Camp, wrote: "I have been looking at your very splendid *Footings* . . . and admiring the most beautiful way in which it has been researched, set out, printed, illustrated and bound. You are to be congratulated on a very fine achievement."[9]

Bodleian Library at Oxford, county record offices, and many others wrote to acknowledge her work.

Elder Dallin H. Oaks wrote about the accuracy of her research: "I salute you for your superior grasp and use of such obscure legal terminology as "seized" and "enfeofed" and for your use and explanation of legal records. Your handling of the legal vocabulary and attainments in connection with the office and activities of Sir Thomas Fleming, Lord Chief Justice, has the feel of a veteran legal scholar."

He continued, "I profited by your essay on the Wiltshire Village, where I learned for the first time of the 1537 law that required parishes to keep registers of births, etc."[10]

The title of Sister Packer's book came from her husband's poem, "Ancestral Home," written about Groombridge Place the night before a visit there in April 1987. The full text appears in her book. A few verses give a sense of place and of his reverence for family heritage:

> With dusk at Groombridge, peacocks call,
> For foxes are abroad.
> Their plaintive cry stirs memories
> Of those who prayed to God,
> Then built and kept this tranquil place
> And left their spirit here.
> What man thought changed, or lost and gone,
> Has always lingered near.
>
> The house is not our heritage,
> For others held the deed.
> It is their home, and rightly so—
> It does not fill our need.
> The heritage we each may own,
> Each in full measure claim:
> Their faith, their love, their sacrifice,
> Their service to His name.
>
> Our heritage, like life itself,
> We keep and yet pass on.
> In doing so, we pay the debt
> We owe to those now gone.
> What came from them, we hold in trust—
> Stored treasure that will last.
> Like Groombridge Place, our lives are built
> On footings from the past.[11]

As they had explored not only Elder Packer's British roots at Groombridge, Donnington Castle, and Bucklebury (home of another Packer-related family) but also Sister Packer's roots in the London area, there had come into their lives an even greater commitment to do the research and temple work for their kindred dead. During the intervening years they performed this service for thousands of their British and American ancestors.

Elder Packer was drawn not only to his paternal line but also to his mother's Scandinavian people who had passed on. This was apparent when he spoke in Stockholm during the Scandinavian Area General Conference for Denmark, Finland, Norway, and Sweden in August 1974. Said he: "I am in fact Scandinavian by ancestry. My maternal grandfather emigrated from Denmark, then worked in the smelters to bring his Swedish wife to America. My father's mother also was Danish," noting that Brigham City, in northern

With Presiding Bishop Victor L. Brown, author Alex Haley, and President Dallin H. Oaks at BYU graduation exercises

Utah where he was raised, was settled almost entirely by converts coming from Scandinavia.

At Brigham Young University on 19 August 1977 President Dallin H. Oaks had awarded an honorary doctoral degree to Alex Haley, author of best-selling *Roots* and "the great-great-great-great-grandson of Kunte Kinte."[12] At that convocation Elder Boyd K. Packer had given the commencement address. His talk reflected a commitment not only to ancestral lines but also to the spiritual beginnings of all of Heavenly Father's children. He told the degree recipients: "Remember who you are, remember your roots. Hang on to them, your spiritual ones. You are a child of God. . . .

"There is a vital difference between your mortal genealogy and your spiritual one. Your mortal genealogy goes back generation after generation after generation, your spiritual genealogy but one. . . . The whole effort of the university is to teach you to find your identity. You are a child of God. That is your spiritual ancestry."[13]

In November 1974 President Spencer W. Kimball dedicated the Washington, D.C., Temple. Many of the General Authorities were present. Elder and Sister Packer were among them when, on 22 November 1974, the prophet testified: "The day is coming, not too far ahead of us, when all the temples on this earth will be going night and day. There will be shifts, of course, and people will be coming in the morning and in the hours of the day and throughout the day and we will have no vacations for the temples. But there will be a corps of workers night and day almost to exhaustion, because of the importance of the work and the great number of people who lie asleep in the eternity and who are craving, needing, the blessings we can bring them."[14]

In October 1975 Elder Packer referred to President Kimball's talk: "This represents our signal that the great work necessary to sustain the temples must be moved forward.

"Genealogical work has, I fear, sometimes been made to appear too difficult, too involved, and too time-consuming to really be inviting to the average high priest." Elder Packer quoted one of their number who, having time and ability, could have done much in this work but had been doing nothing. Asked why, the brother responded: "When I look at the pedigree chart with all of the blank spaces and all of the numbers on it, it reminds me more than any-thing else of an income tax form! And so I do like I do with my income tax. I pay someone else to make that out for me. I'm thereby spared getting involved in that. I pay a little money into the family organization, hoping to get my genealogical research done in the same way."[15]

Elder Packer and the other members of the Temple and Geneal-ogy Executive Committee had studied and prayed to understand why the work was not going forward. President Kimball supported and gave approval to long-term efforts to make a major course correction and accelerate the work for the dead. In these efforts Elder Packer worked closely with Elder Bruce R. McConkie in exploring and dis-cussing the scriptural basis for the sure direction in which the com-mittee was moving.

By assignment from the First Presidency, Elder Packer addressed the employees of the Genealogical Department on 18 November 1975 and pleaded for their cooperation: "Now I'm appealing to you all to set your minds to the task of simplifying basic genealogical research and of streamlining, in every way possible, the process by which names come from members of the Church and are ultimately presented in the temple for ordinance work."[16]

Effecting simplicity in paperwork and personalizing the work for kindred dead became a vital interest for Elder Packer. What he asked of others, he and Sister Packer did for their family, living and dead. Despite the responsibilities of his ministry he led the way by putting his own documented life story into a book of remembrance; by writ-ing his parents' history, "The Best Team," and by supporting and helping Donna in her research and writing. This required that they begin their days an hour earlier than their already early rising time. Of Donna's interest and diligence in all aspects of family history he said, "These deepened my love and appreciation for her in un-bounded, eternal terms."

From her research they have learned that inspiration comes with the doing. Once they began and persevered, they found that infor-mation, details, and names proliferated.

In January 1977 Elder Packer reported: "Several months ago I took to the Genealogical Department eight large volumes, manuscript genealogical work, consisting of six thousand family group sheets of very professional genealogical work, all on the Packer family. All of it was compiled by Warren Packer, originally from Ohio, a schoolteacher, a Lutheran. He has spent thirty years doing this work, not really knowing why."[17]

Significant to the work of salvation for the dead was the announcement at general conference on 3 April 1976 that two revelations were to be added to the latter-day canon of scripture. They were Joseph Smith's vision of the celestial kingdom and Joseph F. Smith's vision of the redemption of the dead (D&C 137 and 138). Responding to the prayerful preparation among the Brethren, and to the historic announcement, Elder Packer spoke of it at a Church Education seminar in the Assembly Hall on Temple Square on 14 October 1977:

"I was surprised, and I think all of the Brethren were surprised, at how casually that announcement of two additions to the standard works was received by the Church. But we will live to sense the significance of it; we will tell our grandchildren and our great-grandchildren, . . . that we were on the earth and remember when that took place."[18]

The two new additions to the scriptures were then included in the cross-referencing of the King James Version of the Bible with all of the standard works which was presently under way.

As he worked in temple and genealogy assignments received from the First Presidency, Elder Packer's vision broadened to encompass all of Heavenly Father's family. In a very personal way the enormous task of bringing the saving ordinance of baptism to them became a reality for him.

On 2 October 1975 he said: "The Lord was neither hesitant nor apologetic in proclaiming exclusive authority over those processes, all of them in total, by which all may return to the presence of our Heavenly Father. . . . In His name rests the authority to secure the salvation of mankind, 'for there is none other name under heaven given among men, whereby we must be saved'" (Acts 4:12).

He continued, "Even the Lord was not exempt from the essential ordinance of baptism, the *strait and narrow gate* through which every soul must pass to obtain eternal life." He then asked a disturbing question: "What power would establish one Lord and one baptism as essential and then allow it to be that most of the human family never came within its influence?" He answered with the Apostle Paul's words: "Else what shall they do which are baptized for the dead, if the dead rise not at all? why are they then baptized for the dead?" (1 Corinthians 15:29.)

"The knowledge of this work represents the signature of authority upon this Church."[19]

The Brethren came to know the magnitude of the task ahead and to understand the doctrinal foundation for the work, as contained in section 128 of the Doctrine and Covenants. They moved on with the pure aim of redeeming the dead out of their prison, following the injunction to "go forward and not backward," and "as a church and a people . . . offer unto the Lord an offering in righteousness" (D&C 28:22, 24). This message reached a Churchwide audience with Elder Packer's general conference talk in October 1975, "The Redemption of the Dead."[20]

In 1977 the Temple and Genealogy Executive Committee was chaired by Elder Howard W. Hunter, with Elders Boyd K. Packer and Marvin J. Ashton, members; Elders Theodore M. Burton and O. Leslie Stone, executive directors; and Elder William Grant Bangerter, managing director. By April 1 that year they had gained approval from the First Presidency for long-range goals that would move "a church and a people" nearer to what the Lord expected of them in redeeming their dead. The Genealogical Department was tooling up to enter the age of computers, and in order to become conversant with them Elder Packer attended a one-week crash course at IBM in San Jose, California.

By assignment from the committee, Elder Packer in a talk titled "That They May Be Redeemed," said: "Billions have lived and we are to redeem all of them. . . . Overwhelming? Not quite! For we are the sons and daughters of God. He has told us that He would give 'no commandments unto the children of men, save he shall prepare a way for them that they may accomplish the thing which he commandeth them'" (1 Nephi 3:7).

We come now to that time . . . when we must step back and consider the full proportions of the work.

> If we are staggered by it, we must catch ourselves and straighten ourselves up and face it.
>
> When we contemplate how big it is, it is astonishing; it is past astonishing, it is overwhelming!
>
> But it is not discouraging!
>
> Whatever the number [of our dead] we can love them, and desire to redeem them. Any one of us has within us the power to expand our concern to include them all. If a billion more are added, we can care for them also.
>
> If the numbers seem staggering, we will move ahead. If the process is tedious, we will move ahead anyway. If the records have been lost, if the obstacles and opposition are overwhelming, we will move ahead anyway.

Elder Packer then talked of new technological advances that allowed for different attitudes and different procedures, saying, "It is as though someone knew we would be traveling that way . . . and we find provision, information, inventions . . . set along the way waiting for us to take them up, and we see the invisible hand of the Almighty providing for us."[21]

Given these helps, Elder Packer then outlined long-range goals for temple and genealogical work: The department would no longer do genealogical work for the Church but would assist members to do their own. Computers, then used solely for the department, would be available to members. When simple criteria had been set, decisions on ordinance work for the dead would be placed in the hands of local Church leaders as for the living. Done by computer, the clearing of names for temple ordinance work would be instant. And to keep more temples in operation, name extraction, previously done by Church employees, would be done in the homes by volunteers. Then, as the number of names warranted in any temple district, more temples, smaller and less costly, would be built.

"We can see into the eternities and contemplate all of God's creations," Elder Packer continued. "Worlds without number and the innumerable hosts of heaven who have lived one day upon this earth. They are eligible to at least make a choice as to whether they will or will not accept baptism."

He spoke of President Kimball's renewed emphasis on temple

building in order to hasten the work. The temple in Washington, D.C., had been dedicated. Those to follow were São Paulo, Brazil; Tokyo, Japan; Seattle, Washington; and Mexico City. In addition, the temples in Mesa, St. George, Hawaii, and Logan were to be remodeled. That was only the beginning.

Elder Packer then recalled the lesson he had learned as a young father from Elder Harold B. Lee, who quoted Ether 12:6: "Wherefore, dispute not because ye see not, for ye receive no witness until after the trial of your faith." Elder Lee then said, "My boy, you must learn to walk to the edge of the light, and perhaps a few steps into the darkness, and you will find that the light will appear and move ahead of you."

"And so it is with this work," Elder Packer affirmed. "We can build those thousands of temples and we can redeem our dead by the thousands and tens of thousands and millions and billions and tens of billions. We have not yet moved to the edge of the light."[22]

Chapter Sixteen

The Holy Temple

 For Boyd K. Packer, walking to the edge of the light was and is toward the light of the temple. Said he, "The house of the Lord, bathed in light, standing out in the darkness, becomes symbolic of the power and the inspiration of the gospel of Jesus Christ standing as a beacon in a world that sinks ever further into spiritual darkness."[1]

"Although the temple is but a building framed up of the same materials used to build other buildings, it is not the same. It is separated from all of the others by the intensity of the light of which we have been speaking."[2]

Of temple work he wrote: "No work is more of a protection to this Church than temple work and the genealogical research which supports it. No work is more spiritually refining. No work we do gives us more power. No work requires a higher standard of righteousness. Our labors in the temple cover us with a shield and a protection, both individually and as a people."[3]

Thus Elder Packer has invited, in fact pleaded with, every member of Heavenly Father's family to prepare, to become worthy, and to come to the temple. "Firmly resolve now," he wrote, "that you will do everything you can do to aid temple work and the genealogical work that supports it and to assist every living soul and every soul beyond the veil in every way you can with every resource at your disposal. Come to the temple!"[4]

Elder Packer quotes the Prophet Joseph Smith, who acknowledged the difficulty when he said: "I have tried for a number of years to get the minds of the Saints prepared to receive the things of God; but we frequently see some of them, after suffering all they have for the work of God, will fly to pieces like glass as soon as anything comes that is contrary to their traditions: they cannot stand the fire at all. How many will be able to abide a celestial law, and go through and receive their exaltation, I am unable to say, as many are called, but few are chosen."[5]

Shortly after Brother Packer had, by assignment, given to Regional Representatives his address "That They May Be Redeemed," he was called as adviser to the Temple Sites and Construction Committee. The construction and operation of temples is kept under the direction of the President of the Church and his counselors. They assign members of the Twelve and other General Authorities to assist them in this most sacred of all work. Committee chairman was H. Burke Peterson, First Counselor in the Presiding Bishopric, who worked directly with President Spencer W. Kimball in all matters dealing with temple planning and building. Elder William Grant Bangerter was managing director of the Temple Department. Also on the committee were the Church architect and key men over buildings, physical facilities, and real estate.

As Brother Packer sought to know his responsibility as adviser to the committee, he sat through their meetings mostly listening. Then he began asking himself, "Why is temple construction being treated here as though it were the same as any other kind of building effort?" He also asked what the committee members knew about Elijah's mission, about sections 110 and 124 of the Doctrine and Covenants, about Wilford Woodruff's announcement about work for the dead. Some of them seemed quite unfamiliar with these basic teachings. So there was a need to instruct those who planned or designed and constructed temples as to the central purpose for them, aside from physical buildings.

With this in mind he had made relevant comments. Bishop Peterson asked him to explain more fully. "I will," Brother Packer responded, "if you will give me time." The chairman readily agreed to devote a meeting to the spiritual purposes for temple construction.

In that meeting Elder Packer, the teacher, wrote on the blackboard words he had seen on a sign: *Will Build to Suit Owner.* These words immediately suggested an attitude toward temple building that would focus upon the true owner.

"We are dealing with temples," he said. "The owner is not the committees you represent; the owner is not the Presiding Bishopric; nor the Brethren. We are building houses of the Lord and they are His. Ought we not then to ask, "What is His will?"

He then reasoned that in order to know the Lord's will they must approach temple building with an understanding of its central purpose: to provide sacred housing wherein the sealing power which the Prophet Elijah restored through Joseph Smith can be operative; a place where the saving ordinances of baptism, confirmation, endowment, eternal marriage, and the sealing of parents and children into lineage-linked families can be performed. This, he affirmed, constitutes the *invisible temple.* The structure itself is but the housing wherein these things can be accomplished. He further stated that magnificent sites and excessively large structures are not needful to accomplish the Lord's purposes.

He quoted President Wilford Woodruff's words spoken not long before his death: "At this period we want to go on and fulfill this commandment of God given through Malachi—that the Lord should send Elijah the prophet, 'and he shall turn the heart of the fathers to the children, and the heart of the children to their fathers, lest I come and smite the earth with a curse' " (Malachi 4:6).

President Woodruff also said: "Were it not for these principles, you and I would not be here today. We have had prophets and apostles. President Young, who followed President Joseph Smith, led us here. He organized these temples and carried out the purposes of his calling and office. He laid the foundation of this great temple on this block, as well as others in the mountains of Israel. What for? That we might carry out these principles of redemption for the dead."[6]

Elder Packer then spoke of the Transfiguration of the Lord,

wherein the Savior, and Moses and Elijah (both translated beings), conferred priesthood keys upon Peter, James, and John, who would be the leaders of the dispensation of the meridian of time. He concluded with the latter-day appearance of Elijah to the Prophet Joseph Smith and Oliver Cowdery and with that ancient prophet's bestowal of the sealing power upon them.

Elder Peterson remembers the impact of Elder Packer's teaching upon him and the other brethren as Brother Packer wove incidents together into an orderly, easily understood tapestry.

The keen interest of Elder Packer's listeners caused him to realize that there was an empty space in the literature of the Church about the mission of Elijah and its significance for temple work. Elder James E. Talmage's book *The House of the Lord* was mainly a history about the construction of temples and only touched upon the doctrine. Beyond this one work there were only a few Church-produced pamphlets regarding temples. None of them adequately covered Elijah's mission and the doctrines that were crucial to it.

Brother Packer then considered the possibility of his writing such a work. As he filled his many assignments, he continued to ponder the idea. Finally he determined to do it. Accordingly he and Sister Packer gave up whatever summer vacation time they might have had and began their days even earlier than they had done to write personal and family histories. In every way possible, Sister Packer freed him for his research and writing. Their son Lawrence, who had looked forward to a summer job in preparation for school in the fall, changed his plans and accepted the responsibility of doing home-and-garden tasks that his father would otherwise have done.

As Elder Packer focused his energies on writing *The Holy Temple*, Sister Packer felt its importance to the Church and to their family.

Elder Packer reviewed with Elder Bruce R. McConkie many scriptures relating to the doctrines of sealing power and temple ordinances and to the history of temples throughout the ages, and found his counsel valuable. He also valued Roy W. Doxey's meticulous research for the project.

Of the experience Brother Doxey said: "Elder Packer was always open to suggestion and counsel, always ready to learn something he did not know, and he was prayerful in his approach. He was precise in his writing, making many drafts and corrections as he went along."

From the book's beginning, Elder Packer intended it to be for the member going to the temple for the first time. With this in mind he wrote informally, directly, and personally to the reader, as if he were sitting down to talk to a son or a daughter. While he would not describe the sacred ordinances and ceremonies of the temple in more detail than had previously been published by the Church, he would answer many questions that a thoughtful member would have.

He quoted: "It may seem to some to be a very bold doctrine that we talk of—a power which records or binds on earth and binds in heaven. Nevertheless, in all ages of the world, whenever the Lord has given a dispensation of the priesthood to any man by actual revelation, or any set of men, this power has always been given." (D&C 128:9.)

Elder Packer had never forgotten an experience he and others had with President Spencer W. Kimball, the man who then held that position and those keys. After the area conference held in Copen-hagen, Denmark, in 1976, President Kimball expressed a desire to

Thorvaldsen's Christus in the Vor Frue Church in Copenhagen, Denmark

visit the Vor Frue Church, where the Thorvaldsen statues of the Christus and the Twelve Apostles are housed. Elder Packer remembered:

> Most of the group were near the rear of the chapel, where the custodian, through an interpreter, was giving some explanation. I stood with President Kimball, Elder Rex Pinegar, and President Bentine, the stake president, before the statue of Peter. In [the Apostle's] hand, depicted in marble, is a set of heavy keys. President Kimball pointed to them and explained what they symbolized. Then, in an act I shall never forget, he turned to President Bentine and with unaccustomed sternness pointed his finger at him and said with firm, impressive words, "I want you to tell every Lutheran in Denmark that they do not hold the keys! I hold the keys! We hold the real keys and we use them every day."
>
> This declaration and testimony from the prophet so affected me that I knew I would never forget it—the influence was powerfully spiritual and the impression was physical in its impact as well.
>
> We walked to the other end of the chapel where the rest of the group were standing. Pointing to the statues, President Kimball said to the kind custodian who was showing us the building, "These are the dead Apostles. Here we have the living Apostles." Pointing to me he said, "Elder Packer is an Apostle." He designated the others and said, "Elder Monson and Elder Perry are Apostles, and I am an Apostle. We are the living Apostles. You read about seventies in the New Testament, and here are living seventies, Brother Pinegar and Brother Hales."
>
> The custodian, who to that time had shown no particular emotion, suddenly was in tears.
>
> As we left that little chapel where those impressive sculptures stand, I felt I had taken part in an experience of a lifetime.[7]

Elder Packer wrote of the opposition and the persecutions of the Saints which took their temple in Kirtland and the later one in Nauvoo, both of which were built out of their poverty and sacrifice. Of this loss Elder Packer said:

> Those who joined the unholy power to prevent temple work seemed to win. Time after time they had their way. They ended up, for a time at least, with the sites—leaving to the persecuted Saints nothing. Nothing? No! We have the keys, the ordinances. We have everything.

They have nothing. They cannot baptize nor ordain. They cannot wash nor anoint nor endow nor seal. We came away with everything, and they have nothing. Our forebears were compelled, because of those deprivations in the early years, to focus on the things that mattered most.[8]

Elder Packer gave a promise: "No one takes hold of this work without being susceptible to the blessings of the Lord. If you have problems with your own immediate family, do all you can for them. Begin working in behalf of the Lord's family and good things will start to happen."[9]

He described how the Spirit of Elijah was at work both in the Church and out, fulfilling that prophet's prophecy of turning the heart of the children to the fathers and the heart of the fathers to the children.

Concluding his book, Elder Packer wrote: "I cannot close this chapter and this book without bearing you my testimony concerning temple work and the genealogical work associated with it. . . . I know as surely as I know that I live that the work relating to the temples is true. I know that it was revealed from beyond the veil."[10]

Having read *The Holy Temple*, Elder H. Burke Peterson said:

> I had never forgotten Brother Packer's talk to us of the Temple Sites and Construction Committee in 1978; his teachings of that day were amplified in this great book. When I became president of the Jordan River Temple in 1985 and worked to fulfill that sacred calling, I hungered to be further taught by him. I expressed this to him, and not long after, he visited me there.
>
> He expanded my spiritual understanding to a remarkable degree. My life has never been quite the same. It was not a course change, but a deeper, wider comprehension of the sacred, saving work of the temple that I find difficult to describe. How grateful I am for his power to teach by the Spirit those things for which words alone are inadequate.[11]

Two years after *The Holy Temple* was published the First Presidency had a forty-page condensed version of the book printed. Copies were distributed to all stakes and wards in the Church, to be read by those going to the temple for the first time. Since then, many bishops recommend to first-time temple attenders a total reading of the book.

In the late 1970s Elder Packer was in Tonga to reorganize a stake. After he had come to know whom the Lord wanted for the stake president, he extended the call to that brother. The new president was a mature man and the father of nine children. Elder Packer asked whether he had been sealed in the temple. Yes, he had. Had his children been sealed to him? At this question the president wept openly. Only one of the nine had been born in the covenant.

Brother Packer asked no further questions along that line, knowing that the airfare from Tonga to New Zealand, the site of the nearest temple, was several times the man's annual income. He recalls thinking, "To make that flight with his other eight children would be as impossible as reaching Mars in a canoe."

"During the same conference I met a handsome young Tongan who had recently returned from a mission. In the course of our conversation I asked if he was dating. 'No,' he responded. 'Why not,' I asked. He gave two reasons: 'Were I to find the right girl, there would be no place to live; and I could not get to the temple.'"

That evening Brother Packer, speaking at a youth fireside, found himself unable to talk about temple marriage. On his return flight he wrestled the question: "Where are we as a Church that I would feel restrained from speaking about temple marriage to our young people?"

That question and its implications troubled him deeply. He had numerous conversations with President Kimball about the need to get smaller, less costly temples to the peoples of developing countries. As he had worked with others to move the work of family research and history forward, he now labored in company with his brethren to advance and expand temple building. Every step in that direction was approved by the First Presidency and the Quorum of the Twelve, and out of their prayers, faith, and labor came an unprecedented temple-building era.

The subject was a major topic of concern and discussion among the Brethren in their weekly temple meetings. President Spencer W. Kimball gave special support and encouragement to the concept of taking temples to *all* people.

Elder and Sister Packer attended the dedication of the Washington, D.C., Temple in November of 1974. At President Kimball's invitation, Brother Packer stood with him to greet the dignitaries who filed through to view that building before its dedication: the wife of President Gerald R. Ford, the Russian Ambassador, the Chief Justice of the Supreme Court, congressmen, and many others.

On 30 October 1978 Elder Packer participated in the dedication of the São Paulo, Brazil, Temple, at which President Kimball again presided.

Although he did not attend the dedication of the Tokyo Temple in October 1980, again conducted by President Kimball, it fulfilled a longing in his heart for the Japanese members to receive their temple blessings.

Elder Packer taught that those who could not go to a temple could still participate in the sacred work. His words were reported in a *Church News* article: "We are trying to establish family history as a cottage industry where members of the family can work it in, along with everything else there is to do. A young mother, for instance, can simply keep the records of the children, such as their ordination certificates, and that's a worthy contribution to family history. It is not required that she drop everything else in order to participate."[12]

Chapter Seventeen

The New LDS Edition
of the Scriptures

 The publication in 1979 of the new LDS edition of the King James Version of the Bible was of great historic importance. It was followed in 1981 with new editions of the Book of Mormon, Another Testament of Jesus Christ; the Doctrine and Covenants; and the Pearl of Great Price. All of these had been linked with footnotes, cross-references, a dictionary, and a six-hundred-page topical guide. What had been estimated as a four- or five-year project had taken nearly ten.

For this monumental task, which had been approved by President Harold B. Lee and guided by his successor, President Spencer W. Kimball, three members of the Quorum of the Twelve had been assigned to see it through to completion: Elders Thomas S. Monson, Bruce R. McConkie, and Boyd K. Packer. The other Brethren had been kept abreast of its progress while they had carried on their own individual work.

No other assignment from the First Presidency had meant more to Elder Packer than this one. Said he at its completion:

> During the last twenty years I have had a variety of assignments. I
> have regarded all of them with respect. Some very few I have regarded

with deep reverence. One of these has been the assignment to have something to do with the publication of the scriptures. . . .

This exertion is a monumental protection and preservation for the Church and kingdom of God upon the earth.

I bear my humble witness that the inspiration of the Almighty has attended this—that we have not been alone.[1]

Elder Packer saw the work partly from the perspective of a teacher of the scriptures who valued the simple but comprehensive reference systems used in the new standard works and what they could do for the growing membership of the Church. During the last phase of preparing these reference materials he had given over his summer vacation time to proofread the eight-inch-thick printout of the Topical Guide, in the process discovering some crucial omissions. Of this exercise he said, "It was like proofing the dictionary." This was but one of the technical, time-consuming tasks he performed in the work that was so dear to him.

He loved and revered the project as a bringing together of "the library of the Lord." For him, it was the treasure house of God's dealings with, and promises for, His children: transcendent promises for the obedient, and stern discipline for the rebellious.

The 1981 edition of the
Book of Mormon

His love and reverence for the scriptures had grown and expanded over a forty-year period since his lonely, consistent study of the Book of Mormon while serving in the military. He would later testify: "I have asked if the scriptures are true. And I have a witness and a testimony, and I give it unto you: That Jesus is the Christ, the Son of God; that He is our Redeemer and our Messiah; that there was the fall of man; that He is our Mediator and our Redeemer; that He wrought the

Atonement; that He is our Lord. I know Him. I bear to you a witness of Him, a special witness of Him."[2]

As a young man Elder Packer had covenanted with the Lord to be true to that sacred witness, to voluntarily surrender his agency to Him, and to be forever obedient to all that it required. He had continued to study not only the four standard works but also the history of the Church and the teachings of the prophets from Joseph Smith to this time in such depth that he could effectively teach them. The knowledge he gained is reflected in each carefully crafted talk he has given. And, as with the other Brethren, when such scriptural knowledge and understanding are quickened and magnified by the spirit of revelation the resultant words are elevated to the stature of modern scripture.

President Harold B. Lee affirmed this point when, as prophet, he quoted from the Doctrine and Covenants: "And whatsoever they shall speak when moved upon by the Holy Ghost shall be scripture, shall be the will of the Lord, shall be the mind of the Lord, shall be the word of the Lord, shall be the voice of the Lord, and the power of God unto salvation" (D&C 68:4).

Elder Packer had borne witness of that quickening, amplifying help: "I know that voice when it speaks."[3]

One of the sources of his knowing is attested to in another section of the Doctrine and Covenants. It is a source open to all who will search and listen:

> These words are not of men nor of man, but of me; wherefore, you shall testify they are of me and not of man;
>
> For it is my voice which speaketh them unto you; for they are given by my Spirit unto you, and by my power you can read them one to another; and save it were by my power you could not have them;
>
> Wherefore, you can testify that you have heard my voice, and know my words (D&C 18:34–36).

With the mammoth scripture project complete and in hand, the three Apostles who had served on the Scriptures Publication Committee addressed a meeting of the General Authorities on 2 October 1981.

Elder Thomas S. Monson, who had spent years in the printing

and publishing business prior to his call as a General Authority, had overseen matters related to the technical aspects of the project. Said he, "As we undertook the gigantic task of correlating the standard works of the Church, we knew that we had to reprint the King James Version of the Bible—one of the most staggering typesetting jobs in the world."

Monotype, a typesetting system in which each character is individually cast and set on a lead slug, was selected because of its full flexibility. "It is," Elder Monson said, "costly and time-consuming. It is a product of the old craftsmanship of typography."

> The company that was selected . . . was the Cambridge University Press of England, one of the three publishing houses in Great Britain that has the Seal of the Crown to print the King James Version. . . .
>
> We used a style in footnoting which has really revolutionized scripture setting worldwide. We used to have superior figures, and by the time we got up to 23 or 24 we could not even read the tiny little superior figures. We have revolutionized that concept by alphabetically listing every reference to a particular verse.

Elder Monson continued, "Cambridge University was awarded the top graphics arts award in 1980 in all of Great Britain on the basis of the typography and work done on the Latter-day Saint edition of the King James Version of the Bible."[4]

Next to address those assembled was Elder Bruce R. McConkie, who, as one of the foremost scriptural scholars and doctrinal authorities, had supervised all text and reference matters and had written the chapter headings for the new editions. Said he, "I do not have any language to indicate how strongly I feel or how much I am assured that the work that has been done will benefit and bless the members of the Church and hosts of people who yet will hear the message of the Restoration."

He then spoke of the men whose work he had directed. "These brethren—Robert J. Matthews, Ellis T. Rasmussen, Robert C. Patch, and William James Mortimer—have literally been raised up by the Lord at this time and season to do the particular, difficult, and technical work that has been required. The Lord's hand has been in it.

"And there is no question that major decisions were made by the spirit of inspiration and that the conclusions reached accord with the mind and will of the Lord."[5]

Elder Boyd K. Packer was next to address the gathering. He had worked closely with Elders Monson and McConkie, especially with Elder McConkie, and comprehended the far-reaching blessings the work would have upon generations to come. Adding to his statement given earlier, he said:

> If the doctrines of the Church could be put in boxes of various sizes and shapes to fit them . . . I would find the box labeled "agency" and set that in place first. . . . As we examine this foundation doctrine, we find such words as "choice," "freedom," "liberty," and we quickly learn that our God intends that we should be free to choose good on one hand and evil on the other.
>
> There is a test involved, crucial to our eternal progress, and we learn that if men are to be free they must know the truth. . . . It is essential, therefore, that every member of the Church become acquainted with the revelations, that every member "speak in the name of God the Lord, even the Savior of the world" (D&C 1:20).

He later said, "As a very direct outgrowth of the scripture project, two revelations were added to the Doctrine and Covenants [sections 137 and 138]. That had not occurred in over a hundred years. And before the books were closed, there came the glorious revelation on the priesthood, just in time to be bound with all else that the Lord has revealed to His Saints in this, the dispensation of the fulness of times."[6]

Because the Apostles travel much and see conditions in the world as they really are, and because the most serious problems within and without the Church are constantly before them, they are burdened as are few other men. Brother Packer expressed his feelings about this to a gathering of Church Education teachers. He had been reading the prophetic description of the evil circumstances that would encircle those living in the latter days: "For men shall be lovers of their own selves, covetous, boasters, proud, blasphemers, disobedient to parents, unthankful, unholy, without natural affection, trucebreakers, false accusers, incontinent, fierce, despisers of those that are good, traitors, heady, highminded, lovers of pleasures more than lovers of God" (2 Timothy 3:2–4).

After reading to that point he sat pondering about all the evidence around us that confirms every element in that prophecy. Said he: "There was a mood of very deep gloom and foreboding, a very ominous feeling of frustration, almost futility. I glanced down the page, and one word stood out, not accidentally I think. I read it eagerly and then discovered that the Apostle who had prophesied all of that trouble had included in the same discourse the immunization against all of it: 'But continue thou in the things which thou hast learned and hast been assured of, knowing of whom thou hast learned them; and that from a child thou hast known the holy scriptures, which are able to make thee wise unto salvation through faith (2 Timothy 3:14–15).' "[7]

Thus he taught that the scriptures are the anchor, the compass, the shield, the corrector, the instructor, and the perfecter for all men in all times. It is little wonder that the new LDS editions of the scriptures meant so much to him.

In its preparation and publication hundreds had served laboriously and unsung, with a conscientious diligence much as had the scholars who had produced the original King James Version of the Bible. There were no stars; no one person's work was of greater value to the whole than another's; it was teamwork of the highest order, with each using his or her particular skill for the accomplishment of the whole.

When the work was complete, every phase of its production was reported in Church publications. Each author told with insight and clarity something about what had been done. Each report had a specific, non-personal purpose: to acquaint Church members with the new edition's purpose and format and to instruct them in its use.

In Elder Boyd K. Packer's October 1982 general conference address, "Scriptures," he stated that the scripture project "had its beginning in Old Testament times and is the fulfillment of a prophecy by Ezekiel, who wrote:

> The word of the Lord came . . . unto me, saying, Moreover, thou son of man, take thee one stick, and write upon it, For Judah, and for the children of Israel his companions: then take another stick, and write upon it, For Joseph, the stick of Ephraim, and for all the house of Israel

his companions: And join them one to another in one stick; and they shall become one in thine hand (Ezekiel 37:15–17).

"The sticks, of course, are records or books. . . . Two events connected with the fulfillment of the prophecy were centered in print shops."

Brother Packer referred to these events. Though skeptical of the project and challenged by opposition and thievery, Egbert B. Grandin, a religious twenty-three-year-old man, finished the printing and binding of the Book of Mormon in March of 1830. "One hundred forty-seven years later, in June 1977, again in a print shop, another step in the coming together of these two sticks occurred."

Early in the project, James Mortimer and Ellis T. Rasmussen had called at the Cambridge University Press in Cambridge, England, which had been publishing the King James Bible since the first edition in 1611.

> They met with Mr. Roger Coleman, director of religious publishing, to discuss the publication of a most unusual edition of the King James Bible. The printers were quite as skeptical about this proposal as Mr. Grandin had been nearly 150 years before. . . .
>
> The text was to remain exactly as it was, no changes, not one. But all footnoting, cross-references, chapter introductions, indexes, and so on, were to be replaced. Only the chapter and verse numbering for the sixty-six books would be retained.
>
> And that was just the beginning. This edition of the Bible would be cross-referenced with three other books of scripture: the Book of Mormon, the Doctrine and Covenants, and the Pearl of Great Price. The printers had barely heard of them.

The technical problems seemed insurmountable to these men. Clearly, "it could not be done," Elder Packer related. "But in that meeting also was Mr. Derek Bowen, editor, a most remarkable man. . . . He was, perhaps, the one man in the world who could direct such a printing project."[8]

Brother Packer quoted Jim Mortimer: "During his service in England's armed forces during World War II, he was seriously injured when he stepped on a land mine. Among his injuries was a complete

Derek Brown (second from right), English editor,
at Cambridge University Press

loss of hearing. Because of his physical limitations he chose not to marry, and lived rather a Spartan life. . . . I had tried during the years to convince him of the truthfulness of the gospel, and he did read everything I sent him about the Church. I reminded him on our last visit that he knew so much about our Church that 'someday he'd be one of us.' He smiled in a beautiful way and we said our goodbyes. Three months later [after he had completed his work on this project] he died."[9]

So impressed was Elder Packer with the spirit of this British gentleman that on 19 May 1988 he personally performed the temple work for him.

On 10 March 1985 a Churchwide satellite fireside had been held, with President Gordon B. Hinckley and Elders Thomas S. Monson, Bruce R. McConkie (who was ill and in great pain at the time), and Boyd K. Packer commenting on the new scriptures and their use.[10] Elder Packer's presentation was later made into a video-training film by Brigham Young University and has been widely used in institutes and seminaries across the Church.

Elder Ezra Taft Benson was ordained President of the Church on 10 November 1985, and almost immediately he began to plead with

Church members everywhere to read the Book of Mormon daily so that, as a people, the Church might not remain under condemnation of the Lord for taking this precious book of scripture for granted.

For general conference April 1986 Elder Packer chose the Book of Mormon as his subject and titled his talk "The Things of My Soul." This talk was later produced as a videotape and used widely in the seminaries of the Church.

He traced the sacred records as they were kept and added to from the time of Lehi until they were hidden up by the prophet-leader Moroni. He then linked the prophecies contained therein so that the Lord's purpose concerning these records was unmistakable, their purpose being threefold: "First, to show what great things the Lord hath done for their fathers; second, that they might know the covenants of the Lord; and third, to the convincing of the Jew and the Gentile that *Jesus is the Christ*, the Eternal God, manifesting himself to all nations" (Book of Mormon title page).

All during the scripture project the friendship between Elder Packer and Elder McConkie had deepened, and an easy bantering manner had developed between them. It was, nevertheless, a friendship undergirt with seriousness, respect, and affection. Of Brother McConkie, Elder Packer said:

> During the long scripture-publication process, the anchor to the spiritual significance of it all was Bruce McConkie. We know from the revelations and from reading Church history that . . . some men are raised up unto a specific purpose, and Bruce McConkie in this great scriptural project was obviously one of them.
>
> It could not have been done without him. Few will ever know the extent of the service he rendered. Few can appraise the lifetime of preparation for this quiet crowning contribution to the on-rolling of the restored gospel in the dispensation of the fulness of times.
>
> Then came the time when Elder McConkie appeared to be tired, worn, and emotionally on edge; not irritable at all, but emotionally drained and less likely to extend a debate or conversation.
>
> One day, he talked to me. He had received from his doctor the result of a recent test. There was a malignancy. It was estimated that he had about two months to live. I said, "You can't do that to me," and I forbade him to die. We were both chuckling but both of us were very

serious over such a matter. There was work that had to be done that only he could do.

About that time Elder Packer gave his friend a blessing. "The work on chapter headings was essentially done," Brother Packer recalled, "but Bruce had worked with the Translation Department to develop a lexicon for translating the new editions of the scriptures into other languages. We went over to see how they were coming with it. They had over nine hundred pages prepared on the first two books of Nephi alone. Since there were thirteen books yet to be done, we knew this would not do."

Accordingly they directed that the work begin again, giving to it an entirely different direction. Brother McConkie then followed the project through personally and helped to prepare an effective lexicon and guide to translation. Again the other brethren were kept informed of the work being done.

In 1990 Elder Packer reported what had been accomplished:

> From the beginning of the Church, in 1830, through 1988, the standard works had been translated into thirty-five languages, with seven other languages in process. During the last year, approval has been given and budgets established to translate and publish the standard works in fifty-one additional languages.
>
> Years of tedious work lie ahead, for each translation must be done as though it alone is important.
>
> When completed, these translations will extend the possible readers of the scriptures in their native tongue to an additional 2,254,000,000 people—half the world population. And other translations will follow.[11]

Elder McConkie's groundwork had truly been of immense value to this aspect of missionary work. Elder Packer said: "This was only possible because Brother McConkie's cancer went into remission. Miraculously, he returned to full service."

During that period he traveled with Elder McConkie to South America. Elder Packer recalled: "Bruce had organized more stakes there than any two of us and had pressed for a different pattern for stakes in those developing countries. As they were approved, the work flourished."

Friends and brothers, Elders Packer and McConkie

Brother Packer continued, "Then when the cancer returned again, he just soldiered on until that April when he barely found the strength to come to conference and give his marvelous testimony."

That testimony serves as a powerful and fitting climax to the publication and the expanded use of the new editions of the scriptures, which so richly testify of Jesus the Christ and of His atoning sacrifice about which Elder McConkie spoke:

> And now, as pertaining to this perfect atonement, wrought by the shedding of the blood of God—I testify that it took place in Gethsemane and at Golgotha, and as pertaining to Jesus Christ, I testify that he is the Son of the Living God and was crucified for the sins of the world. He is our Lord, our God, and our King. This I know of myself independent of any other person.

I am one of his witnesses, and in a coming day I shall feel the nail marks in his hands and in his feet and shall wet his feet with my tears.

But I shall not know any better then than I know now that he is God's Almighty Son, that he is our Savior and Redeemer, and that salvation comes in and through his atoning blood and in no other way.[12]

Shortly after conference Elder Packer visited his friend and found him "resting on the bed, dressed, alert, patient." They expressed their deep love for one another and Bruce asked Boyd to give him a final blessing. He quoted the words of President Joseph F. Smith:

I beheld that the faithful elders of this dispensation, when they depart from mortal life, continue their labors in the preaching of the gospel of repentance and redemption, through the sacrifice of the Only Begotten Son of God, among those who are in darkness and under the bondage of sin in the great world of the spirits of the dead (D&C 138:57).

On 19 April 1985, just twelve days after bearing his great testimony, Bruce Redd McConkie left this mortal life for his new field of labor.

Chapter Eighteen

The New Revelation
on the Priesthood

 At the same time the LDS edition of the scriptures was being prepared for publication another matter was weighing heavily upon the soul of one of the Lord's great watchmen, President Spencer W. Kimball. Other latter-day prophets had wrestled with the same dilemma: that of obeying the divine command to preach the gospel to *every* kindred, tongue, and people, while being keenly aware that, because of race, some of those people were denied the full blessings of the gospel—that is, denied the priesthood and the temple ordinances. Thus these prophets had pleaded mightily with the Lord for answers to the problem, and none of them more intensely than President Kimball. Yet always the Spirit had indicated that the time had not yet come.

Now this prophet, small in physical stature but a spiritual giant, wrestled again, seeking and pleading in behalf of the faithful among all priesthood-denied people. Not only did he struggle, seek, and plead, but his brethren in the highest councils of the Church did so as well.

One day, during the Thursday temple meeting with his Counselors and the Twelve, President Kimball, who was pondering that matter, discussed it with his brethren. When it was Elder Packer's turn to speak, he read a scripture: "Verily, verily, I say unto you, that when I give a commandment to any of the sons of men to do a work unto my name, and those sons of men go with all their might and with all they have to perform that work, and cease not their diligence, and their enemies come upon them and hinder them from performing that work, behold, it behooveth me to require that work no more at the hands of those sons of men, but to accept of their offerings" (D&C 124:49).

A few days later President Kimball asked Brother Packer where he would be the next Saturday. Elder Packer told him he would be speaking Friday evening at the Dixie College baccalaureate but would return by plane early on Saturday.

"Will you come to my office?" the President asked.

"Of course," Elder Packer responded.

Upon his return about one o'clock on Saturday, Brother Packer went directly to the Church Office Building. The security officer on duty said that the President was at home and wished Elder Packer to call as soon as he came into the building.

Reaching President Kimball by phone, Elder Packer offered, "I'll come right up."

"No, I'll come down and meet you."

Arriving shortly after this, the President entered his office. Elder Packer recalls his saying that he had "this thing" on his mind and wanted to talk about it. "There was no need to explain what this thing was," Elder Packer recalled. "We both knew how it was weighing upon him.

"He handed me his scriptures and said he'd like me to read to him from the revelations. So we started with the one from Doctrine and Covenants 124:49 that I had read in the temple. For a couple of hours we just moved back and forth through the Doctrine and Covenants, the Book of Mormon, and the Pearl of Great Price, and then talked about what we read.

"The spirit of revelation seemed to be brooding upon the prophet that day. He asked me, assuming that the revelation was to come, how it might best be announced to the Church, and asked that I put something in writing. This I did and handed it to him a day or two later. He had asked one or two of the others to do the same."

On Thursday, 8 June 1978, in the Salt Lake Temple, the revelation was reaffirmed when the First Presidency and the Twelve approved the announcement that was to go out to the world. It was further reaffirmed in the temple on 9 June 1978 by all of the General Authorities available. They too unanimously approved the announcement.

The long-sought pronouncement that "all worthy male members of the Church may be ordained to the priesthood without regard for race or color" had become official.[1]

On 30 September 1978, at general conference, the assembled Saints voted unanimously to sustain the motion.[2]

Those of the Lord's watchmen who were present at those historic times will recall and have borne witness to the Spirit of revelation that attended them, and each has expressed gratitude for being part of the momentous experience. And none of the Twelve was more grateful for that day than Elder Boyd K. Packer.

From early on, his heart had gone out to faithful priesthood-denied people wherever they resided in the world. Close at hand were the black members of the Church in the Salt Lake Valley—the Genesis Group—whom he knew and encouraged. In the early '70s he was attending their Christmas social with his family. He told his brethren of the incident during their quarterly meeting on 17 December 1972. His youngest son had, much to his relief, climbed up on the lap of a big black Santa Claus, who said to the child, "I'll bet you have never seen a black Santa before, have you?" The three-year-old shook his head.

"Well, now," the Santa said, "I will tell you something. The white Santa is from the North Pole and the black Santa is from the South Pole."

Elder Packer continued: "We shook hands with all of them there, our brothers and sisters in that Genesis Group. They need our help, they need our prayers and our blessings and they need our attention. They really need our attention."

One who had received his help and attention was a tall black boy who reminded Elder Packer of one of his own sons. Another to whom he was drawn was the leader of the Genesis Group, Ruffin Bridgeforth, a faithful man.

Elder Packer said: "During President Harold B. Lee's administration he authorized us to have the brethren who belonged to the Genesis Group attend the priesthood session of general conference."

Shortly after the Official Declaration was ratified, Elder Packer recalls: "I went to President Kimball's office early on Friday morning. I told him that Brother Bridgeforth had not yet been ordained. He seemed surprised, knowing that of all these brethren, this man was the example, the pioneer. Then I asked how he would feel if we presented Ruffin to be a high priest instead of an elder? He pondered for a few minutes and said, 'Yes, that's right. You do that.'"

On Sunday during the sacrament meeting, when it came time for Brother Bridgeforth to be sustained and the stake president was about to stand, Elder Packer said, "President, have him presented to be a high priest.

"He was taken aback, but I assured him, 'President, it's all right.'

"After the meeting, we went to the Relief Society room for the ordination," Brother Packer continues. "Brother Bridgeforth invited members of the family whom he wished to be there."

After the ordination, Ruffin said that his wife would like to have a blessing. She was very feeble and had been brought in a wheelchair. Elder Packer readily agreed, but just as he was placing his hands upon her head he caught himself and said, "Ruffin, you now can give this blessing." And this he did.

There were many individual blessings proceeding from the new revelation, but Elder Packer later acknowledged in general conference an even more far-reaching blessing—that of having "the glorious revelation on the priesthood [come] just in time to be bound [in the new edition of the LDS scriptures] with all else that the Lord has revealed to His Saints in this, the dispensation of the fulness of times."[3]

It may be noted that precedent for its inclusion in the Doctrine and Covenants as Official Declaration—2 was President Wilford Woodruff's Declaration—1 on plural marriage, given eighty-eight years before.[4]

Helping to fulfill the priesthood promises of the new revelation in a land where they were singularly needed, President Kimball dedicated the São Paulo Temple in Brazil on 30 October 1978.[5] Because peoples of widespread racial mixture reside in that country, it was especially gratifying that this prophet, who so loved all people, could be the one to open the doors of this new temple to all worthy members.

Elder Packer had carefully prepared his talk and then had it translated so that he might read it in Spanish. Before the dedication, however, President Kimball held a regional conference in Montevideo, Uruguay, Elder Packer being there with him. The priesthood meeting was held in a theater where they and other leaders were seated in large overstuffed chairs on the stage. Brother Packer sat next to the President.

With President
Spencer W. Kimball

Just as the meeting was about to begin, President Kimball, not feeling well, handed his conducting book to Boyd, saying, "Would you mind conducting?" Elder Packer hastily tucked the binder containing his talk for the temple dedication down beside the cushion of his chair before standing to conduct the meeting.

Returning to the hotel, he suddenly realized that in the press of conducting he had left his talk tucked in his chair at the theater. "Well," he recalls, "the talk could not be found and we were to leave early the next morning for São Paulo, where we would go directly to the temple dedication.

"Before going to bed I quickly wrote the story of my experience with the little Indian boy in Cuzco, Peru. Elder Robert E. Wells and his wife, Helen, then translated it for me and left it under the hotel room door about 2:00 A.M., enabling me to read it in Spanish at the dedication."

Learning enough Spanish to function in Latin America had been a long-term desire of Brother Packer's. He had determined to learn enough Spanish to get by as he traveled and ministered in those countries. For a three-week period during one summer vacation he had a young man tutor him for a couple of hours each week. Elder Packer made up cards and memorized some fundamental words. Then each time he was sent to Latin America he picked up and retained others. He had hoped to take a crash course in Spanish at the Language Training Center, but travel and meeting schedules prevented him.

Early in President Kimball's administration Elder Packer met Regional Representative Angel Abrea when in Argentina to reorganize the Mendoza Stake. They were interviewing together, but time ran short and it became necessary for them to split up in order to handle all of the interviews. Brother Packer felt fairly comfortable asking the usual questions in Spanish, but after a while one of the bishops spoke earnestly about a major problem. Elder Packer listened for about ten minutes and then called Brother Abrea to come in. "This bishop has a problem," he said. "Let me tell you what I think it is."

Brother Abrea talked with the bishop in Spanish and then said to Elder Packer, "You've got it exactly."

"This gave me courage," Elder Packer says. "I interviewed in Spanish and understood what was said that day. I felt overwhelmed by the experience, and when I came back I mentioned it in our report meeting at the temple. In the hall afterwards President Kimball sought me out, saying, 'I want to tell you what happened to you. You were given the gift of tongues. That gift has many expressions.' I was very touched by what he said. From that time on, although my Spanish is only about a quarter of an inch deep, I have tried to communicate with Spanish-speaking people in their language."

Chapter Nineteen

Order, Ordain, Ordinance

 Along with his brethren, Elder Boyd K. Packer has given countless hours of study, prayer, and pondering to understand the simple yet comprehensive principles of priesthood order—the governing order and power of the kingdom. Not only does he have reverence for that governing order but he also teaches it in easily understood terms.

When Brother Packer performs a marriage ceremony in the temple for a family member or a close friend, he teaches the principles of order, ordain, and ordinance as they pertain to priesthood. And, not assuming that they already know, he teaches from the Prophet Joseph Smith that either a man receives the fulness of the priesthood in companionship with his wife in the temple or he does not receive it at all.

Of ordinances he says: "When you receive an ordinance, whether it be baptism, the sacrament, an ordination or setting apart, an endowment, or a sealing, you receive an obligation. Thereafter, you are under covenant not to steal, nor to lie, nor to profane, nor to take the name of the Lord in vain. You are obligated to maintain the moral standard. This standard, by commandment of the Lord,

requires that the only authorized use of the sacred power of procre-
ation is with one to whom you are legally and lawfully wed. You have
responsibility to support every principle of the gospel and the servants the Lord has ordained to administer them."

He continues: "Thirteen years after Moroni appeared, a temple
had been built adequate for the purpose, and the Lord again appeared
and Elijah came with Him and bestowed the keys of the sealing
power. Thereafter ordinances were not tentative, but permanent. The
sealing power was with us. No authorization transcends it in value.
That power gives substance and eternal permanence to all ordinances
performed with proper authority for both the living and the dead."[1]

"It is knowing and obeying the principles and covenants of the
temple that make the Church operate in the pattern that has been
set by revelation."

Elder Packer is formal where priesthood order is concerned.
When he goes out to reorganize a stake, he teaches a primer lesson
about presidency. The stake president is instructed to sit with his first
counselor on his right and his second counselor on his left. They are
then a presidency and are ready for further instruction.

In ministering with his brethren to the worldwide Church, Elder
Packer had learned that many local leaders lack understanding about
some things pertaining to priesthood. For example, many do not
know that the priesthood is indivisible. So he explains: "When a man
receives the Melchizedek Priesthood, the youngest elder ordained has
as much priesthood as the President of the Church. It is afterwards
divided into offices; but the priesthood is not divisible."

He also teaches the difference between ordinations and settings
apart. "A man is *ordained* a patriarch, for that is an office, as *elder* or
high priest or *bishop* is an office. The ordained offices are for life, unless
they are taken away for transgression. Yet they are cumulative, so
that every high priest is a deacon, teacher, priest, and elder, all at
once. A high priest can perform anything that pertains to those other
offices.

"A stake president is not *ordained*, but is set apart and given the
keys of the presidency, because already he is a high priest, or if he is
not, we ordain him a high priest, because that is the office of administration."

Thus in the stakes, temples, councils, and privately, Elder Packer teaches. As one of the Lord's watchmen, the responsibility to teach is constantly upon him. Accordingly, whenever he finds a listening spirit he takes opportunity to share the unwritten, unrecorded store of knowledge that is his.

Long before his call to the Quorum of the Twelve, Elder Packer had made an exhaustive study of the priesthood and the offices of the priesthood. He first collected every scriptural reference to each of the priesthood offices. With the help of Dean Jessee, a friend who worked in the Church historian's office, he then added the statements of the Brethren of the past. Among these were statements of President John Taylor. So penetrating were his insights and so inspired were his writings on the subject that Elder Packer came to refer to him as the architect of priesthood government.

Through Brother Packer's scholarly study and his spiritual grasp of the material, he gained a deep reverence for both the Aaronic Priesthood and the Melchizedek Priesthood, for their structures, and for the nature of priesthood offices and priesthood keys, all of which helped to prepare him for the role he was to fill in the Quorum of the Twelve.

When he became an Apostle in 1970 he already understood the proper composition of the Church. Of this he later said: "For any of us to serve well there must be both a recognition of and an acceptance of the Church as a spiritual kingdom. It can be governed only according to the laws and principles which are spiritual. However useful methods and procedures which govern temporal matters may be, they must not dominate our way either of preaching the gospel and establishing the Church or of reacting to those influences which are calculated to delay or prevent us from doing so."

He also comprehended the priesthood dimensions of his sacred call in a singular way and determined that he would diligently seek "to be good at what he was called to do." In other words, he would seek to magnify the call as defined by Brigham Young, who had been tutored by the Prophet Joseph Smith: "The keys of the eternal Priesthood, which is after the order of the Son of God, are comprehended by being an Apostle. All the Priesthood, all the keys, all the gifts, all the endowments, and everything preparatory to entering into the presence of the Father and of the Son, are in, composed of, circum-scribed by, or I might say incorporated within the circumference of the Apostleship."[2]

After his call to the apostleship Elder Packer began to observe some patterns in priesthood order that seemed, if they were allowed to continue, might alter the course of the Church. In this he was assuming the apostolic responsibility of watchman. He came to know that, to be valid, God's government and the source of power and authority it represents must be transmitted from its source, through an orderly, unbroken conduit of ordained men, until it reaches the individual family through its priesthood leader, the father. Only in this way can family members fully receive the Savior's teachings and His saving ordinances.

There was, however, a problem in priesthood structure that was interfering with that orderly conduit intended to reach the family. To understand the problem-solving process as it pertains to the leader-ship of the Church, there is a truth that needs emphasis: The full organization of the Church was not revealed in the beginning. It has come line upon line as the leaders have asked for direction. As the needs of the Church require, changes in pattern of administration are to be expected. But while neither the doctrines, nor ordinances, nor the fundamental organization change, the Brethren have not only the freedom but the obligation, as watchmen, to meet the needs of the growing Church.

Thus the Brethren sought answers to problems within the priest-hood structure of the elders quorums throughout the Church, answers that would set the matter right.

An examination of Elder Packer's talks during the 1970s shows the intense effort he had given to the matter: "The Path to Man-hood" (April 1970), general priesthood meeting; "The Plight of the Elders" (July 1970), seminar for Regional Representatives; "The Quorum" (1973), seminar for Regional Representatives; "An Appeal to Prospective Elders" (April 1975), general conference; "Statement on Quorums of Elders" (1979), to the Council of the Twelve and again in general priesthood meeting; "The Aaronic Priesthood" (October 1981), general priesthood meeting.

Through his efforts and those of his fellow watchmen, the solution was found. Previously the elders quorums had been functioning under the direction of the bishops, whose priesthood assignments covered Aaronic Priesthood quorums. Now the elders quorums were set in their proper order, to function under their rightful Melchizedek Priesthood heads, the stake presidents.

As a result the combined efforts of the Brethren caused the Church to be strengthened at its core—the family—as it entered an unprecedented period of expansion and growth.

Another area of concern with which many of the former Church leaders had worked, and to which Elder Packer and the Brethren gave concerted attention, was that of the proper role and place of the Seventy. Their concern came at a time when, even with the combined support groups of Assistants to the Twelve, Regional Representatives, and the Seventy, they were taxed to the limit in administering what had become a worldwide church.

The need to provide increasing General Authority leadership for the Church had become crucial. In order to meet the challenge, the Brethren sought the will of the Lord. As in other seekings, great faith and diligent labor would be required before the answer came.

Confirming this approach was a revelation given to President John Taylor in April 1882 pertaining to the future of the Seventies. In part, it reads: "Fear me and observe my laws and I will reveal unto you, from time to time, through the channels that I have appointed, everything that shall be necessary for the future development and rolling forth of my kingdom, and for the building up and the establishment of my Zion. For you are my Priesthood and I am your God, Amen."[3]

The Brethren continued to seek the Lord's will in the scriptures, in prayers of faith, and in discussion among themselves. All knew that the Seventy, as they were organized on a stake level, could not fill their prophetic roles. They must somehow be brought into closer compliance with the scriptural charter.

One who had given much thought and study to those scriptures and to the solution they surely must contain was Elder Boyd K. Packer. He felt both the urgency and the weight of the matter. Finally his brethren assigned him to prepare a document briefing the discussions and decisions of the Church leaders with reference to the Seventy from the beginning.

As the work progressed, and in a marvelous way, unexpected visitors dropped by his office to leave materials that might interest him. One brought notes from the personal papers of President George Albert Smith on the Seventy; another, President Harold B. Lee's personal notes on the same subject.

Laboring in faith and diligence, Brother Packer continued the quest, to know the Lord's will. He studied and pondered the passages in Doctrine and Covenants 107 that pertain specifically to the Seventy. As he read and reread, verse 10 suddenly stood out as if it had been newly placed there: "High priests after the order of the Melchizedek Priesthood have a right to officiate in their own standing, under the direction of the presidency, in administering spiritual things, and also in the office of an elder, priest, . . . teacher, deacon, and member" (D&C 107:10).

Elder Packer tells of the impact upon him:

> It suddenly occurred to me that *that* was a verse on the Seventy that should be added to the others. The reason it had never been considered was that it did not mention the Seventy. And the significance of it was that it did *not* mention the Seventy.
>
> I took it to Bruce McConkie first and read it to him in that context. It was the first time that he had ever seen it in that light. Because it very declaratively said that a high priest could not officiate in the office of a Seventy.

Traditionally, the order of priesthood leadership had been listed deacon, teacher, priest, elder, seventy, high priest, Seventy, Apostle. Now the brethren could see how the Lord intended it to be: deacon, teacher, priest, elder, high priest, Seventy, Apostle, with the Seventy being listed only once. In that sequence, all scripture with reference to the Seventy quickly fell into place.

From that newly highlighted scripture there came to the Brethren the understanding of the Lord's will relative to the Seventy. The call of a Seventy was not a local priesthood call; rather, it was henceforth to be as the Lord had said; the Seventy "form a quorum equal in authority to that of the Twelve special witnesses or Apostles" (D&C 107:26).

The Lord further stated that the Seventy were "to act in the name of the Lord, under the direction of the Twelve or the traveling high council" (D&C:107:34). This was to be in the same sense that the Twelve act in the name of the Lord under direction of the First Presidency. Thus the Brethren, through revelation to one of their number, were provided with the answer: "It is the duty of the [Twelve] to call upon the Seventy, when they need assistance, to fill the several calls for preaching and administering the gospel, *instead of any others* " (D&C 107:38, emphasis added).

Elder Dean L. Larsen, then serving as Senior President of the First Quorum of the Seventy, spoke of Elder Packer's ability to look downstream as it related to the role of the Seventy. "Elder Packer is visionary in the positive sense of that term. He is not only gifted in that way, but he applies himself to it. He thinks deeply and consistently about the future of the Church, about where we are moving and what changes it is going to require, . . . for this reason he has been extremely interested . . . in the development of the Seventy and the role of the Seventy, and he continues to be so."[4]

As an obedient instrument in the hands of the Lord, and under direction of the Brethren, Elder Packer with his diligent study and spiritual effort became a significant factor in the changes that followed.

In perfect unity the Twelve presented their recommendations to the First Presidency. After much prayer and deliberation, the prophet and his Counselors began to implement orderly changes relative to the Seventy.

On 1 October 1976 the First Quorum of the Seventy was expanded by the release of all twenty-one Assistants to the Twelve and their call as Seventies, and by the calling of four new Seventies.

President Kimball stated that the establishment of the First Quorum of the Seventy as one of "the three governing quorums of the Church defined by the revelations" was a great milestone in priesthood government at the general Church level and "will make it possible to handle efficiently the present heavy workload and to prepare for the increasing expansion and acceleration of the work, anticipating the day when the Lord will return to take direct charge of His Church and Kingdom."[5]

On 1 April 1989 the organization of the Second Quorum of the Seventy was announced. It was comprised of thirty-six members who were called to serve for five years. The policy for members of the First Quorum of the Seventy is that they serve until age seventy, at which time they go on emeritus status. The seven Presidents of the Seventy rotate, and they preside over both the quorums.[6]

Elder Dean L. Larsen bore his testimony regarding the remarkable developments that had taken place: "The revelations in Doctrine and Covenants 107 relative to the role of the Seventy are a great testimony of the inspiration of Joseph Smith. There was no way in the world he could have anticipated all of this, yet as you go back and carefully study what the Lord outlined through him, the pattern was given for the Church as it has grown in tremendous dimensions, both geographically and numerically."[7]

Chapter Twenty

Perspective on
Church History

 The First Presidency and the Quorum of the Twelve, the Lord's watchmen on the tower, are thoroughly conversant with the holy scriptures and the teachings of the prophets, and they bear powerful witness of their verity. In the scriptures Brother Packer and his brethren feel the firm ground of truth beneath their feet on any issue involving the doctrines of the kingdom and the government of the Church.

Prior to their calls, each of the Brethren had a background and career different from those of the others. Each excells in his area of expertise and so serves in his calling. Because Elder Packer's orientation is that of student and teacher, he is both scholarly and spiritual in the process of gaining knowledge. Through intense study he has become well informed in Church history from the earliest years of the Restoration to the present. He has studied in detail the writings and addresses of the Prophet Joseph Smith, Brigham Young, John Taylor, Wilford Woodruff, Lorenzo Snow, and Joseph F. Smith, as well as those of the more recent prophets. His experience in teaching Church history to seminary students reinforced his knowledge. Those earlier Brethren as well as today's bear powerful witness that the restoration of the Church in these latter days was brought about by the Father and His Son Jesus Christ through the Prophet Joseph Smith. They also witness that priesthood authority has been handed down to prophets in an unbroken line from Joseph Smith to the present.

A further source of Elder Packer's knowledge is contained in the *unwritten* history of the Church and the workings of Church government as carried in the minds and experience of Church leaders. This knowledge gives him a perspective enjoyed by few men outside the circle of the General Authorities.

Each of these leaders has been influenced and tutored by senior brethren with whom they have worked. Those who taught and encouraged Elder Packer (some from his Brigham City years on) were Joseph Fielding Smith, Henry D. Moyle, Marion G. Romney, LeGrand Richards, Harold B. Lee, and Spencer W. Kimball. Added to these were the late Joseph Anderson, a Seventy, formerly secretary to the First Presidency for nearly fifty years (1922–1970), and Belle S. Spafford, general Relief Society president for twenty-nine years (1945–1974) and one of the great women of modern times.

Of LeGrand Richards, he said:

> It was not kindness alone that motivated me to be caring toward him. It was also a hunger to know the history of how the gospel came to us. Through the eyes of this beloved man, we have looked back across the history of the Church. When he was born, President John Taylor presided over the Church. When he was seven years old he attended the dedication of the Salt Lake Temple. He remembered President Wilford Woodruff very clearly; he remembered everything very clearly.
>
> From his memory we could read between the lines the whole history of the Church. What he did not see himself, he learned from others who saw it back to the very beginning of this dispensation.[1]

From Elder Marion G. Romney, Elder Packer learned a valuable lesson: "Of this we may be sure: to make the proper choice on any issue is of far more importance to us personally than is the immediate outcome of the issue upon which we make a decision. The choices we make will affect the scope of our agency in the future. As of now, we have the right of decision. What we will have tomorrow will depend upon how we decide today."[2]

Elder Packer drew strength from his brethren of the Twelve,
past and present

From Elder Harold B. Lee, Elder Packer learned details about Church government that he would not otherwise have known. Once when they were returning by plane from a servicemen's seminar in Chicago, Brother Lee suddenly said, "Boyd, it's a great event when the President of the Church dies."

"I knew he was going to tell me something," Brother Packer says, "so I listened."

Elder Lee began: "The first experience I had was when Heber J. Grant died." He then explained the event in such detail that Elder Packer says: "I can tell you the room they were in and how they were seated around the table. I can tell you that the senior Apostle, George Albert Smith, was on a train going to the East, and that J. Reuben Clark, Jr., had been a counselor in the recent First Presidency. It was an awkward situation with the senior Apostle gone. It was then that Elder Albert E. Bowen said, 'Brethren, why don't we ask President Clark to chair this meeting.'" Elder Lee then told Boyd in detail the conversations that took place, and he recorded it in his mind.

"Their telling contains powerful testimony and priceless lessons in the application of gospel principles in the administration of the Church," Elder Packer says. "These senior Brethren have told me so many things that I am a product of their conveying to me the unwritten history of the Church."

When Brother Packer says, "unwritten history of the Church," he means it. He does not keep a journal. He says that collectively his talks are his journal. In them are found experiences with members of his family, whom he does not name, lessons learned from friends and mentors, his approach to challenges that have confronted him, his feelings of compassion for the poor and suffering, his firm stand on moral issues, his views on doctrinal and organizational matters within the ministry, his observations of peoples within the worldwide Church, and his powerful witness of Jesus Christ, of the Prophet Joseph Smith and his successors, and of the Book of Mormon and the other standard works of scripture. Collectively these create a base for assessing the man and his ministry.

One area of assessment is found in his approach to problem solving. He seeks to understand a problem by understanding the principle behind it through study of the scriptures and of related materials. To any issue relating to the Church, he may give hundreds of hours in reading, analyzing, and praying. In the process he seeks counsel and information from his Brethren and from other experts in the particular area of his inquiry. Only after doing so will he raise a voice of concern in council meetings.

If the councils of the Church functioned as secular bodies do he might have gathered a committee of like minds and lobbied for the support of others, but this is not the way Church decisions and policies are made. Concerning decisions of the presiding authorities he quotes from scripture:

> And every decision made by either of these quorums [the First Presidency, the Quorum of the Twelve, and the Quorum of the Seventy] must be by the unanimous voice of the same; that is, every member in each quorum must be agreed to its decisions, in order to make their decisions of the same power or validity one with the other. . . .
>
> Unless this is the case, their decisions are not entitled to the same blessings which the decisions of a quorum of three presidents were anciently, who were ordained after the order of Melchizedek, and were righteous and holy men (D&C 107:27, 29).

He explains: "It would be unthinkable deliberately to present an issue in such a way that approval depended upon how it was maneuvered through channels, who was presenting it, or who was present or absent when it was presented.

"There is a rule we follow: A matter is not settled until there is a *minute* entry to evidence that all of the Brethren in council assembled (not just one of us, not just in committee) have come to a unity of feeling. Approval of a matter in principle is not considered authority to act until a minute entry records the action taken—usually when the minutes are approved in the next meeting."

Those who do not know of Elder Packer's thorough homework, or how he feels as he wrestles through to a principle, may perceive him only as stubborn and immovable. Nevertheless he stands steady and, as a watchman, points out soft spots in our defenses—"a trend that will take us where we do not want to go; a teaching that seems harmless and appealing on the surface but will destroy the faith of our youth; individuals who cannot take counsel nor get beyond ego, and thus will drag themselves and others down."

No concern for personal popularity nor fear of criticism will deter him. He bears the battering and the derision of his critics with steadiness. Elder Packer readily admits that he is not always a diplomat. He once wrote: "I think that very often I do not do very well in speaking in council meetings and perhaps my shortcomings there do injury to the very position I am trying to endorse. . . . It is the principle that concerns me."3

An example of his concern, of his studied warnings, and of his withstanding criticism is demonstrated in the events that were published about the Historical Department of the Church. These changes had nothing to do with personalities but only with the principle being addressed. He never wittingly seeks to diminish another. If it sometimes seems he is doing so, looking beyond his forthrightness to the principle he is upholding will clarify his purpose. For example, he wrote:

> On several occasions I have expressed in our council meetings my concern for some projects being undertaken by the Church Historian's Office and some of those who have been engaged to work on the projects. May I state with emphasis, as I have in our meetings, that my concern does not deny in any way that these brethren are active members of the Church. . . . I think our brethren in the Historical Department are wonderful men. . . . It is the principle that concerns me.
>
> It is a matter of orientation toward scholarly work—historians' work in particular—that sponsors my concern. I have come to believe that it is the tendency for most members of the Church who spend a great deal of time in academic research to begin to judge the Church, its doctrine, organization, and history, by the principles of their own profession. Ofttimes this is done unwittingly, and some of it perhaps is wholesome. However, it is an easy thing for a man with extensive academic training to consider the Church with the principles he has been taught in his professional training as his measuring standard.
>
> In my mind it ought to be the other way around. A member of the Church ought always, particularly if he is pursuing extended academic studies, to judge the professions of men against the revealed word of the Lord.

I do feel, however, and feel very deeply, that some tempering of the purely historical approach needs to be effected. Otherwise these publications will be of interest to other historians and perhaps serve them well, but at once may have a negative effect upon many. *Particularly can they affect our youngsters*, who will not view the publications with the same academic detachment that a trained historian is taught to develop.[4]

In his address "The Mantle Is Far, Far Greater Than the Intellect," Elder Packer spoke of a historian whose purpose apparently had been to show one of the Presidents of the Church to be "a man subject to the foibles of men. He introduced many so-called facts that put that President in a very unfavorable light, particularly when they were taken out of the context of the historical period in which he lived."

He continued: "What that historian did with the reputation of the President of the Church was not worth doing. He seemed determined to convince everyone that the *prophet* was a *man*. We knew that already. All of the prophets and all of the Apostles have been men. It would have been much more worthwhile for him to convince us that the *man* was a *prophet*, a fact quite as true as the fact that he was a man."[5]

To understand Brother Packer's approach to these details is to remember his certain witness that the prophets, ancient and modern, are chosen and ordained of God. His reverence for them is profound. He will not slur them nor have anyone else do so; rather he will defend them. The principles of loyalty and reverence toward the Lord's anointed, as taught in the scriptures, are central to the character of Boyd K. Packer.

For him, it matters little what the human foibles and frailties of one of the Lord's anointed may be. Each one of them is in the Lord's hand, and if any such should prove unworthy, he will in the Lord's due time be removed from his place.

When using materials that detract from a leader, a historian making a case for realism or showing that the leader is a man with whom his readers can more easily relate will often cite examples from the Old Testament. Elder Packer has one response to this: he would not have written those accounts; rather, he would have focused upon the leader's inspiring works.

In following principles of reverence for and loyalty to the prophets, he endorses another—the scriptural mandate governing the responsibility of a Church historian. "There is no such thing as an accurate, objective history of the Church without consideration of the spiritual powers that attend this work."[6]

Whether the historian is one individual, as at the beginning of the Restoration, or whether he serves as adviser to the Historical Department of the Church, as at the present time, the mandate is the same. In this context Elder Packer pointed to the commandment of the prophet-leader Nephi to his brother Jacob, as recorded in the Book of Mormon.

> And he gave me, Jacob, a commandment that I should write upon these [small] plates a few of the things which I considered to be *most precious*; that I should *not touch, save it were lightly* concerning the *history* of this people. . . .
>
> For he said that the history of his people should be engraven upon his other [large] plates, and that I should preserve these [small] plates and hand them down unto my seed, from generation to generation.
>
> And if there were *preaching which was sacred, or revelation which was great, or prophesying*, that I should engraven the heads of them upon these [small] plates, and touch upon *them* as *much* as it were possible, *for Christ's sake*, and for the sake of our people. (Jacob 1:2–4.) [The emphases and brackets are Elder Packer's.]

And he adds, "Did you notice that he was '*not* to touch (save it were lightly) on *the history* of the people' but he *was* to touch upon the *sacred things* 'as much as it were possible!' To know that is to know how the prophets and Apostles of today must regard the records of our people and whether or not we are obliged to please the world in what we do with them."

Elder Packer continued, "Nephi made this clear statement on the relative value of the two histories: 'For the fullness of mine intent is that I may persuade men to come unto the God of Abraham, and the God of Isaac, and the God of Jacob, and be saved.' (1 Nephi 6:4.)

"And notice why he did as he did," Elder Packer continued: " 'I have received a commandment of the Lord that I should make these plates, for the special purpose that there should be an account engraven of the *ministry* of my people' " (1 Nephi 9:3, emphasis added).

He then quoted a passage with which he deeply identifies: " 'And upon these [small plates] I write *the things of my soul*, and many of the scriptures which are engraven upon the plates of brass. For *my soul delighteth in the scriptures*, and my heart pondereth them, and writeth them for the learning and the profit of my children. Behold, my soul delighteth in the things of the Lord.' " (2 Nephi 4:15–16, emphasis added.)[7]

Wilford Woodruff said: "I will here say God has inspired me to keep a Journal and History of this Church, and I warn the future Historians to give Credence to my History of this Church and Kingdom; for my Testimony is true, and the truth of its Record will be manifest in the world to Come."[8]

These principles are deeply rooted in Elder Packer and his brethren, and so they continued to watch the trend of research being done in the archives of the Church. They also watched the openness with which materials were being made available to certain individuals other than those authorized. The motives of many of these individuals were later proven not to be worthy.

To some, such concerns seemed to inhibit honest research and foster censorship; but what they did not understand was that the Brethren, knowing where alternate trends could lead, were watching over the Church, defending the Lord's anointed, and protecting a sacred stewardship.

Chapter Twenty-One

Simplification and Reduction

 The families that make up the membership of the Church are the central concern of the Brethren, who are charged with the responsibility to watch over the Lord's people. Because of the breakdown in families, however, some fathers or mothers are left to raise their children alone. Other brothers and sisters are unmarried. These also have the concerned watchcare of the Brethren. All are loved of the Lord, are part of His family, and are blessed by the three-fold mission of the Church: perfecting the Saints; taking the gospel to all the world; and redeeming the dead. These truths are the basis for, and substance of, *simplification and reduction*, which were implemented in our day to bless the Church families throughout the world. As Elder Boyd K. Packer stated: "The family is apart from and above the other organizations and, under the sealing authority, more enduring than them all."[1]

Tithing sufficiency had been a long-hoped-for goal of former Church Presidents. As early as 1907 President Joseph F. Smith stated: "We may not be able to reach it right away, but we expect to see the day when we will not have to ask you for one dollar of donation for any purpose, except that which you volunteer to give of your own accord, because we will have tithes sufficient in the storehouse of the Lord to pay everything that is needful for the advancement of the kingdom of God."[2]

The historic day he envisioned came nearer in November 1989. The implementation of the program, however, did not simply happen. While simplification and reduction had been an item on the agenda of this generation's First Presidency and the Twelve, the issue was often postponed or set aside in favor of more pressing matters. By reason of his experience coupled with his gift for discerning drifts and sensing where they could take the Church, one of their number, Elder Boyd K. Packer, saw the issue as not only pressing but also urgent and crucial.

Elder Dallin H. Oaks speaks of Brother Packer: "In the setting of his work [among his brethren], he is one of a kind. I think that he has more vision, or at least more willingness to share his vision, than any other. He sees ahead and then exerts his personal authority and influence in a leadership way that is very much felt in the Council of the Twelve."

At first Brother Packer broached the subject in their meetings quietly, persuasively, and repeatedly. Encouraged by President Spencer W. Kimball, he began to recommend principles of simplification and reduction in money and time demands upon Church members worldwide—recommendations to do away with member assessments and to make the Church tithing-sufficient. The others did not yet share his vision.

After one of their temple meetings he asked President Spencer W. Kimball, "Shouldn't I just mimeograph my speech and save time in meetings?"

To this the President replied: "No! You are never to let go of it and never give it up." Later that day President Kimball made a rare visit to Elder Packer's office and gave him notes he had written on this subject but had not yet found occasion to use.

Thus, as one among the watchmen on the tower, Elder Packer continually sought to convince his brethren that the time had come to apply the principle of simplification and reduction in money and time demands so that the families of the Church worldwide could have their testimonies strengthened and their lives materially blessed.

He reasoned: "When we overemphasize programs at the expense of principles, we are in danger of losing the inspiration, the resourcefulness, that which should characterize Latter-day Saints. Then the very principle of individual revelation is in jeopardy and we drift from a fundamental gospel principle!

"For generations we have taught that the temporal salvation of the Saints depends upon independence, industry, thrift, and self-reliance. On the other hand, is it possible that we are doing the very thing spiritually that we have been resolutely resisting temporally; fostering dependence rather than independence, extravagance rather than thrift, indulgence rather than self-reliance?"

The issue was one about which he had strong personal feelings and for which his background and experience had schooled him. As next to the youngest in a close-knit family of eleven children who were raised during the years of the Great Depression, he knew that outside monetary demands upon his parents meant sacrifice, not of luxuries but necessities. Then in their marriage and the raising of their ten children he and his wife, Donna, knew what financial restraint was while he worked as both student and teacher. They adopted as their way of life the saying, "Eat it up, wear it out, make it do, or do without."

Later, when he was called into the leading councils of the Church, he, with Elder Thomas S. Monson, was part of the early Priesthood Correlation movement, which was guided by Elder Harold B. Lee, its architect. From its inception, Correlation was designed to strengthen the home and bless families. By means of consolidating auxiliaries, programs, and curricula under unified priesthood administration it laid the groundwork for the step forward to which Elder Packer was bending his efforts.

There were yet further reasons for his sense of urgency. His compassion for the poor and oppressed had remained with him from his military days in occupied Japan. It increased vastly as he ministered with others of his brethren among poor members in Mexico, Central and South America, Polynesia, Asia, and Africa, and among Native Americans. It also extended to the poor who live among prosperous peoples. In 1981 he related a few of his experiences among the poor that had great impact upon him: "I was the first General Authority to stay in the home of a stake president in South America. I know what it is to fold my clothes carefully and lay them on the floor when I occupy a bedroom in the home of a stake president, because there is not one stick of furniture other than the bed and a small table with a lamp on it."

In the home of another stake president the family had chicken stew for the evening meal on Saturday after the meetings. The next morning the small son of the stake president held Brother Packer's index finger and pulled him around the yard to show him a small wire cage with a chicken in it. Said Brother Packer, "My Spanish is good enough to have caught his comment, 'Yesterday we had two chickens.'"

In a home in Lima, Peru, he found a father, a mother, two teenage daughters, a married son and daughter-in-law and their three small children. The father had heart trouble. The son was out of work. The total income for that family depended upon the two teenage girls knitting sweaters on little hand looms that rested on the

Conversing with Indian children in Guatemala

top of a table, and one meal a day the family provided for two missionaries who paid them for it.

He told of an experience in yet another developing country:

> I saw in the Saturday meeting a fine-looking man, about sixty, sitting in the audience, conspicuous because he was the only one without a suit coat. His shirt sleeves were rolled above the elbows. I quickly surmised that he had no coat, and that his sleeves were rolled up to hide the ragged ends. When he smiled he had no front teeth, top or bottom.
>
> That night found him on the stand with his family of nine children. They were to present the family genealogical message. He came to the pulpit wearing a raincoat.
>
> It was very hot to be wearing a raincoat, but I immediately knew that he wore it because he was ashamed to appear behind the pulpit without the dignity of a coat.
>
> When I asked the stake president who he was, he told me that this was the stake patriarch who was "Muy pobre" (very poor). To support his large family he sold peanuts on the street.

Brother Packer also told of seeing a little church building up in the mountains. He looked at it carefully. He thought at first it was made of bamboo. There was a dirt floor, rude furniture, rusty tin roof; and the walls, rather than bamboo, were made of cornstalks. "A chapel!" he said incredulously.[3]

His experiences have developed within him compassion for all who suffer, whether from poverty or from the ills of affluence; from the curse of self-indulgence or the infirmities of age; from the ravages of disease or the pangs of bereavement. Many times he has wept in the night for the poor and the suffering.

Because of his compassion, the material affluence of members within the center stakes of the Church concerned him. He sensed danger in the comforts, the adornments, and the worldly successes that often attend affluence. He felt that if awareness of and consideration for the poor were not constant, and if wealth were not regarded as a stewardship with which to do good, it might breed the same pride and immorality that marked the apostasy of Book of Mormon peoples. In that book he found a concise summary of the cycle of wealth and poverty:

And thus we can behold how false, and also the unsteadiness of the hearts of the children of men; yea, we can see that the Lord in his great infinite goodness doth bless and prosper those who put their trust in him.

Yea, and we may see at the very time when he doth prosper his people, yea, in the increase of their fields, their flocks and their herds, and in gold, and in silver, and in all manner of precious things of every kind and art; sparing their lives, and delivering them out of the hands of their enemies; softening the hearts of their enemies that they should not declare wars against them; yea, and in fine, doing all things for the welfare and happiness of his people; yea, then is the time that they do harden their hearts, and do forget the Lord their God, and do trample under their feet the Holy One—yea, and this because of their ease, and their exceedingly great prosperity. (Helaman 12:1–2.)

Then these words of Moroni: "For behold, ye do love money, and your substance, and your fine apparel, and the adorning of your churches, more than ye love the poor and the needy, the sick and the afflicted" (Mormon 8:37).

Elder Packer drew a distinction, however, between the uncaring wealthy and the righteous whom the Lord blesses with abundance but who remember His goodness and use their stewardships to bless others. The Lord promises those who are faithful in paying their tithes and offerings, "I will . . . pour you out a blessing, that there shall not be room enough to receive it" (Malachi 3:10).

And from the Lord's words in our dispensation:

For have I not the fowls of heaven, and also the fish of the sea, and the beasts of the mountains? Have I not made the earth? Do I not hold the destinies of all the armies of the nations of the earth?

Therefore, will I not make solitary places to bud and to blossom, and to bring forth in abundance? saith the Lord.

Is there not room enough . . . that you should covet that which is but the drop, and neglect the more weighty matters? (D&C 117:6–8.)

Despite his concern for the poor, Elder Packer has never advocated the dole to provide for them. Rather, he has favored self-reliance at every level and in every instance. To Regional Representatives and stake presidents from Brazil he said:

I have been to Brazil many times. I have organized some of the stakes there. I have been able to see something about the future of your country and about the future of the Church there. Perhaps it is not unusual for any of us who have been sustained as prophets, seers, and revelators to sense such things when we are in a land.

There are some things that will be phased out. Not only in Brazil, but across the world. We will not build buildings again like those we have built in this last generation. The large, beautiful buildings must now give way to buildings that we can afford.

"If you get something you want that is important to you, that you need, if you get it for nothing you have paid too much for it."

He applied the same principle to missionaries:

Every worthy young man in Brazil should serve a mission. But we must not rob him or his family of responsibility! We have a policy that we will not call a missionary in the Church who is to be fully supported from Church funds. The missionary and/or his family must make a substantial contribution toward his mission. What is substantial? That depends. In one case it may be very little—hardly any. In another case, it should be the whole funding of the mission. But whatever it is, it is, and he and his family must not be excused from their part.

We must put in place a basic principle of financing the Church: We cannot expend any money for any purpose except for the purpose for which it was contributed. We cannot spend tithing or fast offerings to support missionaries. Every branch president must know this.[4]

After many more talks, pleadings, and presentations on basic and related subjects, his brethren finally caught the vision of simplification and reduction and, in unity, determined policies to implement the needed changes.

On 15 November 1989 the First Presidency—Ezra Taft Benson, Gordon B. Hinckley, and Thomas S. Monson—sent a letter of announcement to priesthood leaders at every level. In part it stated:

Effective January 1, 1990, all of the operating costs of wards and stakes will be financed from the general funds of the Church, thus relieving the members of budget assessments. The governing principle is that members who pay their tithes and offerings may expect that from these contributions the other expenses incident to membership will be met.

With this policy change, budget funds should no longer be raised, nor should there be other assessments or fund-raising projects. Rather funds will be made available through two procedures; first, the direct reimbursement of costs related to the construction and operation of buildings and certain standard programs; and second, the providing of an allowance based on the number of members regularly attending Sacrament meeting.

On 18 February 1990, via satellite broadcast, Elder Packer and Presidents Hinckley and Monson spoke. Said Elder Packer:

> I could not express to you, my brethren and sisters, the depths of my feeling about what has been announced. It is a course correction; it is an inspired move. It will have influence upon the Church across the world, not just in our generation but in the generations to come. I have the certain conviction that it is pleasing to Him who is our Lord and our Redeemer, even Jesus Christ, our Savior.
>
> The scriptures speak of tithes and of *offerings*; they do not speak of assessments or fund-raising. To be an offering, it must be given freely—offered. The way is open now for many more of us to participate in this spiritually refining experience.
>
> You must devise ways of letting those who have drawn back because of expense know about the change. . . . Tell them what the prophet said: "Come, my brethren, every one that thirsteth, come ye to the waters; and he that *hath no money*, come buy and eat; yea, come buy wine and milk *without money* and without price" (2 Nephi 9:50).

He quoted President Brigham Young, from *Journal of Discourses* 18:354: "I have told you many times, the property which we inherit from our Heavenly Father is our *time*, and the power to *choose* in the disposition of the same. This is the real capital that is bequeathed unto us by our Heavenly Father."

"This change in budgeting," Elder Packer added, "will have the effect of returning much of the responsibility for teaching and counseling and activity to the family where it belongs. While there will still be many activities, they will be scaled down in cost of both time and money. There will be fewer intrusions into family schedules and family purses."[5]

President Monson continued this theme:

> The primary responsibility for building testimonies and providing faith-building experiences in our members, including our youth, resides in the home. The Church should continue to support the determination of the family to do this. Priesthood leaders will wish to increase their efforts to build strong gospel-centered homes. Families vary in size and composition. All are to receive our devoted attention. The building of testimonies is not related to financial costs. It is not necessary to buy the activity of our youth. Our youth activities depart from the pattern of the world.

He then read a member letter in grateful response to the new announcement. One paragraph expressed the father's feelings: "Yes, we too are grateful to the Lord for this blessed and inspired day—not so much for the financial relief, but more for the hopeful reduction in ward and stake activities that will allow families to return home."[6]

President Hinckley concluded the broadcast:

> I am grateful for what Elder Packer and President Monson have said, and commend their words to you.
>
> I bring you the love and blessing of President Benson, who has expressed his full approval of the program of which we speak.
>
> I stand before you as one who is filled with a tremendous sense of gratitude and thanksgiving. I am thankful for the bedrock of faith on which Latter-day Saints stand and build their lives. I am confident that the Lord loves His people for the goodness of their lives and the generosity of their hearts as they consecrate of their means in the payment of tithes and offerings. I am grateful for the faith of the wealthy who give generously of their abundance. I am equally grateful for the faith of the poor who likewise contribute with a great spirit of consecration.
>
> I am thankful for the law of tithing. Surely it is divine. The Lord has made it universal in its application among all of His people. It is miraculous in its simplicity. No certified public accountant is needed to determine what is owed to the Lord. . . .
>
> What we have recently done in the institution of this new program is, I am satisfied, an expression of that inspiration. What we have done is an act of faith.

Then a word of caution:

> The Church is not so wealthy that it can indiscriminately scatter its resources. We must be extremely careful and wise, and I believe inspired, if this program, which involves many millions of dollars of added expense, is to function. . . . We may be as free as we wish with our own funds, but not with the Lord's.
>
> We want our buildings to be comfortable and well lighted. We want them to be well maintained and attractive in the communities in which they are located. But we must not be wasteful. . . .
>
> As servants of the Lord, endowed with His holy priesthood, we bless you that as you walk in faith and faithfulness, the windows of heaven may be opened and that there may be showered upon you those precious gifts which come from the God of heaven, who is our Eternal Father, and His divine Son, who is our Redeemer and who declared, "Seek ye first the kingdom of God, and his righteousness; and all these things shall be added unto you" (Matthew 6:33).[7]

Elder Packer had said that few could know the gratitude he felt over what had been done. But when the vision of it had come to all of his brethren, and the inspired decision to act had been reached, he went alone to the temple to *express* what he felt, and the Lord knew.

Chapter Twenty-Two

Boyd K. Packer and Church Education

Through the years of Elder Packer's ministry the theme of education has been constant in his numerous talks at BYU and to the Church at large. All are based on the scriptural principle, "seek learning, even by study and also by faith" (D&C 88:118). It is a principle grounded in conversion to the gospel and commitment to the Savior. Thus he would agree with the statement by Arthur Henry King: "When we have laid down at Christ's feet all our scholarship, all our learning, all the tools of our trades, we discover that we may pick them all up again, clean them, adjust them, and use them for the Church in the name of Christ and in the light of his countenance. We do not need to discard them. All we need to do is to use them from the faith which now possesses us."[1]

As a member of the Board of Trustees and of the Executive Committee of Brigham Young University, Brother Packer has sought to know what goes on at all levels, for he is aware of the tremendous investment the Church has made in effort and money to provide the physical facility, faculty, and personnel for BYU and its sister institutions in Hawaii and at Ricks College. In this he has fulfilled the role, along with his brethren, of a thoroughly informed watchman on the tower, noting trends and drifts and speaking out to entreat and to warn. At BYU in February 1991 he said:

> Now listen carefully! . . . There is danger! Church-sponsored universities are an endangered species—nearly extinct now. Recently the administration of Baylor University announced that it was severing ties with the Baptist Church, which founded it 145 years ago. Other Baptist schools—Furman, Mercer, and Wake Forest—are going through the process. They join Harvard, Yale, Princeton, Chicago, Columbia, and a long, long list of others which have severed ties from the churches which founded and financed them.
>
> Last month's journal of the New York-based Institute on Religion in Public Life was devoted to the de-Christianizing of American universities. I quote from their editorial entitled "The Death of Religious Higher Education."
>
> "The beginning of wisdom on this subject is to recognize that the road to the unhappy present was indeed paved with good intentions. To be sure, there were relevant parties who made no secret of their hostility to religion. But, for the most part, the schools that lost, or are losing, their sense of religious purpose, sincerely sought nothing more than a greater measure of 'excellence.' The problem is that they accepted, uncritically, definitions of excellence that were indifferent to, or even implicitly hostile to, the great concerns of religion. Few university presidents or department chairmen up and decided one day that they wanted to rid their institutions of the embarrassment of religion. It may reasonably be surmised that most believed that they were advancing a religious mission by helping their schools become like other schools—or at least more like the 'best' of other schools. The language of academic excellence is powerfully seductive."

Elder Packer's analysis of the problem and his counsel for its solution are crucial to an understanding of his perspective on Church education.

> If we succeed in keeping BYU in faith with the founders, we will do something very few others have done. . . . Our best protection is to ensure that the prerogatives of this unique board of trustees are neither diluted nor ignored. Boards of Education, Trustees, and Regents are venerable and indispensable institutions in education in the free world.

They are not to be taken lightly. Theirs, and theirs alone, is the right to establish policies and set standards under which administrators, faculties, and students are to function. . . . The future of education in the free world, and of this unique university, depends on safeguarding the prerogatives of boards of education.

He added: "When [BYU's future] role is finally defined, it will be determined by the Board of Trustees, whose fundamental credentials were not bestowed by man and whose right and responsibility it is to determine policy and 'approve *all* proposed changes in basic *programs* and *key personnel*' and establish standards for both faculty and students."

Elder Packer continued:

The ties between universities and the churches which founded them have been severed because of the constantly recurring contention between the spiritual and the temporal; the never-ending controversy between a narrow view of science and religion; the ancient conflict between *Reason* and *Revelation*.

There are two opposing convictions in the university environment. On the one hand, *Seeing Is Believing*; on the other, *Believing Is Seeing*. Both are true! Each in its place. The combining of the two individually or institutionally is the challenge of life. Neither influence will easily surrender to the other. They may function for a time under some sort of truce, but the subtle discord is ever present.

Some scholar-teachers have seen no way of resolving the conflict. Elder Packer, however, suggests that the two opposing convictions mix the way oil and water mix—only with constant shaking or stirring; and that when the stirring stops, they separate again. But he also knows what is needed to reconcile them. "It takes a catalytic process to blend them. This requires the introduction of a third ingredient, a catalyst, which itself remains unchanged in the blending process." He identifies that requirement: "The essential catalyst for the fusion of reason and revelation in both student and faculty is the Spirit of Christ. He is 'the true light that lighteth every man that cometh into the world' (D&C 93:2). The blending medium is the Holy Ghost, which is conferred upon every member of the Church as a gift."

He further explains: "Each of us must accommodate the mixture of reason and revelation in our lives. The gospel not only permits but *requires* it. An individual who concentrates on either side solely and alone will lose both balance and perspective."[2]

To give balance and perspective to Elder Packer's lifelong career as a teacher, and more particularly to his views on Church education, consideration is here given to those who take issue with his academic views.

As with others of his brethren, Elder Packer's addresses at universities and at general conference occasionally draw forth the response, *anti-intellect*. Thereafter some of the area's publications write about them in negative terms. One such example was headlined "Elder Packer Provokes Academics." Its unsigned author named four talks. "Behind the scenes," the author wrote, "faculty members strongly discussed the talks. Some were saddened at Elder Packer's approach to empirical research. Others lamented the polarization they were causing."[3]

At a BYU graduation ceremony in April 1994

This subject he determined to speak on had been on his mind since his days as a supervisor of seminaries and institutes, when he had seen so many alert young Church members in college subtly directed along a path that weakened or destroyed their faith.

He prepares his talks with more than usual care. Seeking to expand his knowledge, he counsels with authorities in various fields. As is his way with experts in any area of inquiry, he asks many simple questions and presses authorities to reduce their extensive knowledge into the simplest terms, hoping to lift the table of inquiry above academic terminology to a common ground of understanding, where the principles underlying a concept may be discussed to the profit of each.

Elder Packer also counsels with several of his brethren, who read his talks and make suggestions to him.

What is it that causes some members of the academic community to take issue with Boyd K. Packer? Perhaps one who has known and observed him over a period of many years, from both the academic and the ecclesiastic perspective, is qualified to respond to this question.

Former Brigham Young University President Dallin H. Oaks, now a member of the Quorum of the Twelve, spoke of Elder Packer in these terms, first as a member of the Board of Trustees during the 1970s: "I had two impressions of Brother Packer at that time. One was that he was one of the most gifted teachers that I had ever known. The second was that, although I had a profound respect for him, I thought him less than diplomatic in the board meetings and I was not particularly drawn to him. In contrast, however, my feelings for him are very different now since my own call to the Quorum of the Twelve. My respect for him as a teacher is undiminished, but my respect for him as a person and my enjoyment of his company have changed entirely."

As he works with Elder Packer in the councils of the Church Brother Oaks observes him closely and feels that he is much like Harold B. Lee was in the previous generation—bold, assertive, and task-oriented.

Asked about those who perceive Elder Packer as austere, Elder Oaks responded: "They are right and they are wrong. He is austere in the sense that he does not invite familiarity, but Boyd Packer is interested in principle and does not hesitate to make himself understood when one is at stake."

Asked about the effect of his orthodoxy within the intellectual community, Brother Oaks said: "Well, Boyd Packer is the prototypical person who, in the words of Neal A. Maxwell, 'has his citizenship in the kingdom and is a temporary traveler in the intellectual world.' That is one reason that those who have their citizenship in their professions take issue with him. Some have their primary orientation in the arts, the law, or the sciences, especially the biological sciences. When some academicians in these fields come in contact with Elder Packer, they feel uncomfortable because he will remind them that they are first Latter-day Saints and second, professionals in their fields. They are good people, but they have their citizenship in their professions and still have some growing to do in the principles and doctrines of the gospel."

Elder Oaks concluded: "Now, just to put this in perspective, I would estimate that during my administration the people who took issue with Brother Packer, or who didn't understand his intent, were only 5 to 10 percent. Perhaps another 30 percent didn't listen with comprehension, so had no problem. The remaining 60 percent listened carefully, understood what was intended, and said: 'Amen. That was great!' "[4]

Like his brethren, Elder Packer is totally grounded in the scriptures; he has the sure witness of their truth; and he likens them in all things pertaining to both life and learning. He takes literally these words of the Lord: "What I the Lord have spoken, I have spoken, and I excuse not myself; and though the heavens and the earth pass away, my word shall not pass away, but shall all be fulfilled, whether by mine own voice or by the voice of my servants, it is the same" (D&C 1:38).

Thus what the Lord has spoken on past or present issues is immutable truth to Elder Packer, and His words are not to be adjusted by experiments or theories of men. Brother Packer has perfect confidence that for anything to be true in any field of learning it must ultimately square with the revealed word of the Lord. Until that time so-called facts, particularly in the scientific field, need to be measured against the word of the Lord. If these are at variance with His word, they should be taught as tentative and temporary and not as established truth.

Through long experience Brother Packer has seen many good and well-meaning men and women, either unwittingly or intentionally, drift into intellectual attitudes that are in subtle or in direct opposition to revealed truth. His keen spiritual perception is quick to detect such drifts, and he will caution, even warn of dangers ahead.

He does not object to highly educated individuals discussing their opinions among themselves; but he does object to, and counsels against, teaching opinion as truth, or teaching that there are no absolute truths except those which can be empirically proven.

As an assistant administrator of seminaries and institutes of the Church (1955–1961) along with A. Theodore Tuttle he acquired not only the wariness of a watchman on the tower but also the daily-shared responsibility for what LDS teachers were teaching the youth of the Church. Their years together gave him and Brother Tuttle valuable experience in sizing up the spiritual and doctrinal tenor of LDS teachers of youth worldwide. In the process they gained absolute trust in the Brethren, followed them to the letter, and represented them honestly to the teachers they supervised.

Through those years Boyd and Ted, as they were known by their colleagues, developed into men of sound understanding in principle, doctrine, and priesthood government by the same formula as that followed by the sons of Mosiah: "They had searched the scriptures diligently, that they might know the word of God. But this is not all; they had given themselves to much prayer, and fasting; therefore they had the spirit of prophecy and the spirit of revelation, and when they taught, they taught with power and authority of God." (Alma 17:2–3.)

Subsequently the two men were themselves called into the governing councils of the Church—Brother Tuttle as a member of the First Council of the Seventy (1958) and Brother Packer as an Assistant to the Twelve (1961), then an Apostle (1970). These calls, their expanded responsibilities, their intensive study of the scriptures, and their tutoring by the Brethren bound them even more surely to the revealed word of the Lord.

When Elder Packer was called to the Quorum of the Twelve he brought with him what had been developing over a period of years: keen spiritual perception, expanding prophetic power, and the courage to speak out on issues where principles were involved. His talks have been listened to and appreciated by members throughout the Church. But in the minds of some few he has been viewed as controversial, dogmatic, bigoted. Most often, however, his critics have taken issue with him as *anti-intellectual.*

Ironically, those who know Elder Packer well and at close range see him as a thorough scholar and researcher with a brilliant mind which is lightened by an engaging sense of humor. He has remarkable recall and is a prodigious worker who, if he were to give himself over

to any academic field, would be very competitive with the most qualified people in that community. As with his brethren who have left
distinguished careers in business management, education, law, and
medicine, Elder Packer gives full measure of strength and talent to
the ministry whereunto he and they have, by revelation, been called
of the Lord.

Generally he has taken criticism calmly; but after one particularly harsh piece, and in a jocular mood, he found solace in writing a
poem:

Academic Freedom
They say we're anti-intellect,
Afraid to even think—
Our paranoid, deep fear of truth
Has caused our minds to shrink.

We're bigoted and prejudiced,
Withdrawn, afraid, regressive.
They must speak out and save the Church;
Someone must be progressive.

But them! How could we dare believe?
No! No! They're nowhere near it.
For shame that we should think the thought
That they are anti-spirit.[5]

He signed it "A Narrow-Minded Bigot" and put it in his files.

Although personally painful, taking criticism has been preferable
to not speaking out. And his personal discomfiture has been nothing
compared to the pain he has felt when one of his brethren of the First
Presidency or the Quorum of the Twelve has come under critical fire.

His ministry has deepened his commitment to the Savior and to
the example of His selfless life, freely given for all of His Father's children. That commitment is reflected in the lives of all the Brethren. It
is a quiet ministry wherein acts performed are rarely seen by other
than the one ministered to or by those near the one. As with them,
Elder Packer's quiet ministry lends balance to his public ministry of

which his interest in and contribution to Church education is only a small part.

As earlier mentioned, Elder Packer's talks are, in a sense, his journals. Perhaps in no general conference address did he reveal the spirit of his quiet ministry as in "The Moving of the Waters" (April 1991). There he expressed deep love and understanding for the unsung care-givers of the Father's children who are handicapped or terminally ill. The talk was in no way hypothetical, but was a reflection of his and Sister Packer's tender care for terminally ill members of their families.

Nowhere in his silent ministry is his tenderness more in evidence than among the poor of developing countries around the world. But it is also seen in ordinary settings, as when a child, about to trip over his unlaced shoe in a conference crowd, found a smiling, grandfatherly man stooping down to tie it.

Elder Packer's quiet ministry is not limited to children, however, but extends to all who suffer, from whatever cause or circumstance. Most of the older senior Brethren have received his solicitous watch-care. He steadied Elder LeGrand Richards as he walked to and from temple meetings, or he pushed his wheelchair. Brother Richards, in turn, often referred to him as "Boyd, my guardian angel." This same Boyd was at President Hunter's side through all the years of his illnesses.

Some of the Brethren have told how Boyd has visited them in the hospital or at home. Morning and evening he has stopped to encourage them and to keep them up to date on quorum business. Or he has persuaded them to let him take one of their assignments as a favor to him.

As in his public ministry, his wife, Donna, is a supportive and often a participating partner. A friend whose husband was dying of cancer acknowledged with deep gratitude their constant thoughtful acts and frequent phone calls, which continued beyond the husband's passing. Donna was again a part of his quiet ministry on the day of President Benson's funeral. Her husband and others of the Brethren had handled details incident to the services at the Tabernacle; to the funeral-cortege trip to Whitney, Idaho; and to grave-side proceedings there. Finally, they could leave for home. They were very weary and he felt pain in his hip and shoulder, yet they detoured to the hospital so that he could give a blessing. Such quiet acts are as much a part of his and Donna's lives as are the administrative responsibilities, travels, problem-solving, and speaking assignments of his apostolic call.

Stress-filled travel, tight schedules, and heavy responsibilities are the lot of all his Brethren. Each needs and each must find his respite from them, whether in music, painting, gardening, tennis, or spectator sports. Each may then return to his work refreshed and refueled.

Brother Packer finds his respite from the demands of the ministry by painting or carving. This is part of his and Donna's private world. It has been very useful in drawing close to his children and grandchildren as he has taught them to appreciate nature and to find their own means of creative expression. He has been reluctant to include a chapter on his work in this book. Donna, however, persuaded him that without it a significant dimension of his life would be missed.

While a serious pursuit of art is closed to him, he does envision limitless possibilities for others. He has said that the greatest Latter-day art and music is yet to be produced. And he predicts that when it is, it will be created by those who excel not only in talent but also in humility and faith.

Chapter Twenty-Three

The Art of Boyd K. Packer

Although Elder Packer's artistic talent has matured gradually, his subjects, themes, and inherent characteristics remain quite unchanged and are traceable from his youth. His subjects are family, animals, flowers, and the sites and associations of his boyhood home—but most often birds.

The membership of the Church has had brief glimpses of his paintings. In 1977 Deseret Book Company published *Mothers*, a booklet he wrote and illustrated with five sensitive bird paintings to honors mothers for their special day. In 1979 his book *Teach Ye Diligently*, was published, also by Deseret Book. Its jacket design was taken from his painting of eight family members, and its inside showed a number of his black-and-white sketches. In 1993 his small, charmingly illustrated *A Christmas Parable* was published by Bookcraft.

Brother Packer laments his lack of formal art training. He has moments of frustration over his lack of technical knowledge that sometimes makes it impossible for him to complete a subject as he visualizes it. When this happens he seeks help from those whose expertise exceeds his own in one phase or another of his work.

Peacocks in autumn

"Brigham City is a pretty little town"

One time he came to such a point and did not know how to proceed. He sought help from James Christensen, who has made an
international name for himself with his exquisite fantasy paintings.
Jim told about it:

"He had three or four paintings for me to see. 'Look,' Brother
Packer said, 'I don't need to be taught painting from the ground up.
What I've got is what I've got; I know what I want to do, and what I
want from you is a little help. What can I do better?'

"I gave him colors, I gave him brushes. Basically, then, I showed
him some techniques. Then I looked at his paintings and said, 'This
is a problem because of this; do this instead.' Then he said, 'What I'd
like you to do is just paint on it a little and show me what you mean.
Don't talk to me, show me.' So I did, and it was amazing. I came back
three months later and he had applied everything I had shown him
and more. You only have to tell that man something once. I wish I
had him in one of my classes at BYU."

Brother Packer likes to paint, would like to paint better, but feels
that his painting is adequate for its home application. But by those

*The town of Willard was named after Willard Richards, who was a
counselor to President Brigham Young. The mountain peaks above the town
were known to the early pioneers as* The Presidency.

Lazuli bunting with iris

Blue jay with maple leaves

who know it is generally agreed that it is in his bird art that he reaches the apex of his artistic expression.

People hearing that Elder Packer carves birds sometimes think of decoys, as did a woman from California. But when she actually saw his bird carvings she said, "It was like seeing the Grand Canyon for the first time—so far above my expectations that it took my breath away." His carved birds in their settings of leaves or flowers often have that dramatic an effect upon the viewer.

A bird-carving friend, Lance Turner, who has won prizes in world competitions, said of Brother Packer's work: "Boyd is a great student of nature and particularly of birds. He has an acute sense of observation. He sees a lot of the subtleties that I would overlook—turning a

Yellow throat
with lobelia

House wren family
with honeysuckle

foot, for instance, or having one foot down, or understanding the physical reasons that a bird hangs on a branch so it doesn't fall off. He is a master of the natural attitudes of birds and animals. His compositions and his bird attitudes are just beautiful."

Continuing, he said: "In carving, as in all else Boyd does, he attacks things with vigor; he has to. He can only snatch a few minutes here and there to do what he does."

His friend's comment explains why a bird carving often takes a year to complete. And Brother Packer's accuracy of detail, proportion, and attitude are hard won. He is a lifelong observer of birds, but also a lifelong student of their habitats, flight patterns, and characteristics. His reference books on birds number close to a hundred. And he does not depend upon observation and study alone, but he works from museum specimens—counting and measuring every feather. Of this his artist friend said, "If you get the proportions right and if you get the attitudes right, then the sheer mechanics of carving becomes secondary."

What the observer of his bird carvings experiences, however, is not the mechanics but sheer wonder that a piece of basswood and some brush loads of paint can be so constructed that it seems actually to breathe.

From boyhood his art has been characterized by strength and action. Even in repose, his subjects are never static. His keen sense of observation allows him, as his friend said, to capture the telling movement, the identifying attitude, and the accurate detail that give his subjects their aliveness. Even at a great distance he can identify a species by its flight pattern. "Are those geese?" a fellow observer asked about a formation in the distant sky. He replied, "No, they are ibis, a wading bird, related to the heron; the sacred ibis (*threskiornis aethiopic*) was venerated by the ancient Egyptians."

Underlying the visual expression of his art are basic qualities of character that guide the creative process beyond the media used. His reverence for life is apparent in his visual creations. At his touch, the physical is raised to the level of the spiritual. Being in tune with the source of inspiration, not only does he draw upon it to guide his hands but, while his hands create, his mind is refueled and refreshed, making of his art a welcome respite from travels, pressures, and challenges that are an ongoing part of the ministry. Also in the Packer

Meadow lark with sego lilies

home is the peace and quietude he requires, so that while his hands create, thoughts and insights come for problem solving, for pure knowledge to flow, and for revelation to come, not for his art alone but also for his talks, his teaching worldwide, and his input within the General Authority councils.

Basic to his creative process is Elder Packer's love of work, his total disregard for tedium, his discipline, and his efficiency. When he tackles something there is no wasted motion. Even in ordinary chores his approach is direct and knowing. He picks berries and fruit with two hands. He orders seeds for spring planting in January and plants before the recommended time. He and the grandchildren rake winter

Detail of relief carving
on fireplace mantel

Fireplace
mantel

leaves between spring snows so early bulbs can shoot up free. For
early spring color he plants primroses and pansies in outdoor tubs
before the snow has left the ground.

Preparation is basic to his approach. Whether for a chore, a talk,
or a painting, he lays it out in his mind, has materials at hand, and
begins at the first opportunity. When a task loses luster, he takes a

walk to the pond, has a word with a grandchild, or observes a bird's flight. These refresh him and unstop temporary blocks to his creative power so that he can return with fresh perspective to whatever he left. Then, too, prayer and pondering provide inspired impressions.

Elder Packer's artistic bent is as integral a part of him as are spirituality, compassion, steadiness, and humor. All are interwoven into a rich and complex entity that is constant yet ever-changing under the light of inspiration and revelation.

A chapter on the art of Boyd K. Packer would be incomplete without the homespun creativity of his companion, Donna, for she is artistic and innovative in making home a delight as well as a refuge. The casual observer's eye may rest upon Elder Packer's painting of the Savior and totally miss Donna's fabric-covered wall upon which his picture is displayed. Or the viewer may see only his blue jay carving or his painting of mountain peaks and not be aware of her handiwork with lace valances, pillows, and afghan throws that give the exact feeling of warmth and homeyness that are the perfect foil for his art. Her flower arrangements and table settings reveal her creativity. And if aware, one has not far to look for upholstered chairs, quilts, or children's toys that bespeak Donna's talent.

Her homemaking skills have developed out of the necessity to create beauty with meager means. As a result she still loves to remake, recycle, and redo. Both she and Elder Packer find satisfaction in working with used materials. Their creative imaginations see possibilities for enhanced rejuvenation in the old or the used. In this their creativity harmoniously dovetails.

Donna also encourages him to paint or carve as respite from the heavy pressures of the ministry. She helps make time for these by saving him from tasks that she can do. And she is uncritical. As a result he can always come home, to work, to eat and rest, or to create in an atmosphere of encouragement and peace. She is an eternal gift to him, and often he will say, "Without Donna I am nothing."

Chapter Twenty-Four

The Language
of the Spirit

 The Lord's watchmen on the tower—His witnesses—know the language of the Spirit. It was requisite to their call as prophets, seers, and revelators. As one among them, Elder Boyd K. Packer has, by constraint of the Spirit or by assignment, taught what spiritual communication is and how to prepare to receive it. Whether the classroom is a seat on the plane, a hotel room, a home, a chapel, the Mission Training Center, the Salt Lake Tabernacle, or a satellite audience, reverence and a receptive heart must be present if this teacher is to teach and the learner learn.

As a senior member of the Quorum of the Twelve, Elder Packer has felt the burden of responsibility to pass on to new General Authorities things—many of them spiritual—which he knows but which are not recorded. He has made it a point to travel with them, stay with them, and teach them. Younger members of the Quorum of the Twelve and many of the new Seventy affirm the value of his one-on-one instruction.

By assignment he also taught new mission presidents and their wives about spiritual communication that they would need as they, in turn, would teach and supervise the thousands of missionaries worldwide.

"As an Apostle," said Brother Packer, "I listen now to the same inspiration, coming from the same source, in the same way, that I listened to as a boy. The signal is much clearer now."[1]

Thus a lifetime of expanding spiritual comprehension and experience has passed between his boyhood and the occasions when he shares with new mission presidents things he has learned about the Spirit and how to prepare to receive it:

"We do not have the words (even the scriptures do not have words) which perfectly describe the Spirit," he told new mission presidents and their wives at a seminar on 19 June 1991. "The scriptures usually use the word *voice*, which does not exactly fit. These delicate, refined spiritual communications are not seen with our eyes nor heard with our ears. . . . It is a voice that one *feels* more than one *hears*.

"Once I came to understand this, one verse in the Book of Mormon took on profound meaning and my testimony of the book became fixed. The verse had to do with Laman and Lemuel, who rebelled against Nephi. Nephi rebuked them and said: 'Ye have seen an angel, and he spake unto you; yea, ye have heard his voice from time to time; and he hath spoken unto you in a still small voice, but ye were past feeling, that ye could not feel his words' (1 Nephi 17:45)."[2]

"I have come to know that inspiration comes more as a feeling than as a sound," Elder Packer repeated in general conference, October 1979. He then counseled: "Ponder and pray quietly and persistently. . . . The answer may not come as a lightning bolt. It may come as a little inspiration here and a little there, 'line upon line, precept upon precept' (D&C 98:12).

"Some answers will come from reading the scriptures, some from hearing speakers. And, occasionally, when it is important, some will come by very direct and powerful inspiration. The promptings will be clear and unmistakable."[3]

He recalled what the Prophet Joseph Smith said:

A person may profit by noticing the first intimation of the spirit of revelation; for instance, when you feel pure intelligence flowing into you, it may give you sudden strokes of ideas. . . . And thus by learning the Spirit of God and understanding it, you may grow into the principle of revelation, until you become perfect in Christ Jesus. (*Teachings of the Prophet Joseph Smith*, p. 151).

"We cannot express spiritual knowledge in words alone. We can, however, with words show another how to prepare for the reception of the Spirit. The Spirit itself will help. 'For when a man speaketh by the power of the Holy Ghost the power of the Holy Ghost carrieth it unto the hearts of the children of men'" (2 Nephi 33:1).

He spoke then of Nephi's profound sermon of instruction in which that prophet explained that "angels speak by the power of the Holy Ghost; wherefore, they speak the words of Christ. Wherefore, I said unto you, feast upon the words of Christ; for behold, the words of Christ will tell you all things what ye should do." (2 Nephi 32:3.)

"Should an angel appear and converse with you," Elder Packer continued, "neither you nor he would be confined to corporeal sight or sound in order to communicate. For there *is* that spiritual process, described by the Prophet Joseph Smith, by which pure intelligence *can* flow into our minds and we can know what we need to know without either the drudgery of study or the passage of time, for it is revelation."

He quoted further from the Prophet Joseph Smith:

All things whatsoever God in his infinite wisdom has seen fit and proper to reveal to us, while we are dwelling in mortality, in regard to our mortal bodies, are revealed to us in the abstract, . . . revealed to our spirits precisely as though we had no bodies at all; and those revelations which will save our spirits will save our bodies (*Teachings of the Prophet Joseph Smith*, p. 355).

Elder Packer then cautioned against talking freely of unusual spiritual experiences, which he said are "generally for our own edification, instruction, or correction." He reminded the mission presidents of Alma's words: "It is given unto many to know the mysteries of God; nevertheless they are laid under a strict command that they shall not impart only according to the portion of his word which he doth grant unto the children of men, according to the heed and diligence which they give unto him" (Alma 12:9).

He further counseled: "You cannot force spiritual things. . . . Do not be impatient to gain great spiritual knowledge. Let it grow, help it grow, but do not force it or you will open the way to be misled."

He continued: "We should go about our life in an ordinary, workaday way, following the routines and rules and regulations that govern life. . . . [These] are valuable protection. Should we stand in need of revealed instruction to alter our course, it will be waiting along the way as we arrive at the point of need."

He then encouraged the presidents in their new call: "Now, do not feel hesitant or ashamed if you do not know everything. . . . There may be more power in your testimony than even you realize." And he quoted: "Whoso cometh unto me with a broken heart and a contrite spirit, him will I baptize with fire and with the Holy Ghost, even as the Lamanites, because of their faith in me at the time of their conversion, were baptized with fire, and with the Holy Ghost, and they knew it not" (3 Nephi 9:20).

Elder Packer continued:

> Oh, if I could teach you this one principle. A testimony is to be *found* in the *bearing* of it! Somewhere in your quest for spiritual knowledge, there is that "leap of faith," as philosophers call it. It is the moment when you have gone to the edge of the light and stepped into the darkness to discover that the way is lighted ahead for just a footstep or two. "The spirit of man," as the scripture says, indeed "is the candle of the Lord" (Proverbs 20:27).
>
> Can you not see that [the witness] will be supplied as you share it? As you give that which you have, there is a replacement, with increase. For as Moroni said, "wherefore, dispute not because ye see not, for ye receive no witness until after the trial of your faith" (Ether 12:6).[4]

Each Apostle is ordained as a prophet, seer, and revelator. Some of his brethren affirm that Elder Packer has remarkable spiritual perception and the ability to know, by the Spirit in advance, what is to be.

In the fall of 1982, winter came early to northern Utah, and the snow began to lay heavily in the mountains. Brother Packer was concerned. "Since we live on Little Cottonwood Creek, I knew something of the patterns of high water in the spring because we had experienced them on irregular occasions. I sensed that we were in for something unusual. I was the supervisor of the Utah Area with Carlos E. Asay of the Seventy."

Brother Asay had recorded in his journal, 28 September 1982, "The rainfall in the last few days has exceeded anything this part of the world has seen in the last 100 years." On 2 December 1982 he wrote, "More snow fell during the day. . . . The snow level on our front lawn measures between 25 and 30 inches."

Elder Packer said: "I kept indicating that we should do something and suggested that Brother Asay not only contact the county but also get the Church organized to meet the possible emergency. He began in a casual way to organize. Along about February, they were still taking it up in this or that meeting."

Meanwhile Elder Packer had deep feelings of impending trouble and finally told his assistant and those working with him: "Now, you brethren are not listening. We are in for a terrible circumstance unless we prepare. We have got to move and prepare for something big. We must get all of the stakes along the Wasatch Front prepared to react immediately when this happens, because it is going to happen as certainly as we are sitting here. You emergency planners are taking a casual approach to it and we have got to put it on a red alert basis."

Those responsible then began to move. Elder Asay wrote: "There was a flurry of activity in the late spring and summer of 1983 as some flooding emergencies were averted [by creating] a sandbagged river down State Street and sandbagging on other streets in Salt Lake City. . . . Priesthood lines of communication and priesthood organization operated smoothly in meeting challenging emergencies. And, it was a time when seeric and prophetic powers displayed by Church leaders helped the people prepare for a crisis and work a miracle."[5]

At the time Elder A. Theodore Tuttle left for South America for his first assignment as a Seventy, Brother Packer was still a seminary supervisor.

"Before Ted left," he said, "we talked and we prayed together. When we were through praying I said, 'I have the feeling that you and I will stand together to bear witness of the restored gospel on the soil of South America.' Now, that was as improbable as anything, because we had no seminaries there and no reason for me to travel down there.

"After Ted left, I went to work on my doctorate and did what was needed for seminary and institute opening in September. Yet I had the gnawing feeling, 'What does it matter? You are not going to be here.'"

On 30 September 1961 Brother Packer was called as an Assistant to the Twelve. Of the call he said: "There was a spiritual prophecy that preceded it by a few hours. It happened this way: After the conference announcement I tried to reach Ted in Montevideo and they said he was in Peru. Late that afternoon I got through to him and said, 'I have something to tell you.' He said, 'I already know.' And I said, 'Did somebody call you?' and he said, 'I've learned it otherwise.' Ted had had a dream the night before."[6]

Elder Packer rarely speaks of foreknowing events, but when the Spirit prompts he will tell of a significant experience. On such an occasion he said: "Not long ago I was in Otavalo, Ecuador, where we have a branch of four hundred members. They were completing a chapel and they took me up into the mountains to look at a site for another chapel.

"The site was not as big as this room. It was on the edge of a cornfield way up on the mountainside. It now belongs to the Church; we traded a sewing machine for it because a sewing machine was worth a good deal more than the money involved. The Indian member, part of whose inheritance the site represented, wanted more than anything else to have a sewing machine."

Elder Packer said he walked over that site and was about to leave when he noticed something. "I saw in the middle of that little pasture a stake about as big around as your wrist and protruding from the ground about sixteen inches."

He continued: "As I saw that, it was as though lightning struck me, for there in that little pasture was a stake! I knew as surely as I have ever known anything that one day another kind of stake would be there.

"Some would ask, 'Even there, way up in the mountains above Otavalo?'

"And to them I say, 'Oh, yes. One day. Maybe that piece of wood was put there to tether a calf, but to me it was a great prophecy.'"[7] (By

1991 there was a stake in Otavalo, two in Quito, not far away, and six more in other parts of Ecuador.)

In October 1978 he attended a mission presidents seminar in Hong Kong. There he first met President David Chen of the Hong Kong Mission.

"Before I left Hong Kong we were in Brother Chen's office, where he briefly told me the story of his life and about his family in China, whom he had not seen since 1947. He began to weep openly. There was no chance that he could see his family nor any way he could get into China. He had not heard from them in many years. He did not know whether they were alive or dead. Neither did he dare write to them.

"I promised him that he would go back. We then had a prayer together. In the prayer I invoked the blessings of the Lord upon him and upon China and upon restoring him to his family. After the prayer, I told him that he would go to China and that we would be in China together."8

In an address given at BYU in March 1991 Elder Dallin H. Oaks talked of China. He recalled an "electrifying message" given in 1978 by President Spencer W. Kimball to the Regional Representatives of the Church, of whom Brother Oaks was one. President Kimball pleaded for those leaders to move forward, saying, "It is better for something to be *under way* than *under advisement.*"

Elder Oaks continued: "He referred to various nations where we had not yet taught the restored gospel." He singled out China for special praise, saying:

> By comparison with the widespread breakdown of morality and discipline in the western world, the Chinese are a disciplined, industrious, frugal, closely-knit people. Their moral standards are very high by modern western standards. . . . Family life is strong, with old family members still given great respect and care.
>
> When we are ready, the Lord will use us for his purposes. There are almost three billion people now living on the earth in nations where the gospel is not now being preached. If we could only make a small beginning in every nation, soon the converts among each kindred and tongue could step forth as lights to their own people and the gospel would thus be preached in all nations before the coming of the Lord.

When President Oaks returned to BYU from that meeting, he asked his assistant, Bruce L. Olsen, to begin planning for a BYU performing group to go to China.

In his 1991 address Elder Oaks talked of a miracle. "Just two months later, in December 1978, President Jimmy Carter unexpectedly announced that the United States and China would exchange formal diplomatic recognition on the first day of 1979. With that announcement, a BYU trip to China became at least a theoretical possibility."9

The miracle became a reality when BYU performing groups began annual visits to China in July 1979, at which time Elder James E. Faust rededicated China for the preaching of the gospel. In January 1981 the Chinese ambassador, Chai Zemin, visited Church headquarters. Then in May 1981, with the blessings of President Kimball and the other Brethren, Elder and Sister Packer, with BYU President Jeffrey R. Holland and his wife, Patricia, went to China with BYU's

With Dr. David Chen on the Great Wall of China

International Folk Dancers on a goodwill performing tour for the Church. And in Hong Kong Dr. David Chen joined them to aid in translating and helping in whatever way he could.

Brother Packer reported that he had sensitively introduced gospel possibilities to their Chinese hosts. But one of the most significant experiences for him was the Sunday that he stood on the Great Wall of China with David Chen and together they remembered the promise to David made three years before. David's mother had died a short time before, but he was reunited with his two sisters, one a doctor and one a peasant.

Occasionally Elder Packer has shared spiritual experiences of a personal nature at funerals of family or friends. "Funeral talks are often isolated, separate, and apart from anything else we say. They are times of emotion and in a way there is a little more freedom to speak on deeply spiritual things.

"We are close, very close, to the spirit world at the time of death. There are tender feelings, spiritual communications really, which may easily be lost if there is not a spirit of reverence."[10]

At the funeral of his brother, General Leon Claron Packer, he said: "I saw Mother once since she passed away. I saw her as clearly as I see any of you. There was nothing said. For a time I didn't understand why I had been permitted to see her. And then President Kimball told us in the temple that he had seen his father . . . whom he knew had come to say that he approved of what was happening to his son. Then I knew why my mother had come. It was to say she approved of my life. She was glorious, as others have been who have come to visit."[11]

On 5 February 1982 Elder Packer spoke at the funeral of his and Donna's great friend, Belle S. Spafford, former general president of the Relief Society (1945–1974). He told of a sacred personal experience. "On Sunday morning 18 September 1977 I awakened in the early hours of the morning greatly troubled over a dream that concerned Sister Spafford. My wife also awakened and asked why I was so restless.

" 'Sister Spafford is in trouble. She needs a blessing.'

"When morning came I called her. She was deeply troubled indeed. I told her I had a blessing for her. She wept and said it came

Elder and Sister Packer with Belle S. Spafford,
General President of the Relief Society,
in a Relief Society Conference

as an answer to her fervent prayer the night long. She had not been well. There had been tests. The day before, the doctor told her the results. They were frightening. There was a tumor and other complications. An attentive young neighbor assisted me in the blessing. It was most unusual. Her life was not over. Her days were to be prolonged for a most important purpose. Promises, special promises were given. . . . All of them now have been fulfilled, and she has accomplished those things so dear to her. When further tests were made that next week, the tumor was not there."[12]

Sometime before the fatal illness of his friend A. Theodore Tuttle was diagnosed, Elder Packer had a dream. He never spoke of it in detail, but he told Sister Packer, "Ted will not be with us much longer." She asked if something had been said. He responded, "No. Just that." She understood.

And so it was. Great blessings were given Elder Tuttle, and many prayers were offered in his behalf. But he pleaded with the Lord to give them, instead, to poor Saints in South America.[13] Those who were close to Brother Tuttle knew at the time he died that his prayers had been, would be, answered as he wished.

Just three years before Elder LeGrand Richards died, that beloved Apostle raised his bold, inimitable voice to testify in the October 1979 general conference: "To me the gift of the Holy Ghost is as important to man as sunshine and water are to the plants. . . . [This] is God's kingdom. He is the only one that can put his Holy Spirit into the hearts of his people. . . . No wonder Peter said: 'Ye are a chosen generation, a royal priesthood, an holy nation, a peculiar people; that ye should shew forth the praises of him who hath called you out of darkness into his marvelous light' (1 Peter 2:9)."[14]

Chapter Twenty-Five

New Responsibility
Among the Twelve

President Ezra Taft Benson passed away on Memorial Day, 30 May 1994, after a long illness. On 5 June Howard W. Hunter, President of the Quorum of the Twelve Apostles and next in line of succession, was sustained as President of the Church. He named Gordon B. Hinckley as First Counselor and Thomas S. Monson as Second Counselor in the First Presidency. President Gordon B. Hinckley was sustained as President of the Quorum of the Twelve.

Since President Thomas S. Monson was next in line of succession after President Hinckley, the three senior Apostles were now all serving in the First Presidency. As had been the order of things, Elder Boyd K. Packer, next in seniority, was sustained as Acting President of the Quorum of the Twelve and set apart by President Hunter.

He was not the first to serve as Acting President of the Twelve; Presidents Joseph Fielding Smith, Spencer W. Kimball, and Howard W. Hunter had all served in that position. As Acting President, Brother Packer was to assume leadership and conduct all meetings of the Twelve in a fast-growing Church.

The responsibilities of his new office were not unfamiliar to

President Packer. Because of the occasional and at times extended absence of President Hunter, due to illness, it had been necessary for him to conduct the meetings of the Twelve and attend to the duties of the office in President Hunter's absence.

President Packer was scrupulously careful never to presume upon his leader. When President Hunter was confined to his home, or in the hospital, President Packer would visit him at the end of each day. He would report the meetings of the Twelve to receive approval of and direction from his quorum president. Or he would call him to report on matters of interest or importance. As it became increasingly difficult for President Hunter to walk, Elder Packer was always at his side to be of assistance.

Two of the Apostles spoke of how he handled matters during these periods of President Hunter's illnesses. Elder James E. Faust said: "For the time and period when President Hunter was not as well as he would have liked to be, Brother Packer had to assume leadership in the Twelve, and he was very, very careful not ever to assume President Hunter's prerogatives. But he worked very hard at keeping the Twelve abreast of everything that was going on."[1]

Elder Neal A. Maxwell expressed his impressions: "Elder Packer is by nature task-oriented, moving large issues along to a solution. But while President Hunter was ill, he sensed that he was in a different role. And so he shifted from the role of a driving, leading force to one who paused and did what I would call maintenance work on feelings, and in giving encouragement. He nurtured us, and I thought it a wonderful thing to see how well he did."[2]

While Elder Packer served in that temporary role only those close to him knew the fervor of his

With Presidents Howard W. Hunter and Gordon B. Hinckley

prayers in President Hunter's behalf, or his tender and solicitous watchcare over his senior brother, or the depth of his gratitude when President Hunter was well enough to resume his place once again.

Just one month after President Packer had been set apart the July summer-vacation period began, during which the General Authorities are free from conference or other assignments. President Packer decided to use this relatively free period to prepare himself for the duties that now were his. He determined to read the standard works carefully and draw from them every reference to the Twelve, to revelation, and to several other subjects. He set up his "summer office" under the shade trees at the pond and spent his days in quiet study. In addition to the scriptures he read every reference to the twelve in the seven-volume *History of the Church* and in Orson F. Whitney's biography of Heber C. Kimball to learn more fully of the organization and activities of the Twelve in the early days of the Church. He compiled these scriptures and statements into two large loose-leaf binders. Supportive of his studies and research, Donna would bring him treats or picnic meals to share together.

Frequently one or more of the Twelve would visit him. He would willingly interrupt his study to spend time with them or with children and grandchildren who found him there at work.

During this period he also helped prepare for their annual Fourth of July family get-together. As usual, the families set up camps in the woods and joined in the activities that were organized by family members.

This reunion centered on family heritage. A large tepee was set up under the trees, with a bear skin, baskets of unhusked corn, a totem pole, and a papoose carrier. On the sun-porch "museum," displays of pictures and artifacts from missionary work among the Indians were arranged. During evening firesides adults told the children stories about the missionary work of Joseph Alma and Sarah Wight Packer, who served two missions in the early years of the century among the Sioux Indians at Wolf Point, Montana. Also President Packer related stories of his own work among the Indian peoples.

The grandchildren had carved the totem pole that stood by the tepee. They also did bead work and passed off merit badges on Indian lore. The younger children fashioned tepee centerpieces for the picnic tables upon which were served delicious meals cooked in Dutch ovens.

With Donna's encouragement Brother Packer had earlier determined to attend to some physical needs. Through the years the effect of his childhood polio had become more pronounced. His left leg was an inch shorter than the other. He resorted to a lift inside his left shoe but in time found it necessary to have a thick sole attached to the outside. His limp became more pronounced, his pain more intense, and his need for medication more disagreeable.

By shifting only two regional conference assignments to his brethren and using the Thanksgiving and Christmas holidays in which to recuperate, he could have his hip replaced. He scheduled the operation for 24 October 1994. The surgeon skillfully replaced his hip and lengthened his leg. Brother Packer followed precisely the therapy instructions of his doctors and was soon walking without the pain or the limp. He finally could say with a smile that, at last, he was levelheaded. The operation also helped to relieve the pain in his shoulder which for so many years had disturbed his rest at night.

Through study and prayer he had prepared his mind and spirit for the heavy responsibilities that were now his; through surgery he had prepared physically to better handle the weight of them. Looking ahead, he mused: "Nothing is changed, but everything is changed."

Change is one of the constants in life. Another change came when President Gordon B. Hinckley called him on the morning of 3 March 1995 saying that President Howard W. Hunter had died at home and asking Brother Packer to notify the Twelve. It was with a heavy heart that he did so, but with a grateful one. The Lord had mercifully released a great servant who had endured well his long season of suffering and pain.

The following days were filled with unending detail. The outpouring of love from Church members and from leaders around the world was overwhelming. As a member of the funeral committee and as one of those whom the family had asked to speak, Brother Packer carried his share of the load.

When he spoke on that occasion, 8 March 1995, he avoided personal references to his close association with the former President, except to recall Brother Hinckley's words that "tears come easily to old men," and to say, "President Hunter knew that Donna and I loved him, and we know that that love was returned."

For those who were listening, however, Brother Packer did teach about the Lord's flawless plan of succession from one of His prophets to the next:

> There are those who wonder at the system where the senior Apostle, invariably now an older man, becomes the President of the Church.
>
> Those who do not understand write to us or publish articles saying, "Isn't it time now to do the sensible thing and install a vigorous, young leader to face the challenge of a growing international church?"
>
> They fail to see the divine inspiration in the system established by the Lord. Granted, it does not work as the wisdom of men would dictate. The Lord reminded Isaiah: "My thoughts are not your thoughts, neither are your ways my ways. . . . For as the heavens are higher than the earth, so are my ways higher than your ways, and my thoughts than your thoughts." (Isaiah, 55:8–9.)
>
> See what the Lord has provided. Nowhere on this earth is there a body of men of leadership and authority as completely devoid of aspiring. The very system that seems so strange to many just does not allow it; neither would the Lord permit it. There is no jockeying for position or power, no soliciting for votes, no hint of cultivating influence in any self-serving way.
>
> There is a brotherhood that accommodates differing views and personalities, but we are *one*. The authority in the administration of the Church is independent of any individual and is held in trust by fifteen men who have been ordained as Apostles. President Hunter's life has taught us that regardless of the age or infirmity of any man among them, including the President, the work goes on.[3]

On Sunday, 12 March 1995, Brother Packer met with his brethren in the temple for the reorganization of the First Presidency. It was his fifth time in so participating, the first being when Harold B. Lee became President of the Church.

Now it was Gordon B. Hinckley, the senior Apostle, who, not having sought or wanted it to be so, was ordained and set apart as the Lord's mouthpiece to the over nine million members of His church, and to lead them through one of the most perilous times in the world's history.

To aid him in this awesome responsibility he chose Thomas S. Monson as his First Counselor and James E. Faust as his Second. These were so ordained and set apart. President Monson, as next senior Apostle, was also ordained and set apart as President of the Quorum of the Twelve. Boyd K. Packer was again set apart as Acting President of the Quorum of the Twelve and was given a blessing by the new prophet and President of the Church.

When President Hinckley was asked during the press conference held the next morning, 13 March 1995, in the Joseph Smith Memorial Building, "What do you consider to be the greatest challenge facing the Church?" he answered without hesitation, "The most serious challenge we face, and the most wonderful challenge, is the challenge that comes of growth."[4]

On March 18 President Packer indicated what that growth had come to mean. He spoke in Washington, D.C., to ambassadors from nations of the world who were guests of the BYU Management Group. "There are nearly 22,000 ecclesiastical units speaking 106 languages. We are growing rapidly. Just under 50,000 full-time missionaries preach the restored gospel in 156 countries. There has been nothing to compare with it in the history of the world."

To meet the administrative and spiritual challenges which the new President of the Church faced it was Brother Packer's desire, and that of his brethren, to follow President Hinckley's simple but all-encompassing counsel: "Carry on!" In so doing, he could say as before, "Nothing is changed, yet everything is changed."

Chapter Twenty-Six

A Watchman
on the Tower

In the introduction and throughout this biography of President Boyd K. Packer we have seen him as one of the Lord's watchmen on the tower, working and bearing witness with his brethren in the ministry. This concluding chapter will focus on those traits and attitudes which, though partially shared by the others, are more uniquely his own.

The Lord's watchmen on the tower have consistently counseled Church members to read the scriptures daily so that they might know the word of the Lord for themselves; and not only to read them, but to "liken all scriptures unto us, that it might be for our profit and learning" (1 Nephi 19:23).

From young manhood Boyd K. Packer has followed this counsel and has mined the scriptures for their hidden treasures until they are an integral part of him. In the process he has taken on attributes of certain of the prophets whose lives are recorded therein. But most particularly, through his intensive study of the life, teachings, and teaching methods of the Savior, Brother Packer's own teaching has come to reflect his personal knowledge and spiritual comprehension of the Lord Jesus Christ. This has been the desire of his life, of which he said:

I determined that among all the gifts that might make one useful to the Lord the gift to teach by the Spirit would be supreme. I came to find that if one desired it, asked for it, prayed for it, studied, pondered, and earned it, and believed with sufficient faith that he could possess it, the gift would not be withheld from him.

Accordingly I turned to the New Testament to "associate" with and learn from the Lord, who as a teacher is the ideal. . . . It was a most enlightening experience to "walk" with Jesus and "observe" Him teach. Thereafter, I began with all diligence to pattern my teaching efforts after Him. Through this association I came to know Him—Jesus Christ, the Son of God, the Only Begotten of the Father—and that He lives.[1]

With this personal knowledge of the Master Teacher, Brother Packer has been a student of the Lord's teaching techniques, attempting never to teach except as guided by the Spirit. In doing so, he gives full credit to those other watchmen from whom he has learned, saying, "Most of what I know about the ministry that is really worth knowing, I learned by reading about the Brethren of the past and watching the Brethren I have known since I came as a very young man into the circle of General Authorities over thirty years ago."

Continuing, he adds: "Now, there is a certain loneliness that comes with the realization that most of them are gone. There is no longer the security of talking something over with President Joseph Fielding Smith, whose father was the son of Hyrum, brother of the Prophet Joseph; or with LeGrand Richards, who could remember Wilford Woodruff; or with Joseph Anderson, who came to this building as a replacement for Brother Gibbs who was hired by Brigham Young."

And again, "I have never given a major talk of any kind, conference or otherwise, that I haven't gone over it with somebody of the Bishopric, Seventy, or the Twelve and learned every time from something they have been able to point out."

Howard W. Hunter, as President of the Quorum of the Twelve, expressed similar feelings of gratitude and gave wise counsel to younger men who had received high callings:

> In recent years, my close association with members of the First Presidency and the Twelve has been an exceptional blessing to me in my service. . . .

As you sit with them on various councils and committees or accompany them on assignments, especially in the early stages of your service, I suggest you observe them carefully. Be attentive and teachable. Make notes, mentally and otherwise. You will learn your duty through this process in a powerful way. You will not go wrong if you do as they do, dress as they dress; you will not be in error if you think and speak and pray as do my brethren.[2]

President Packer has felt great responsibility to pass on to the younger men what he has learned. Elder M. Russell Ballard told of the time he served as president of the Canada Toronto mission. For three days he was a listening, learning student as Brother Packer tirelessly taught him things of value for that time and for his calling as an Apostle.

Elder Richard G. Scott also expressed gratitude for Brother Packer's intensive teaching as they traveled together on assignment, staying with him in their hotel rooms so that no opportunity would be lost in passing along things which would benefit Brother Scott in his new calling.

"Be attentive and teachable," President Hunter counseled. These are attitudes which President Packer also deems essential in the process of counseling and correcting.

President Packer's method of correction is direct and based upon a true principle. It is given without rancor and always with the intent to lift the counseled one to greater understanding or higher performance. He does not skirt issues to save feelings; rather, he is a courageous and caring critic who may temporarily jar the one he counsels into recognition of a need to change. But if the counseled one is honest and teachable he will admit in his heart that Boyd Packer spoke the truth as a friend, correcting in the spirit of the scripture: "Reproving betimes with sharpness, when moved upon by the Holy Ghost; and then showing forth afterwards an increase of love toward him whom thou hast reproved, lest he esteem thee to be his enemy; that he may know that thy faithfulness is stronger than the cords of death" (D&C 121:43–44).

One of President Packer's missionaries in New England came from a small town and had not had the school advantages of others. The former missionary indicated that his speech was grammatically wanting. President Packer asked if he was man enough, with desire enough, to overcome his faulty speech. He was. His president coached, encouraged, and occasionally penalized him until he learned. And he followed the young man's later progress with interest and affection as he married, raised a family, and became a stake president and a successful businessman. For such a one, Brother Packer's correction is counted as priceless.

President Packer, however, hesitates to counsel those who are unwilling to change, or those who wish to be made comfortable in low-level performance when they are capable of greater, or those who seek approval for contrary behavior.

A central motivating force in President Packer's life has been his early commitment to obedience. It set him on a course of freedom beyond his highest expectations. He wrote: "Obedience—that which God will never take by force—He will accept when freely given. And He will then return to you freedom that you can hardly dream of—the freedom to feel and to know, the freedom to do, and the freedom to *be*, at least a thousandfold more than we offer Him. Strangely enough, the key to freedom is obedience."[3]

With a commitment to obedience, a personal testimony of the Savior, and a solid grounding in the scriptures, there was little time lost in painful repenting from grievous error. Nevertheless, repentance for him, as for all who are striving toward perfection as commanded, has been a governing, motivating principle of the gospel to be applied daily.

Also among his characteristics is his certainty, along with Nephi's, that one can "go and do" what the Lord commands, even the seemingly impossible, knowing that "the Lord giveth no commandment unto the children of men, save he shall prepare a way for them that they may accomplish the thing which he commandeth them" (1 Nephi 3:7).

This certainty was manifest in Brother Packer as one of those responsible for the Geneological Department (now Family History) of the Church. As he contemplated the redeeming of *all* of the billions of our Father's children who had ever lived upon the face of the earth, he said: "If the numbers seem staggering, we will move ahead. If the process is tedious, we will move ahead anyway. If the records have been lost, if the obstacles and opposition are overwhelming, we will move ahead anyway."[4]

Another characteristic of Brother Packer's is his steadiness in the face of criticism. He has written: "There is a position of truth—strong, powerful, steady. Somebody has to stand, face the storm, declare the truth, let the winds blow, and be serene, composed, and steady in the doing of it. Who are we anyway? Are we the ones who were born to be immune from persecution or from any penalties in connection with living and preaching the gospel?"[5]

In his attitude toward his critics we are reminded of the prophet Nehemiah, whom President Packer admires. When Nehemiah was laughed to scorn, when his enemies tried to take him by subtlety and by lies, when they entreated him to come down and negotiate with them, he answered: "I am doing a great work, so that I cannot come down: why should the work cease, whilst I leave it, and come down to you?" (Nehemiah 6:3.)

As always, when the Lord's work moves forward, Satan conspires within the hearts of men to mock and to fight against the work. Brother Packer has answered: "If you feel that you must answer every criticism and challenge that comes your way, a single critic or one heckler can occupy your full time. I have learned that there is one place to search for approval and that is up—to be approved of our Lord and of our Heavenly Father."[6]

Brother Packer told of a time when he, along with President Ezra Taft Benson, was sharply criticized by the local and national media. President Benson sent him a scripture which strengthened him: "No weapon that is formed against thee shall prosper; and every tongue that shall revile against thee in judgment thou shalt condemn. This is the heritage of the servants of the Lord, and their righteousness is of me, saith the Lord." (3 Nephi 22:17.)

Of the criticism he has endured, a fellow watchman, Elder Neal A. Maxwell, said: "When Boyd is on to something that needs to be said, he is willing to pay the price to address an unpopular subject. A seer must do that, for if he is seeing ahead of the crowd, he is going to speak out and take the criticism that comes. But Boyd subjugates himself to the need and he doesn't ask any of us to defend him or try to explain him. He only wants our love and support."[7]

Face to face with undesirable philosophies and practices that have become ever more prevalent in a permissive society, President Packer wrestles with implications, does extensive research, and ponders and prays to be ready for whatever assignments come to him. One such assignment came from President Spencer W. Kimball in 1978, when he asked him to address a BYU fireside regarding homosexuality. Feeling very inadequate, Brother Packer responded, "President, I just couldn't do it." Then after much soul-searching he repented for having refused an assignment from the prophet. The result of his repentance and his thorough preparation was his talk "To the One," 5 March 1978.[8]

In preparing him for the responsibility that he now carries as Acting President of the Quorum of the Twelve Apostles the Lord tested and tutored President Packer through teachers and mentors by calling him to understudy positions at different periods of his mature life—assistant stake clerk (one year), administrator of seminaries and institutes (six years), Assistant to the Twelve (nine years), substitute President of the Quorum of the Twelve during President Hunter's sometimes long illnesses, then Acting President for nine months prior to President Hunter's death on 3 March 1995. Thus his training has been deep and thorough, even though he had not filled a full-time mission or served as a bishop or a stake president. In each calling he has given complete devotion, has learned in depth what each office encompassed, and has been a highly contributing entity in whatever assignment came to him.

Also, by the sure word of personal prophecy, he was entrusted with a quiet foreknowledge of his later apostolic calling, the burden of which he carried alone for over twenty years, sharing it with no one until it became a reality. Thus the Lord could trust him with his portion of the weight carried by His watchmen on the tower as they administer the affairs of the rapidly growing worldwide Church.

Another of President Packer's traits is his profound reverence for life and for sacred things, including the righteous use of the priesthood. As do his brethren, he strives to exercise his priesthood in the spirit of and according to the principles embodied in Doctrine and Covenants 121:36–46.

Life for the Lord's watchmen is more demanding than most

Church members can ever know; it taxes them to their very limits as long as they live. President Packer's quick wit and spontaneous sense of humor give momentary relief to the burdens carried and act as leaven to the whole man. Rarely does he tell jokes; rather he responds wittily and without sarcasm to the circumstance of the moment.

An account of President Packer would be incomplete without considering home and what has gone into creating its unique aura. He, with his children, has lived by the biblical command to Adam that he should eat his bread "by the sweat of his brow." Because the Packers chose to live in the country and to have acreage that required the children's help to subdue and maintain, the family has labored in much the same way that many of his and Donna's forbears did.

Years ago he and his sons split rails and built a fence around the living portion of the property. It is now weathered and looks as if it grew there with the trees that surround it.

There was no pond in the beginning, so after the family acquired some additional property they dug, dredged, and filled one. Thereafter they stocked it with tame waterfowl, which in turn attracted wildfowl in their migrating seasons.

This blending of the tame and the wild are part of the total scene which is not without its small emergencies: A raccoon lodging in a fireplace chimney for its winter hibernation; a huge snake sunning itself on the front step; a mink attacking a duck; hawks that are protected by law, killing his songbirds; the wind blowing over a heavy tree that grazes the house; or the creek overflowing at flood season. Each of these has been met with steadiness. If the task has been beyond Brother Packer's strength or time frame, the grown sons have come willingly to help.

There is a rhythm to the seasons there: the cleanup and early planting in spring; the maintenance of garden and orchard in summer, highlighted midway by the grandchildren's annual Fourth of July camp-out in the woods; the harvesting, canning, and putting-to-bed in fall; and the snow-plowing and holiday observance in winter. And year round there are the birds, fending for themselves or supplied from feeders.

The Quorum of the Twelve in 1995

And there is a harmony between the land and the home that radiates peace and quiet beauty. It reflects the mind-set and the character of those who live there. Because of the demands of his ministry and the ever-changing needs of a large and ever-increasing family (there are seventy-eight at this writing), the Packers' lives can rarely conform to personal inclination or to settled comfortableness. The telephone constantly interrupts. Grandchildren come and go and yet are never unwelcome to the grounds, or to grandparents. There are emergency calls from headquarters. Yet there is order there; and peace.

President Packer can always go *home*, a reality and a blessing that both anchors and renews him. And of course, central to their home is Donna, as she is central to his life. They have so lived their lives that they have become *one* in the biblical sense, as the Lord intended his sons and daughters to be—"created in His image, male and female," and endowed with divine attributes. They have labored and sacrificed for one another until their love has reached its mature expression of trust and contentment; sweeter, by far, than its earlier flame.

As central to their lives as are family and home there is a deeper center. It is President Packer's call as a witness of the Lord Jesus Christ. It places greater responsibility upon him and his brethren—not more important, President Gordon B. Hinckley says, than that resting upon the least in the kingdom, but greater in the sense that there will be no letup because of weariness, sickness, age, or infirmity.

None among the Brethren has come to this assignment without the deepest soul-searching of which he is capable, knowing that, despite all he is or is not, he is to be a witness of the Savior himself. And it is the Lord who will temper and mold him to the task.

With each change in the Presidency of the Church, the seniority of each Apostle changes. Then new tests confront him and new responsibilities are laid upon him. Sharing in these is his wife and companion.

So it is with President Boyd K. Packer and his wife, Donna. Having yielded their agency to the Lord, and having committed their lives to His service, they have met each test and shouldered each responsibility that has come to them. All they are and ever will be is consecrated to Him and to His redeeming work—the salvation of all the Father's children.

Boyd K. and Donna S. Packer

Notes

Chapter Two
His Ancestry

1. Boyd K. Packer, *The Holy Temple* (Salt Lake City: Bookcraft, 1980), p. 258.

Chapter Three
His Parents

1. Boyd K. Packer, *Improvement Era*, December 1962, pp. 926–27.
2. Talk at Stockholm Area Conference, August 1974, p. 24.
3. *Improvement Era*, June 1962, pp. 460–61.
4. Boyd K. Packer, "The Best Team" (Salt Lake City, 1976), p. 22. Unpublished.
5. Ibid., p. 23.
6. *Ensign*, May 1982, p. 86.
7. *The Source Book* (Chicago: Source Research Council, Inc., 1934).
8. Boyd K. Packer, *Mothers* (Salt Lake City: Deseret Book, 1977), pp. 20, 22.

Chapter Four
Childhood

1. Utah State University, Department of Agriculture, Utah Data Bulletin, September 1924, U.S. Weather Bureau.

2. George Albert Smith's stake conference visits to Brigham City Tabernacle, Church History Library.

3. Unpublished talk, Council of the Twelve meeting, April 1970, ms. p. 2.

4. Brigham City, Central School, report cards 1930–36.

Chapter Five
As a Youth in Brigham City

1. William Lamoin Packer interview, 19 December 1989.

2. Lillian Felt interview, 8 January 1989.

3. Box Elder Junior High term reports, 1936–38.

4. *Brigham City News*, 19 June 1932.

5. Dr. Malcolm S. Jeppsen interview, 12 January 1989.

Chapter Six
Serving His Country

1. *Deseret News 1991–1992 Church Almanac*, p. 336.

2. *Box Elder News Journal*, 11 September 1945.

3. *Ensign*, November 1985, p. 81.

4. *Improvement Era*, June 1970, pp. 52, 54.

5. From a tape from L. T. Saltysiak, 30 March 1989, pp. 1–2, 4 of transcript.

6. *Ensign*, January 1974, p. 25.

7. Boyd K. Packer, personal papers.

8. "To Those Who Teach in Troubled Times," Seminary and Institute Conference, Salt Lake City, 19 June 1970, p. 5.

9. *New Era*, September 1978, p. 33.

10. *Ensign*, May 1984, p. 43.

Chapter Seven
Courtship and Marriage

1. Letter, May 1947.

2. Ira Wight Packer's account of his and Emma's trip to Chicago, Detroit, Nauvoo, and the pioneer trek to Salt Lake City, July 1947.

3. *Utah Centennial Trek*, Souvenir Program and Guide, 14–22 July 1947, pp. 35–37.

4. *Utah Centennial Official Program*, p. 15.

Chapter Eight
Donna

1. Talk, Logan Temple Rededication, 15 March 1979, pp. 1–2.

2. Donna Smith Packer, "The Life History of Rasmus Julius Smith," p. 23. Unpublished.

3. Donna S. Packer, "The Life Story of William W. Smith and Nellie Jordan Smith," pp. 18–21. Unpublished.

4. Ibid., p. 25.

5. Donna S. Packer, Book of Remembrance.

Chapter Nine
Brigham City Days

1. *Ensign*, November 1987, pp. 17–18.

2. Donna S. Packer, personal history, p. 22.

3. *Box Elder News Journal*, 3 June 1949, p. 1.

4. Ibid., 19 October 1949, p. 1.

5. *Church News*, 28 April 1979, p. 3.

6. Donna S. Packer, personal history, p. 22.

7. *Box Elder News Journal*, 7 November 1951.

8. LDS Seventh Ward Chapel, Brigham City, Utah Dedication Program, 24 August 1952.

9. "An Evaluation of the Teaching of Jesus in Terms of Selected Principles of Education" (Logan: Utah State Agricultural College, 1953).

10. *Teach Ye Diligently* (Salt Lake City: Deseret Book, 1975).

11. *Teach Ye Diligently*, p. 133.

12. *Box Elder News Journal*, 21 January 1955, p. 1.

Chapter Ten
A Supervisor of Seminaries and Institutes

1. *Instructor*, November 1962, p. 390.

2. Boyd K. Packer, "Manual of Policies and Procedures for the Administration of Indian Seminaries of The Church of Jesus Christ of Latter-day Saints."

3. *Teach Ye Diligently*, p. 176.

4. Ibid., pp. 307–21.

5. Ibid., pp. ix–x.

6. Letter from Hermine Briggs Horman, 28 January 1989, p. 3.

7. Letter to the First Presidency, 24 October 1974. Unpublished.

Chapter Eleven
Assistant to the Twelve

1. William E. Berrett interview, 8 November 1988.

2. Boyd K. Packer, talk, General Authority Board Meeting, 3 October 1973, p. 117. Unpublished.

3. *Improvement Era*, May 1941, p. 269.

4. Ernest L. Wilkinson, Introduction to BYU Fireside talk "Eternal Love," 3 November 1963.

5. Talk, General Authority Board Meeting, 3 October 1973. Unpublished.

6. Boyd K. Packer, *That All May Be Edified* (Salt Lake City: Bookcraft, 1982), pp. 134–36.

7. Richard O. Cowan, *Every Man Shall Hear the Gospel in His Own Language: A History of the Mission Training Center and Its Predecessors* (Provo: Missionary Training Center, 1984), p. 18.

8. Belle S. Spafford interview, 3 November 1980.

9. Boyd K. Packer, *That They May Be Redeemed* (Salt Lake City: Corporation of the First Presidency of The Church of Jesus Christ of Latter-day Saints, 1977), p. 8.

Chapter Twelve
President of the New England Mission

1. Wilbur W. Cox interview, 9 August 1988.

2. Blessing upon Donna Edith Smith Packer by Elder Spencer W. Kimball, 2 June 1965.

3. Dr. Steven Smith interview, 2 February 1990.

4. Talk, General Authority Board Meeting, 3 October 1973. Unpublished.

5. *That All May Be Edified*, pp. 51–52.

6. Talk, "By the Spirit of Truth," Mission Presidents Seminar, 3 April 1985. Unpublished.

7. Elder Loren C. Dunn interview, 25 January 1990.

8. *That All May Be Edified*, p. 341.

9. Talk to seminary and institute personnel, 19 June 1970. Unpublished.

10. *Balfour Craftsman*, September 1967, p. 4.

11. *Improvement Era*, June 1968, p. 60.

12. Boyd K. Packer, *Let Not Your Heart Be Troubled* (Salt Lake City: Bookcraft, 1991), p. 128.

13. *Let Not Your Heart Be Troubled*, p. 113.

14. Boston Stake Fireside, 5 May 1968.

Chapter Thirteen
Call to the Quorum of the Twelve

1. Neal A. Maxwell interview, 8 December 1989.

2. *That All May Be Edified*, p. 208.

3. Boyd K. Packer, talk to Regional Representatives, 3 April 1970. Unpublished.

4. Talk to Regional Representatives, 11 December 1969. Unpublished.

5. *Church News*, 18 October 1969, p. 3.

6. Talk, General Authorities Board Meeting, 3 October 1973. Unpublished.

7. *Improvement Era*, June 1970, p. 28.

Chapter Fourteen
The New Apostle

1. *That All May Be Edified*, p. 256.

2. *Improvement Era*, May 1970, p. 5.

3. *History of the Church*, vol. 2, pp. 187–88.

4. Address given at Brigham Young University, 14 April 1970.

5. Talk, Council of the Twelve quarterly meeting, 2 April 1972. Unpublished.

6. Talk, 17 December 1972. Unpublished.

7. *Ensign,* December 1971, pp. 41–42.

8. *Ensign,* June 1971, pp. 87–88.

9. Talk to Regional Representatives, 12 December 1970. Unpublished.

10. Address at Logan Institute of Religion, 23 January 1973.

11. Manchester Area Conference, Women's Session, 28 August 1971.

12. "The Edge of the Light," *BYU Today,* March 1991, pp. 42–43. From an address given at Brigham Young University, 4 March 1990.

13. *Ensign,* February 1974, pp. 86–87.

Chapter Fifteen
The Eternal Family

1. Monument Park Stake Conference, general session, 29 April 1990.

2. David L. Kezerian interview, 23 July 1990.

3. Terri Anne Bennett Packer interview, 23 July 1990.

4. Boyd K. Packer, "A Visit to Groombridge Place." Unpublished.

5. Donna S. Packer, *On Footings from the Past: The Packers in England,* pp. 100–101.

6. Ibid., p. 101.

7. Ibid., pp. 103–4.

8. Ibid., p. 98.

9. Letter, Anthony J. Camp, 23 December 1988.

10. Letter, Dallin H. Oaks, 24 March 1989.

11. Boyd K. Packer, "Ancestral Home," in *Footings,* pp. 398–402.

12. *Salt Lake Tribune,* 20 August 1977, p. 1-A.

13. *Deseret News,* 19 August 1977, p. 1-A.

14. Spencer W. Kimball, repeated at Priesthood Genealogy Seminar, 4 August 1977.

15. Talk, Regional Representatives Seminar, 2 October 1975. Unpublished.

16. Talk to Genealogical Department employees, 18 November 1975. Unpublished.

17. *Ensign,* January 1977, p. 12.

18. Talk, Church Education Seminar, 14 October 1977. Unpublished.

19. Talk, Regional Representatives Seminar, 2 October 1975. Unpublished.

20. *Ensign,* November 1975, pp. 97–99.

21. Boyd K. Packer, "That They May Be Redeemed," talk to Regional Representatives, 1 April 1977. Later printed in pamphlet form and distributed by approval of the First Presidency.

22. Ibid.

Chapter Sixteen
The Holy Temple

1. *The Holy Temple*, p. 43.
2. Ibid., p. 44.
3. Ibid., p. 265.
4. Ibid., p. 23.
5. *History of the Church* 6:185.
6. *The Discourses of Wilford Woodruff*, G. Homer Durham, ed. (Salt Lake City: Bookcraft, 1969), pp. 153–54.
7. *The Holy Temple*, pp. 83–84.
8. Ibid., p. 175.
9. Ibid., p. 179.
10. Ibid, p. 267.
11. H. Burke Peterson interview.
12. "Family History: 'A Work Anyone Can Do.'" *Church News*, 26 March 1988, p. 9.

Chapter Seventeen
The New LDS Edition of the Scriptures

1. Talk, General Authority Training Meeting, 2 October 1981. Unpublished.
2. "The Law and the Light," Book of Mormon Symposium, Brigham Young University, 30 October 1988.
3. Talk, Quarterly Meeting of the Twelve, 17 December 1972. Unpublished.
4. Talk, General Authority Training Meeting, 2 October 1981. Unpublished.
5. Ibid.
6. *Ensign*, November 1982, p. 53.
7. Church Educational System talk, 14 October 1977.
8. *Ensign*, November 1982, pp. 51–52.
9. *Ensign*, August 1983, pp. 37–38.
10. *Ensign*, December 1985, pp. 49–53.
11. *Ensign*, May 1990, p. 36.
12. *Ensign*, May 1985, p. 11.

Chapter Eighteen
The New Revelation on the Priesthood

1. Doctrine and Covenants, Official Declaration—2, pp. 293–94.
2. Ibid., p. 294.
3. *Ensign*, November 1982, p. 53.
4. Doctrine and Covenants, Official Declaration—1, pp. 291–92.
5. *Deseret News 1991–92 Church Almanac*, p. 270.

Chapter Nineteen
Order, Ordain, Ordinance

1. "Ordinances," BYU fireside, 3 February 1980, p. 16.
2. Brigham Young, *Journal of Discourses* 1:134–35.
3. Boyd K. Packer, notes from an unpublished document.
4. Dean L. Larsen interview, 25 January 1991.
5. *Ensign*, November 1976, pp. 134, 136.
6. *Ensign*, May 1989, p. 17.
7. Dean L. Larsen interview, 25 January 1991.

Chapter Twenty
Perspective on Church History

1. LeGrand Richards Funeral Address, 14 January 1983.
2. Marion G. Romney Funeral Address, 23 May 1988.
3. Letter to the First Presidency, 24 October 1974.
4. Ibid.
5. Boyd K. Packer, *Let Not Your Heart Be Troubled* (Salt Lake City: Bookcraft, 1991), pp. 106–7, 108.
6. Ibid., p. 104.
7. "The Things of My Soul," *Ensign*, May 1986, p. 60.
8. "Journal of Wilford Woodruff," 6 July 1877, Church Archives.

Chapter Twenty-One
Simplification and Reduction

1. "Let Them Govern Themselves," Regional Representatives Seminar, 30 March 1990, p. 10.

2. Conference Report, April 1907, p. 7.

3. Report to the Committee on the Cost of Church Membership, 27 February 1981.

4. Talk to Regional Representatives and stake presidents from Brazil, April 1983. Unpublished.

5. "Teach Them Correct Principles," *Ensign*, May 1990, pp. 89–91.

6. "The Lord's Way," *Ensign*, May 1990, pp. 93–94.

7. "Rise to a Larger Vision of the Work," *Ensign*, May 1990, pp. 95–97.

Chapter Twenty-Two
Boyd K. Packer and Church Education

1. Arthur Henry King, *The Abundance of the Heart* (Salt Lake City: Bookcraft, 1986), p. 30.

2. "I Say Unto You, Be One," Devotional Talk, Brigham Young University, 12 February 1991.

3. *Sunstone*, July 1988 (delayed publication, actually appearing in November 1988), pp. 50–51.

4. Elder Dallin H. Oaks interview, 15 December 1989.

5. Boyd K. Packer, personal papers.

Chapter Twenty-Four
The Language of the Spirit

1. "Prayers and Answers," *Ensign*, November 1979, p. 21.

2. "The Candle of the Lord," *Ensign*, January 1983, p. 52.

3. *Ensign*, November 1979, pp. 20, 21.

4. *That All May Be Edified*, pp. 334–40.

5. Carlos E. Asay, memorandum, 15 February 1991.

6. Told by Boyd K. Packer at an informal gathering.

7. BYU Indian Week Address, 15 February 1979.

8. Boyd K. Packer, China Report.

9. Dallin H. Oaks, "Getting to Know China," BYU Devotional, 12 March 1991.

10. "Funerals—A Time for Reverence," *Ensign*, November 1988, p. 20.

11. At the funeral of General Leon Claron Packer, Brigham City, Utah, 29 November 1985.

12. *That All May Be Edified*, p. 119.

13. "Covenants," *Ensign*, May 1987, p. 22.

14. LeGrand Richards, "The Gift of the Holy Ghost," *Ensign*, November 1979, pp. 76–77.

Chapter Twenty-Five
New Responsibility Among the Twelve

1. James E. Faust interview, 2 February 1990.
2. Neal A. Maxwell interview, 15 December 1989.
3. *Ensign*, April 1995, p. 29.
4. Ibid., p. 6.

Chapter Twenty-Six
A Watchman on the Tower

1. BYU Commencement, 21 August 1981.
2. Howard W. Hunter, "Counsel to General Authorities," 19 June 1992, pp. 5, 6. Unpublished.
3. *That All May Be Edified*, p. 256.
4. Talk, Regional Representatives Seminar, April 1977.
5. "To Those Who Teach in Troubled Times," talk to seminary and institute personnel, BYU, 19 June 1970.
6. *That All May Be Edified*, p. 249.
7. Neal A. Maxwell interview, 8 December 1989.
8. *That All May Be Edified*, pp. 186–99.

Index